Good Buys in IT

A MANAGER'S GUIDE
TO EFFECTIVE SPENDING

Roger Barnes

McGRAW-HILL BOOK COMPANY

London · New York · St Louis · San Francisco · Auckland
Bogotá · Caracas · Lisbon · Madrid · Mexico
Milan · Montreal · New Delhi · Panama · Paris · San Juan
São Paulo · Singapore · Sydney · Tokyo · Toronto

Published by
McGRAW-HILL Book Company Europe
Shoppenhangers Road, Maidenhead, Berkshire SL6 2QL, England
Telephone 01628 23432
Fax 01628 770224

British Library Cataloguing in Publication Data
Barnes, Roger
   Good Buys in IT: A Manager's Guide to
   Effective Spending
   I. Title
   658.05

ISBN 0-07-709097-7

Library of Congress Cataloging-in-Publication Data
Barnes, Roger.
   Good buys in IT: a manager's guide to effective spending / Roger Barnes.
     p. cm.
   Includes index.
   ISBN 0-07-709097-7 (pbk. : alk. paper)
   1. Information technology–Management. 2. Information technology–Equipment and supplies–Purchasing. I. Title.
HD30.2.B364   1995
658'.05–dc20   95-8873
                                                                                            CIP

Copyright © 1995 Roger Barnes. All rights reserved.
No part of this publication may be reproduced,
stored in a retrieval system, or transmitted,
in any form or by any means, electronic, mechanical,
photocopying, recording, or otherwise, without the prior
permission of the author and McGraw-Hill International (UK) Limited.

12345 BL 998765

Typeset by BookEns Ltd., Royston, Herts.
and printed and bound in Great Britain
by Biddles Ltd., Guildford, Surrey

Printed on permanent paper in compliance with ISO Standard 9706

Contents

CHAPTER 1	**Introduction**	**1**
	Into the next century!	1
	IT decision making	4
	Process overview	4
	Critical success factors	8
	Use of consultants	10
	How to use this book	10
CHAPTER 2	**People**	**13**
	Introduction	13
	Roles	13
	Approach	15
	Conflict	15
	Conclusion	20
CHAPTER 3	**Planning for success**	**21**
	Creating the environment	21
	Planning	27
CHAPTER 4	**Quality**	**43**
CHAPTER 5	**Business needs and benefits**	**46**
	Feasibility phase	46
	Critical success factors	48
	Business needs	49
	Benefits	54
	Business process re-engineering	58
	Identifying business needs and benefits	62
CHAPTER 6	**Summary of requirements (SOR)**	**65**
	Critical success factors	65
	Summary of requirements	66
	Preparing the summary of requirements	68
	Quality review of the summary of requirements	71
CHAPTER 7	**Request for proposal (RFP)**	**72**
	Critical success factors	72
	Request for proposal	72

CONTENTS

	Preparing the request for proposal	77
CHAPTER 8	**Short-listing options and suppliers**	**79**
	Introduction	79
	Critical success factors	81
	Supply options	82
	Identifying suppliers	86
	Issue request for proposal to suppliers	88
	Evaluation models	88
	Evaluate suppliers' responses	91
CHAPTER 9	**Business case**	**95**
	Introduction	95
	Critical success factors	95
	Business case	98
	Preparing the business case	101
	Business case evaluation and approval	107
CHAPTER 10	**Operational requirement (OR)**	**111**
	Selection phase	111
	Critical success factors	113
	Operational requirement	113
	Preparing the operational requirement	116
	Quality review of the operational requirement	118
CHAPTER 11	**Invitation to tender (ITT)**	**120**
	Critical success factors	120
	Invitation to tender	120
	Preparing the invitation to tender	126
	Issue invitation to tender to suppliers	128
CHAPTER 12	**Evaluation**	**129**
	Introduction	129
	Critical success factors	129
	Evaluation planning	129
	Evaluation models	133
	Evaluation procedures	136
	Evaluate invitation to tender responses	138
	Product evaluation	138
	Services evaluation	143
	Supplier evaluation	146
	Final short-list	148
CHAPTER 13	**Decision making**	**149**
	Introduction	149
	Recommendation	149
	Capital request	155

CONTENTS

CHAPTER 14	**Supply agreements**	**163**
	Critical success factors	163
	Best and final offer	163
	Negotiating	164
	Agreements	166
CHAPTER 15	**Implementation considerations**	**178**
	Introduction	178
	Critical success factors	178
	Why projects succeed	182
	Why projects fail	183
CHAPTER 16	**Post-implementation reviews**	**185**
	Introduction	185
	Critical success factors	185
	System review	185
	Benefits review	187
CHAPTER 17	**Two case studies compared**	**190**
CHAPTER 18	**Case studies: selecting IT solutions**	**200**
	BP Oil	200
	Castle Cement	203
	Leicester City Council	206
	Prudential Assurance	209
	Yule Catto	213
CHAPTER 19	**Case studies: IT solutions and business process re-engineering**	**217**
	British Telecom	217
	Pepe Jeans	221
	SmithKline Beecham	224
CHAPTER 20	**Case studies: facilities management and outsourcing**	**229**
	Birmingham City Council	229
	Bolton Metro	235
	Trent Regional Health Authority	240
AUTHOR'S POSTSCRIPT		**247**
INDEX		**248**

Introduction

CHAPTER

1

Into the next century!

Computers! Software! Words guaranteed to evoke a reaction from both management and users. Why? Over the past twenty-five years large sums of money have been invested in information technology (IT), some wisely, some foolishly, and if most reports are to be believed a significant proportion with indifferent results. Yet the investment continues.

The demands of the 1990s on IT are very different from preceding decades. The rate of change in both the public and private sectors is unprecedented. The on-going drive to reduce cost, improve efficiency, increase market share and open new markets has already resulted in:

- The growth of non-proprietary hardware and software (open systems like UNIX) to achieve standards, flexibility of supply and lower unit costs, which is more than adequately illustrated by the number of the case studies researched for this book that are moving to UNIX-based solutions

- A continual decline in high-cost central IT departments and a move towards distributed computing with less in-house technical support and more reliance on suppliers. This decline, that started in the 1980s, was initiated by concern over the cost of running large centralized IT departments combined with a dissatisfaction with the level of service offered. The decline accelerated with the availability of stable and low-cost alternative solutions from the open-systems suppliers. The decline in the relative position of mainframe computers, that were and still are in many cases the traditional technology used by central IT departments, has resulted in the suppliers reducing prices. The cost per user comparison between the competing mainframe, mini and PC/workstation computer configurations is now much more even. This process of rethinking the most effective computer platform or environment on which to run applications has been labelled rightsizing, downsizing and even smartsizing!

- Another trend is the realignment in the way that IT departments are organized. The central IT department is increasingly shrinking. IT staff are being transferred to user departments as users take ownership of IT and bring IT investment more in line with the needs of the business

- A strong demand for new information systems that are usable by all levels of management to speed up the decision-making processes and reduce senior managers' reliance on the information provider

- A continuing demand for software packages with high functional content that can be implemented quickly at low risk

- A demand for outsourcing to offload responsibility for IT and facilitate change

- An on-going demand for easier-to-use workstations to improve desktop productivity

- A demand for independent/multi-vendor hardware and software support to reduce maintenance costs

- An increased role of the user in deciding and taking ownership of IT. This is dramatically illustrated by an analysis of the case studies researched for this book. Nearly all (88 per cent) of the application software projects, one-third of the systems software projects and three-quarters of facilities management/outsourcing projects were user-led

- According to the Price Waterhouse *1994/95 IT Review for the UK*, the total IT expenditure spent by users is 21 per cent and increasing, the amount spent on outsourcing is 10 per cent and increasing with the balance of 69 per cent spent by the central IT department and decreasing. This 69 per cent is made up of 26 per cent for staff, 25 per cent for all computer hardware expenditure including maintenance, 10 per cent for software and 6 per cent for telecommunications, of which only the 10 per cent share for software is increasing. The balancing 2 per cent is made up of miscellaneous and rounding errors. The average spend on IT as a percentage of turnover is 1.5 per cent with the manufacturing sector being below average; retail and distribution, utilities and government about average; and the finance sector above average.

The effect of these trends and pressures on the IT industry has been significant:

- The cost of hardware has continued to decline, as has the number of manufacturers

- A shift by the hardware manufacturers to become service companies offering multi-vendor support (third-party maintenance), system integration and outsourcing in an attempt to maintain growth and margins

- The globalization of the major software houses to support their international customer base and achieve economics of scale in their battle for market share
- The continual growth in the numbers of indigenous software houses to meet the needs of local markets
- The availability of 16 000 software products from 6000 suppliers in the UK alone.

These structural changes within the IT industry have been accompanied by an equally unprecedented rate of technical change. Hardware and software product life cycles are becoming shorter and shorter. The sales life cycle of personal computers and workstations is now 12-18 months. The working life is longer, say three years, before either replacement or upgrade. The two contributing factors to these short life cycles are the rapid advance in technology, making earlier products obsolete, but, more importantly, the ever-increasing computing power and disk storage required by each new release of software. Software is paradoxically becoming both easier to use and more complicated. The additional functionality and mouse-driven user interface demands more and more computing power. Fortunately, the cost of this additional power has been and looks likely to continue to be offset by falling hardware prices. The result is that it has become far more difficult to select an IT solution with a medium- to long-term life cycle, as is typical of most business applications.

Managing computer projects is no longer the sole domain of the IT department. Selection and implementation projects are increasingly led by users with the IT department providing the necessary technical support. The challenge of the 1990s is how to align IT closer and closer to the business to achieve real benefits. This will mean having a clear understanding of the needs and requirements of the business and using rigorous selection techniques to decide which of the increasing range of available options will give most benefit. *The chances are that the results of the selection decisions made in the mid-1990s will be very visible in the twenty-first century.*

Also during the 1990s business process re-engineering will radically change many organizations and their use of IT. In some cases the results of business process re-engineering will change how IT fits into the organization and the systems required. In other cases business process re-engineering will have been made possible only by advances in technology.

EXAMPLE

In some parts of the motor and retail industries paperwork and the reconciliation of documents has all but been eliminated when ordering and paying for goods. This has been achieved by the use of electronic data interchange (EDI) between the customer and the supplier to transmit documents automatically and quickly. Goods are ordered by use of an EDI link between the customers' purchasing system and the suppliers' sales order processing system, without the need to print the purchase orders or call-off notes. Orders can be acknowledged by sending an EDI message the other way from the supplier to the customer. On receipt of the goods the customer raises a self-billing invoice that is posted automatically to the general ledger and accounts payable, sending a copy of it by EDI to the supplier. The customer can then automatically pay the supplier without having to receive, authorize or process a supplier's invoice.

IT decision making

There should be nothing different about decision making in IT. The fundamental questions to be answered when deciding any change forward are:

- Do we need the benefits?
- Can we achieve the benefits?
- What is the risk?
- Are we achieving the benefits at optimum cost?

The objective of this book is to define a business process, addressing these questions, that is applicable to IT.

Perhaps the complex nature of decision making in the first place, combined with the fast-moving and technical arena of IT, has contributed to the sceptical view of IT projects taken by many managers and users. This book is written for the project team, business analyst, user manager, steering committee member, corporate planner and senior management. In short, anyone involved in decision making when selecting IT solutions. The aim is to introduce the reader to a straightforward structured process that is both comprehensive and understandable.

The process is designed for medium and large organizations in both the public and private sectors. However, the principles are equally applicable to a smaller organization, but in practice, as the number of people involved will be fewer and the lines of communication shorter, some of the steps within the process can either be consolidated or omitted altogether.

Process overview

The process described in this book is *solutions oriented* (see Figure 1.1). This means identifying business requirements and testing the market to find the most appropriate solution. The emphasis is on presenting

INTRODUCTION 5

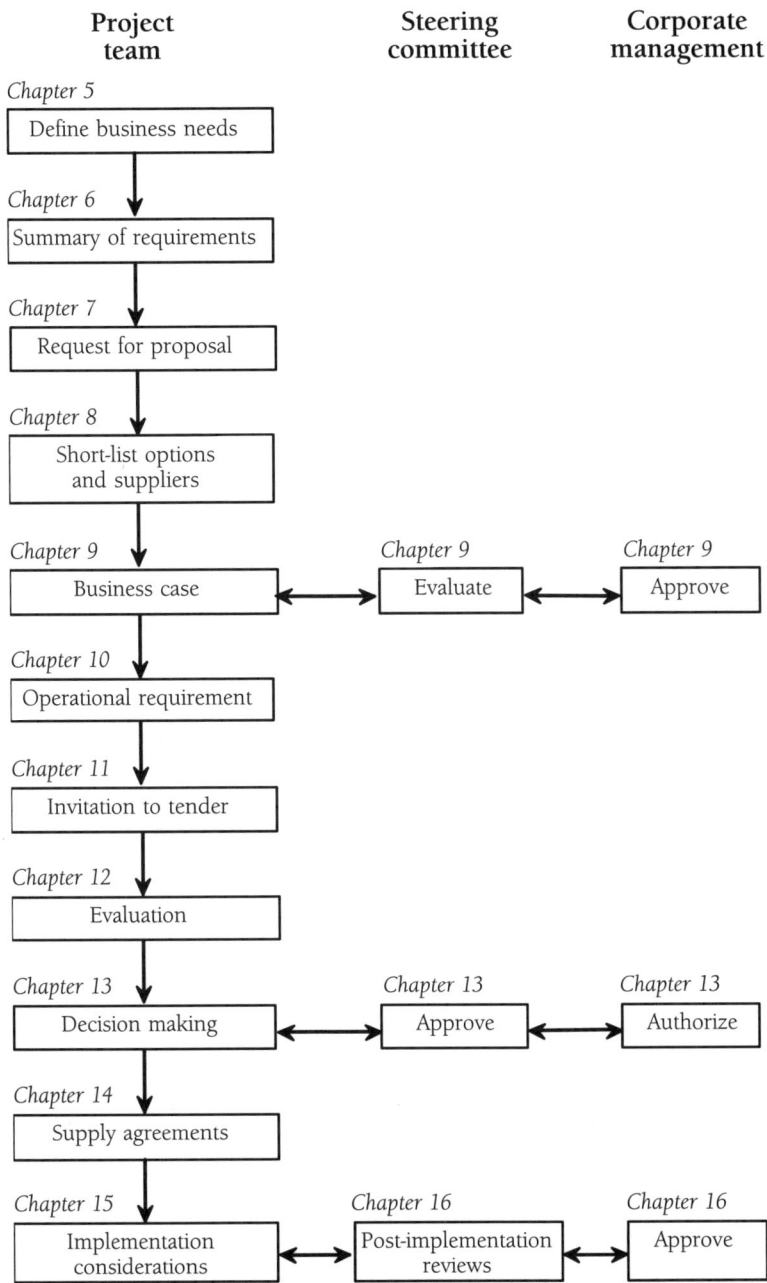

Figure 1.1 *Selection process model.*

business requirements to potential suppliers and inviting suppliers to propose solutions (as against presenting detailed specifications of requirements, products or services). In this context supplier means the solution provider who could be either internal or external.

EXAMPLE When selecting a PC for, say, WORD Version 6.0 simply state the requirement, forcing suppliers to propose solutions and the appropriate configuration. The advantages are that the technical task of determining the configuration is avoided and the suppliers committed to the fact that their proposed configurations will do the job. The alternative of predetermining the configuration and then selecting a PC accordingly does not commit the supplier to the solution.

The advantages of this approach are first, it ensures that all options are explored. Second, it enables results-oriented supply agreements to be negotiated. This is a direct result of presenting the business requirement to the supplier and gaining the supplier's commitment to the solution (and not just to delivering products and services). Third, it avoids the users defining their computing requirements in detail that has proved to be notoriously difficult over the years. Fourth, it satisfies the last of the fundamental decision-making criteria (*Are we achieving the benefits at optimum cost?*) because all options are explored.

EXAMPLE A district health authority, which was devolving budget responsibility to local managers, required a new management information system. The obvious solution was to implement a centralized system to facilitate the collection of data to be accessed by all budget holders. The authority prepared an invitation to tender, outlining their business need and requirement, a management information system (not a specification for hardware and software that is a potential solution). After a rigorous evaluation the authority selected an outsourcing supplier. The authority, therefore, avoided significant capital costs for hardware and software by negotiating a transaction-based charging structure with their outsourcing supplier, who provided the necessary hardware, software and services to implement and support the system.

The process also recognizes the key roles played by a steering committee and corporate management. It is assumed that the project team, which will normally comprise two to six people, reports to a steering committee responsible for the work of the project team. Among other responsibilities the steering committee must address the first fundamental decision-making criterion *Do we need the benefits?* when reviewing the business case built by the project team. Later in the process, the steering committee must also satisfy itself that the project team have adequately addressed the other two fundamental decision-making criteria *Can we achieve the benefits?* and *What is the risk?*

The role of corporate management is identified separately and defined as initially addressing the key question *Does this project fit into corporate objectives?* when approving the business case. Subsequently when authorizing capital and revenue expenditure the key question is simply *Do we need the benefits?* In many cases the functions of the steering committee and corporate management will be executed by the same body. However, it is important to recognize the two different functions.

The evaluation, selection, purchasing and implementation cycle has five distinct phases:

1. Pre-feasibility
2. *Feasibility*
3. *Selection*
4. Implementation
5. Post-implementation reviews.

This book concentrates on the feasibility and selection phases.

The individual steps of the process described in this book are illustrated in Figure 1.1. Table 1.1 analyses the steps in more detail and also indicates responsibility for completing the steps.

Table 1.1

Chapter		Project team	Steering committee	Corporate management
Feasibility phase				
5	Business needs and benefits	Define business needs Agree benefits		
6	Summary of requirements	Prepare summary of requirements	Quality review	
7	Request for proposal	Prepare request for proposal		
8	Short-list options and suppliers	Options Identifying long-list of suppliers Issue request for proposal Evaluation models Evaluate suppliers' responses Initial short-list		
9	Business case	Prepare business case	Evaluate	Approve

Table 1.1 cont.

Chapter	Project team	Steering committee	Corporate management
Selection phase			
10 Operational requirement	Prepare operational requirement	Quality review	
11 Invitation to tender	Prepare invitation to tender Issue invitation to tender		
12 Evaluation	Evaluation planning Evaluation models Evaluation procedures Evaluate invitation to tender responses Product evaluation Services evaluation Supplier evaluation Final short-list		
13 Decision making	Build financial models Recommendation Prepare capital request	Approve Approve	Authorize
14 Supply agreements	Best and final offer Negotiating Supply agreements		
Implementation phase			
15 Implementation considerations	Implementation		
Post-implementation reviews			
16 Post-implementation reviews		System review Benefits review	Approve

Critical success factors

The process defined in this book is designed to:

- Deliver successful projects
- Make *value for money* decisions
- Achieve projected benefits
- Enable the user to manage the project.

It does this by establishing clear guidelines for accountability, responsibility, communications, quality and standards. This provides a sound basis for planning, estimating, evaluating and decision making. The effect of this is to provide a consistent business process that evaluates risk and enables clear critical success factors to be checkpointed. The setting of critical success factors is unique for each project.

The literal use of any process will not guarantee success. Chapter 2 considers the people typically involved a project. Most projects are looking to achieve benefits and move the organization forward. Change involves people and to get people to work together creates the project. The management of the change requires an understanding of both the process itself and the interaction between the players. The setting of critical success factors should reflect this by recognizing both tangible and intangible objectives. Typical critical success factors are listed in Table 1.2.

Table 1.2

Tangible	Intangible
Feasibility phase	
■ Does the project have a sound plan?	■ Is senior management committed to the project?
■ Have we clearly identified business needs?	■ Are the users committed to the project?
■ Does the summary of requirements reflect business needs?	■ Is the IT department committed to the project?
■ Can we adequately resource the project?	■ Have realistic levels of expectations been set to management and users?
■ Have we short-listed the correct suppliers?	
Selection phase	
■ Does the supplier understand our requirements?	■ Is senior management still committed to the project?
■ Do we have a detailed implementation plan agreed with the supplier?	■ Are the users still committed to the project?
■ Do we understand the risk? Can the project be phased?	■ Is the IT department still committed to the project?
■ Do we still need the solution?	■ Have realistic levels of expectations been set to management and users?

The management of expectation is critical. The level of expectation can only be set, or challenged, based on a sound understanding of what is achievable. The setting of expectation is critical to both management and users. Success is judged on it.

EXAMPLE A project manager was asked to undertake a full selection process in three months that he accepted knowing that it would take five months. At the end of five months, having completed a good job, he felt pleased but management was disappointed. He would have been better advised to have argued for more time, based on a sound plan, therefore, managing the expectations of senior management. At a broader level it is sometimes easy for senior management to quantify a project's success, particularly if cost savings were a key benefit. However, it is far harder to judge success at the end-user level when personal satisfaction with a new data entry screen or report writer may be the criterion. Frequently dissatisfaction is caused not by any failure or omission of the solution but because it does not meet an unrealistic expectation.

A tick-list of critical success factors is included in Chapter 3 and used in Chapter 17 to compare the success of one project against another.

Use of consultants

Because of the critical nature of many projects, and the fact that most users only make a selection decision once or twice in their careers, external consultants are frequently used to help in both the selection and implementation. The process described in this book can be used with or without consultants. However, the responsibility for the selection cannot be abdicated to consultants. The aim of this book is to outline an understandable and manageable process. If consultants are used then their role should be defined and they can be selected depending on the skills and experience required.

How to use this book

This book is written in a modular fashion so that each chapter can be read and used in its own right with minimal cross-referencing to other chapters. The process described is generic and potentially suitable for any IT solution. It is anticipated that each organization will adapt the process to their own particular needs depending on size, typical complexity of projects and whether procurement is subject to regulatory authorities (i.e. EU, GATT).

The longer-term benefit of using a defined process to an organization is consistency. Once the process has been tested and adapted to suit an organization's needs, its on-going use will make the management of projects easier. This is because a proven approach will be in place, obviating the necessity of each project team building their own ground rules. Also, at steering committee and corporate management level, it will be easier to compare business case proposals, monitor project performance and complete post-implementation reviews, as each project will have used a similar approach.

The description of the selection process starts in Chapter 5 and finishes in Chapter 16. Before looking at the process in detail, Chapter 2 considers some of the people issues, Chapter 3 project planning and Chapter 4 quality. The case studies in Chapters 17-20 are capable of being read in their own right and are also referenced throughout the book.

The importance of making the right decisions in the early stages of a project cannot be overemphasized. A mistake or omission early in the selection process that results in a change much further into the process can be extremely costly to rectify as has been discovered and rediscovered all too often.

CASE STUDY

Company B commissioned consultants to review their IT strategy as part of their plan to go public. Their report was accepted by the board and an operational plan prepared to downsize the old mainframe-based applications to an open platform over a period of three years. This was to take advantage of a wider choice of products and anticipated cost savings. The first application to be implemented under the new strategy was the sales information management system.

Business pressures had reduced the time scale to three months to implement the new system. This was unrealistically short but the project team agreed to do their best and started work without a project plan and only an outline business requirement.

Company B has a tradition of building systems in-house. The project team quickly came to the conclusion that the new system could not be satisfied by a package and therefore decided to redevelop it in-house. This meant selecting the relational database management system and a UNIX-based computer on which to run it. In order to save time the project team selected, in their opinion, the leading supplier of database management systems and the leading UNIX computer supplier for evaluation.

The project team immediately got to grips with evaluating their selection. Equipment and software were delivered and the project team started a two-week trial to build a prototype of the new application. As problems arose they contacted the suppliers for support. After two weeks they decided that they liked the computer hardware supplier but were dissatisfied with the technical functionality and support from the database supplier. The computer supplier was given preferred supplier status and it was decided to evaluate the next two database suppliers on their list. After a one-day overview from each of the database suppliers they opted for one of them and immediately recommended another two-week prototype build of the application. This went well, and after reference visits and financial health checks on the computer hardware and database management system suppliers both were recommended. The supply agreements were negotiated and signed by the head of IT who was also the project manager.

The development of the application continued as it had started with no clear requirements document. Infrequent meetings were held with the users and the first release of the new application delivered late.

According to the new head of IT, who has been brought in from a line management function to run IT: 'Many lessons have been learnt from this experience. Users are now given ownership of their own projects and must present a sound business case before any expenditure is authorized. Further, products and services must be evaluated in line with the requirements as determined by the business need, scoped correctly and the evaluation and selection process properly planned.'

Lastly, the IT industry is subject to fashion like many other industries. Some ideas and new technologies take hold, thrive and prosper. Some do not and wither on the vine, much to the inconvenience of their users! Outsourcing is currently growing strongly but, at the same time, there is considerable debate as to what long-term benefits it offers to business. UNIX, as an open system, is also growing strongly but there is every likelihood that it will eventually settle down to be one of a small number of open operating systems. Client/server systems are growing strongly with a bewildering number of definitions as to what it means and concerns over the complexity of the technology and costs. The overall message is clear. There is no panacea that suits everyone. There is a right solution for you: it may be the same as someone else has chosen, but equally it may not. The choice of solutions available is wide and potentially confusing. Selecting the right one based on business requirements, not fashion or policy, is what this book is about.

People

CHAPTER 2

Introduction

Most of this book concerns itself with defining the chronological steps to follow in order to make a beneficial selection decision. However, there is no doubt that the individuals involved and their interaction with each other and with the organization will impact the decision and its subsequent implementation. The selection of an IT solution is the effect, not the cause. The cause is the achievement of a business benefit that invariably means moving the organization forward. The management of this change is critical, and to be successful it is vital to understand the people issues involved and create an environment that encourages success.

Roles

The titles of individuals involved in a selection process will vary enormously, and even within similar organizations titles can be very misleading as duties and reporting structures are not consistent. Ignoring titles, certain roles are present, these are as follows.

Sponsor or champion

A sponsor is the person who initiated the project in the first place, who identified the business need and the potential benefits. Typically, this person is trying to move the organization forward and holds its needs foremost. Once the project has started a sponsor is not involved in the project or in the management of the change process created but is satisfied that the objectives are being achieved. A champion, on the other hand, not only sponsors the project but also acts as its champion and promotes the project as and when necessary. A sponsor might not be personally committed to a project but a champion will be personally committed and will be the person with most to lose or gain by its success.

Decision maker

This is the person whose approval is required to initiate the project and subsequently represents the project at a decision-making level and who can control or influence financial decisions. This person may be a member of the project team or steering committee but more typically will delegate most of the detailed selection tasks to *users* and *technicians*. The decision maker could also be the sponsor or the champion of the project.

The concerns of the decision maker with respect to the project are mainly objective:

- What is the return on investment?
- Price/performance issues
- What will be the impact on the organization?
- What is the risk?
- How will it be viewed externally?
- Does it address corporate objectives?
- What are the benefits?

Users

These are line managers, departmental managers and users who will be directly affected by the project, who will develop the business need and benefits and specify the functional requirements. The concerns of users with respect to the project are therefore more subjective:

- How will it affect me?
- How can I use it?
- How will it affect my department?
- How will it affect our performance?

Technicians

These are professional staff who will contribute to the project, adding essential technical expertise in areas like IT, purchasing, legal and personnel, ensuring that any proposed solution complies with standards and procedures. The effect of technicians on the project is normally neutral or negative. It is neutral when the necessary expertise is supplied efficiently and dispassionately and potentially negative when there is a conflict of interest or when the project is reviewing potential solutions that challenge accepted standards and working procedures (see 'Conflict' below).

Consultants

Consultants are professional staff who are external to the organization and who might be fulfilling the roles of users or technicians, inputting ideas, adding expertise or advising on the management of change.

Approach

Each person involved with the selection will approach it differently. Their approach will be influenced by their own personal needs and ambitions, previous experience and positions they are obliged to take in the normal cut and thrust of interdepartmental rivalry present in most organizations. Their approach and reaction to the business issues involved are illustrated in Table 2.1.

Conflict

The solutions-oriented approach described in this book encourages exploring all options in order to select the best solution to meet business requirements. This may well cause stresses and strains within the organization and project teams as existing standards and working practises are challenged. The following are examples of potential conflict areas.

The changing role of the IT department

The last few years have seen a vigorous debate as to the role of the IT department. Concern over the cost and dissatisfaction with results have certainly initiated the changes that are happening. However, the arguments are not all one-sided and the counter-arguments need to be heard in order to take a balanced decision. One of the key arguments from the traditional IT community is the need to maintain standards so that systems and computers can communicate effectively. It is probably true that the rapid growth in the use of PCs and departmental computers has been caused by frustration at the inflexibility of mainframe computers combined with the growing independence of users. One of the results of the growth in the use of PCs has been a fall in standards, making it very difficult to share the data now kept at a personal level. Looking back, there is no doubt that had the IT department been able to control personal computing it would have

Table 2.1

Approach	Reaction
Problem oriented Immediate recognition that real and urgent business issues are involved and something needs to be done about it Examples of these issues are a reaction to competition; compliance with regulatory authorities; changes resulting from deregulation, take-overs, mergers, centralization and decentralization	Supportive and favourable
Growth oriented Recognition that real business issues are involved and something should be done about it Examples of this are plans to meet future growth and efficiency improvements	Supportive and favourable but priority will always be given to projects attracting a problem-oriented approach
Elsewhere Recognition that there might be real business issues involved but currently the project does not have the priority because of other issues Examples of this are pending deregulation, higher priority projects and possible take-overs when management is distracted	Possibly favourable after current business issues and projects have been addressed
No need No recognition that there are business issues and benefits involved Examples of this are a project that is technically driven, looking to take advantage of new technology, but is not really offering any benefit to the organization; or simple resistance to change or not recognizing that change is necessary	Not supportive and unfavourable. However, beware the situation when senior management is supportive, because they see the business benefits but the users do not, or where some members of the project team are favourable and others are not who may be defending a departmental position by resisting change
Consultants Consultants should approach each assignment with an open mind, act dispassionately and make any recommendations in the best interest of their client. However, they in turn will be influenced by their own experiences, their own personal needs and the needs of their own organization	

slowed down progress to the disadvantage of the users. Looking ahead, there is no doubt that for the desktop to continue to bring business advantage it will need to operate in a more controlled environment.

BP OIL **CASE STUDY**

Since 1992 the role of the head office of BP Oil at Moorgate has significantly changed, resulting in a reduction of head count from over a 1000 to around 150. The associated reduction in IT support staff meant that a new approach to the provision of desktop services was needed.

Prior to these reductions, the policy with respect to office automation had been *to give the users what they want*. The result of this practice was five different graphics packages, four word processors and three spreadsheets. Local area networks were mainly used to share printers. Information exchange between individuals within the same building, let alone different geographic locations, was extremely messy and long-winded. The inherent problems and inefficiencies in managing this technical environment had led to a widespread view that the IT department was *late, useless and expensive*.

The project was initiated by the IT department to improve their efficiency and perhaps their image by creating a better desktop environment for the users in head office. The tangible benefits, supported by a cost-benefit analysis, were to reduce the direct costs of the IT department in licensing, maintaining and supporting such a diverse range of products. The intangible benefits were generally to improve the overall efficiency of head office by standardizing on the desktop and making all data compatible; inter- and intra-communications easier; eliminating the necessity to convert or re-enter data from one system to another; and making it easier and simpler for the head office team to work electronically anywhere in the world. As it turned out, the nature of the project changed and it was subsequently viewed as an infrastructure project adding to the overall operating efficiency of head office.

The project successfully met the user requirements and rebuilt the lost credibility of the IT department.

The growth of open systems and the decline of proprietary ones

In the mainframe environment the costs of both systems software and application software are high. It therefore became the norm for the IT department to standardize on a systems software platform (i.e. an operating system and database management system) and then develop or select the application software for that platform. The benefits of doing this were cost savings in licences and support and, hopefully, the opportunity to create an integrated environment to make data and information more accessible. This frequently created a situation when perfectly viable (and cheaper) solutions were declined because they did not fit into the corporate standard. The growth of open systems and user independence has challenged this approach. Taking a solutions-oriented approach to selecting solutions will create a dilemma, balancing, on one side, the advantages of selecting the best-fit solution that might not fit the corporate standards and might seem to create technical problems with, on the other, selecting a second-choice solution that does meet corporate standards.

The possible reliance on small (and sometimes new) software houses for critical business solutions

When selecting an IT solution the organization is frequently looking to benefit from the originality and creativity of the market. However, depending on the nature of the requirement, this must be balanced against the suppliers' ability to supply and support the product or service over its required life cycle. One of the key judgements when selecting a product is *where is the product in its life cycle?* Products that are at the back end of their life cycle are frequently functionally rich but have a limited life. Those at the beginning of their life cycle frequently come from small entrepreneurial companies. A good decision, in selecting a new product from a new company, can be rewarded by many years of good service. A poor decision, in selecting an old product that is phased out or from a supplier that fails, is costly.

CASE STUDY

A good example of a decision to go for a small committed supplier is Pepe Jeans. Pepe Jeans is a very successful 21-year-old company. Based in London, Pepe Jeans created a world brand image in a competitive, fast-moving consumer goods market. Turnover rose to over $200 million and Pepe Jeans became recognized as among the top ten jeans' companies in the world. The Pepe Jeans formula is to be sales and marketing driven, sell via traditional retail outlets, design their own products but subcontract manufacturing. In 1992, however, the company was almost bust. Overexpansion, a world recession combined with overconfident management resulted in losses for two consecutive years in excess of $25 million. De-listing and new owners followed. A new management team was recruited committed to turning the company around.

A detailed specification of requirements was prepared, the critical requirements being:

- A sales order processing system to meet the requirements of the textile trade
- A standard off-the-shelf package operating in a computing and communications environment that could be facility managed
- An international package that could meet the requirements of the European operating companies
- Multinational support from the supplier obviating the need for an IT department to support the solution

- An integrated solution.

Preliminary research had identified about 50 packages. A long-list of 12 suppliers was selected by reading supplier's literature, interviewing potential suppliers and applying the key criteria of the requirement. These 12 suppliers were issued the invitation to tender. Nine satisfactory responses were received and an initial short-list of four selected after each supplier had given a half-day presentation to the project team.

Eventually the project team and users were equally divided between the two suppliers on the final short-list. One supplier was quite small but with a very good sales order processing package developed for the textile trade and the other was an incumbent supplier. The deciding factor was user satisfaction.

The project has been very successful to date. The size of the accounting department has reduced from 100 to 45, the IT department from 16 to two and the company is back in profit. Rob de Meij, the chief financial officer of Pepe Jeans, has some very clear views on why the project has been so successful: 'Selecting a software supplier who is totally committed to our solution, if we fail, he fails.'

Consideration of outsourcing the supply of an IT solution

The selection and implementation of IT solutions affects and is dependent on people. The rise of facilities management and outsourcing has added a new dimension as it affects the IT staff themselves. If facilities management or outsourcing is being evaluated then the consequences on the IT staff are taken into account and their attitude towards the evaluation anticipated.

However, sometimes selecting the best solution is a two-step process, first, to select the products or services that best meet the business need and requirements and second, selecting the best way of achieving them. This could mean using the services of a facilities management company to run the products or services on your behalf instead of the products or services being implemented by in-house staff, or outsourcing the supply and, again, not using in-house staff. The potential conflicts of interest that can arise need careful management.

CASE STUDY

Pepe Jeans first selected the software supplier, then the computer hardware supplier and finally a facilities management supplier to manage the computer hardware and the network. Eventually the project team and users were equally divided between the two suppliers on the final short-list. One supplier was quite small but with a very good sales order processing package developed for the textile trade and the other was an incumbent supplier. The deciding factor was user satisfaction. This was tested during the reference visits by some searching questions and an open and frank discussion with the suppliers' senior management. The decision was for the UNIX- and PROGRESS-based package from Option Systems Limited. Once the software supplier had been selected a very quick hardware evaluation selected NCR with AT&T as the facility's manager for the computer and communications network.

Simple resistance to change

Simple resistance to change must be anticipated. What is important is to understand the reason for the resistance, as this will determine how it is handled. Change equals uncertainty and uncertainty can lead to fear. Recognizing this and building an effective change programme into the project plan can remove the resistance.

Conclusion

The selection and implementation of a new IT solution inevitably involves change. The management of the people issues is critical to a successful conclusion. It is probably now true that the management of these issues is the critical area and is more likely to contribute to the failure of projects than technical problems associated with hardware or software.

Recognizing the roles and approaches of the people involved and how they will be affected by the project is a good starting point to start to manage the change process successfully. The next chapter starts with how to create the right environment to encourage success.

Planning for success

CHAPTER 3

Creating the environment

The object of the selection process is to select and implement the solution that best meets the business requirements. In order to achieve this a variety of skills will be required and probably more than one department of the organization involved. The best way is to create a team representing the interests of the various departments involved that has the best possible balance of skills.

The normal functional responsibilities within the project team are listed in Table 3.1. The individual skills and knowledge required by the various members of the project team are broadly outlined below.

Project manager

The essential skills of the project manager are to be able to lead and motivate the team and communicate effectively with the steering committee, users, the IT department and management. Previous experience in selecting similar IT solutions is useful. However, as more and more projects are user-led this is less likely and the necessary knowledge must be gained from books (like this one), training courses and external consultants. It is, however, essential that by the time the project starts the project manager understands the selection process well enough to be able to build a viable plan and set achievable levels of expectations to both users and management.

The selection process will involve internal business planning workshops to define objectives and identify problem areas; formal interviews with users and management to ascertain requirements; conference room pilots to test out ideas; product workshops with potential suppliers to evaluate products; negotiations with short-listed suppliers; report preparation, report writing and presentation skills. The project manager will need to understand how to manage and conduct all these events.

Table 3.1

Chapter		Users	IT	Purchasing	Legal
5	Define business needs	✓			
6	Prepare summary of requirements	✓	✓		
7	Prepare request for proposal	✓	✓	✓	
8	Supplier long-list	✓	✓	✓	
	Issue request for proposal			✓	
	Build evaluation models	✓	✓	✓	
	Evaluate supplier responses	✓	✓	✓	
	Initial short-list	✓	✓	✓	
9	Prepare business case	✓	✓		
10	Prepare operational requirement	✓	✓		
11	Prepare invitation to tender	✓	✓	✓	
	Issue invitation to tender			✓	
12	Build evaluation model	✓	✓		
	Evaluation planning	✓	✓		
	Evaluation procedures	✓	✓		
	Product evaluation	✓	✓		
	Services evaluation	✓	✓		
	Supplier evaluation	✓	✓	✓	
	Final short-list	✓	✓	✓	
13	Build financial models	✓			
	Recommendation	✓	✓	✓	
	Prepare capital request	✓			
14	Best and final offer			✓	
	Negotiation			✓	✓
	Supply agreements	✓	✓	✓	✓

CASE STUDY

Pepe Jeans and the Prudential Assurance both have clear views as to the requirements of the project manager. Rob de Meij, the chief financial officer of Pepe Jeans says why the project has been so successful: 'Having a multi-lingual European project team, an only English-speaking team would have been a disaster as they would not have understood the different European cultures and would not have been able to communicate effectively.' And according to Ron Skelley, systems development manager of the Prudential Assurance, success is due to '... creating the best team in the first place with particular emphasis placed on appointing a project manager who is business-led, capable of making decisions, recognizing when they do not know the answer and delegating and bringing in expertise as and when required'.

Users

The essential contribution of the users is their understanding of the business issues and functional areas involved. Previous familiarity with analysis techniques to identify business needs and benefits; computer appreciation to enable requirements specification to be prepared; report preparation, report writing and presentation skills are useful but these can be readily learnt.

IT (see note 1 below)

The essential contribution of the IT department to the project is an understanding of the likely technical issues that will arise, i.e. computer and communications hardware, software, an understanding of current systems, interface requirements and implementation considerations. Familiarity with building data models and process models may be required depending on the size of the project and the in-house standards in use.

Purchasing (see note 2 below)

The contribution of the purchasing function to the project is an understanding of the organization's purchasing procedures, whether subject to regulating authorities (i.e. EU, GATT) and expertise in vendor appraisal and negotiating supply agreements.

Legal (see note 2 below)

The contribution of the legal function to the project is the skill and experience in drafting and finalizing appropriate IT supply agreements and, most importantly, for facilities management and outsourcing selections understanding the current legislation with respect to the transfer of undertakings and protection of employment (TUPE).

Note 1

The IT function can be fulfilled by the IT department, users who are computer-literate, support from a central IT department or an external consultant.

Note 2

The purchasing and legal functions are not normally part of the project team and may be fulfilled by specialized departments or suitably qualified individuals.

Project team

Composition

The project team will normally comprise two to six people possibly supported on a large project by subproject teams. The appointment of the project manager is a key decision. In large organizations the project manager has traditionally been an IT department appointee but there is a growing trend for the project manager to be a senior user who can bring business experience to the team to ensure that the solution meets business objectives. The role of the IT department is then to supply the necessary technical expertise to ensure that a viable solution is selected. In smaller organizations, without an IT department, then obviously the project manager has to be a user and the necessary IT technical expertise supplied by computer-literate users or an external consultant.

Terms of reference

The terms of reference of the project during the feasibility and selection phases should be prepared as soon as possible and should include:

- The objectives of the project
- Time scales
- Reporting arrangements to the steering committee and other interested parties
- Lines of communication to users and management
- Limit of authority.

Function

The project team has two key functions. First, it must recognize that the project team is the instrument of change. For the change to be successful, it must gain acceptance of its ideas, sell the benefits of change and motivate management, the IT department and users to work with the project team to achieve the desired result. Second, the project team is responsible for recommending the most appropriate solution to meet the business need (and perhaps implementing the solution).

What makes a successful project team?

- A sound understanding of the organization and business issues involved
- A positive results-oriented approach to the issues at hand
- Leadership
- A clear understanding of the scope of the project
- Balance of skills, i.e. management, users and technicians
- Balance of personalities, i.e. realists, visionaries, pessimists, leaders, doers.

What does a successful project team need?

- Support of senior management
- User commitment
- Clear terms of reference
- Full- or part-time commitment to the project by the individual members and recognition by their management of the importance of this commitment and ensuring that the necessary time is made available.

Steering committee

Composition

The steering committee will normally comprise management representatives of the interested user departments and IT management as well as general management representing the organization itself.

Functions

Project set-up:

- Does the project meet business objectives and corporate priorities?
- How does the project fit into our IT strategy?
- Can we resource the project?
- Decide on the membership of the project team and their training requirements

- Agree terms of reference with the project team
- Agree reporting arrangements with the project team
- Agree critical success factors with the project team
- Agree the project plan with the project team
- Agree the selection processes, procedures and techniques to be used by the project team.

Monitoring the project:

- Is the project meeting business objectives and corporate priorities?
- Has anything changed that alters business objectives and corporate priorities?
- Is the scope of the project still correct?
- Does the project have a viable plan?
- Has anything changed that affects risk?
- Is the project meeting its objectives?
- Is the project on time?
- Is the project following its quality plan?
- Is the project on budget?
- Is the project adequately resourced?
- Initiating and reviewing a post-implementation system review one month after project sign-off.

Decision making:

- Initiating a quality review of the summary of requirements
- Evaluating the business case
- Initiating a quality review of the operational requirement
- Evaluating the project team recommendation
- Approving the capital request
- Initiating a post-implementation benefits review six months after project sign-off.

What makes a successful steering committee?

- A clear understanding of business objectives and corporate priorities

- An understanding of what is achievable, bearing in mind the culture of the organization and approaches of key individuals
- A clear understanding of the organization's IT strategy.

Corporate management

Function

- To set business objectives and corporate priorities
- To approve the business case
- To authorize capital and revenue expenditure
- To approve the post-implementation benefits review.

Planning

The project effectively begins when there is recognition that there is a business issue to resolve. From then on, in order for the issues to be properly addressed, it will need a team with the appropriate skills and a plan. In the early stages of the project the team will probably be informal. As the project develops project team members will have to be released either full- or part-time from their current commitments, the project formalized and planned accordingly.

This book concentrates on the feasibility and selection phases of the total evaluation, selection, purchasing and implementation cycle. The pre-feasibility phase is not covered as it varies greatly depending on organization and project size. It can also be an informal phase with the sponsor *selling* ideas and only as the ideas gain acceptance does work begin as a project. The advantage of this informal approach is that it can be very stimulating, provided that a culture and framework exists within the organization to encourage and consider new ideas before the more formal project process takes over. The step, however, from the pre-feasibility to the feasibility phase needs to be formalized. It is at this point that the project formally comes into being with defined objectives and the commitment of the organization to invest in it.

One of the first tasks is to prepare an outline project plan. At this early stage it is not possible or necessary to plan in detail but it is possible to set objectives. Then, as the project progresses, the plan can be filled out in detail. Key factors to take into account when preparing an outline project plan are as follows.

Legislation

Is the organization subject to the EU and GATT procurement directives?

When planning facilities management and outsourcing selections that will involve the transfer of staff it is essential to take into account the transfer of undertakings and protection of employment (TUPE) legislation. Broadly, this legislation seeks to protect the rights of employees being transferred with an undertaking and other employees who are dependent on them. The legislation is, however, subject to amendment and interpretation and as each facilities management or outsourcing situation is unique it is essential to seek current legal advice. Three areas are of particular importance:

1. Which employees are covered by the TUPE regulations? For instance, if an IT unit of 100 staff is supported by a full-time purchasing officer in the purchasing department and a part-time solicitor in the legal department, then apart from the employees of the IT unit who are obviously subject to the TUPE regulations, what is the position with respect to the purchasing officer and the solicitor?

2. Do the planned staff consultation procedures comply with the regulations?

3. What rights do the regulations give to the employees?

Priority

How important is this project? What will be the approaches of the key individuals? How urgent is it?

Resourcing

Do we have the staff to resource the project? Do we have the time? Do we have the financial resources? What will be the impact on our existing computing and communications facilities? Do we need to buy in the necessary skills to resource the project?

Risk

What are the risks involved? Will the project encounter resistance? What are the technical risks?

Training

What training and user education will be required to prepare the ground and overcome internal objections so that the project team can do its work in a positive atmosphere? What training is required for the project team itself to bring it up to the required skill level? For example, project management; analysis techniques; computer-appreciation courses in fourth-generation languages (4GL); client/server technology; outsourcing and facilities management arrangements.

Pace

What is the optimum pace of the project? How much time do we need to allow to get to know potential suppliers? Do we need to allow extra time for the organization and users to accept change? Do we need to act quickly to meet competitive pressures?

The pace of the project is a key decision. Too fast, and the necessary consensus required for any project to succeed will be put at risk, too slow, and momentum will be lost and any eventual implementation will end up solving yesterday's problem.

Quality

Do we have any quality control procedures? How can we build quality into our plans?

Contingency

How much contingency should we allow in the plan to cater for unforeseen circumstances? Do we anticipate any internal inertia problems?

Critical success factors

What are the critical success factors? How can we identify them? Table 3.2 is a checklist of the critical success factors referenced in this book. Some of the critical success factors appear more than once. This is because they need to be reconsidered at a later step, probably by a different group that considered them the first time.

Decision making

Does the selection process planned rigorously address the four fundamental decision-making questions:

1. Do we need the benefits?
2. Can we achieve the benefits?
3. What is the risk?
4. Are we achieving the benefits at optimum cost?

Table 3.2

Critical success factors	Tick-list

Critical success factors in defining business needs and identifying benefits are:

- Are the business needs relevant to current business objectives and corporate priorities?
- Have the benefits been agreed by the *owning* users and management?
- Do we understand the assumptions made in calculating the benefits?
- Are the benefits achievable?
- Are the benefits measurable?

Critical success factors when preparing the summary of requirements are:

- Does the project team have the correct balance of skills to define the application, technical and management requirements?
- Is the scope of the project defined correctly?
- Do the requirements accurately reflect our business needs?
- Do the technical requirements fit in with our IT strategy?
- Is a quality review part of the preparatory procedures?

Critical success factors when preparing the request for proposal are:

- Does the request for proposal effectively convey our business requirements to potential suppliers, enabling them to respond quickly and efficiently?
- Does the suppliers' section of the request for proposal adequately reflect our requirements from suppliers?

Critical success factors in short-listing options and suppliers are:

- Have we selected the right options?
- Have we long-listed the right potential suppliers to issue the request for proposal?
- Have we followed the correct procedures when we issued the request for proposal (particularly important to the public sector and some parts of industry who are subject to EU and GATT regulations)?
- Have the most likely suppliers responded to the request for proposal?
- Do we understand our key requirements well enough to differentiate between suppliers?
- Will our evaluation model and procedures produce the best initial short-list?

Table 3.2 cont.

Critical success factors	Tick-list

Critical success factors in preparing the business case are:

- Are the business needs still relevant to current business objectives and corporate priorities?
- Have the benefits been agreed by the *owning* users and management?
- Are the benefits achievable?
- Is the scope of the project defined correctly?
- Do the requirements accurately reflect our business needs?
- Do the technical requirements fit in with our IT strategy?
- Have we selected the right supply options?
- Have we followed the correct procedures when we issued the request for proposal?
- Have we selected the best suppliers for the initial short-list?
- Have we considered the organizational impact of the project?
- Have we considered the personnel and training ramifications of the project?
- What management issues does the project raise?
- What change management issues does the project raise?
- Have we considered all the risks?
- Is the level of expectation set correctly to management?
- Is the level of expectation set correctly to users?
- Are management still committed to the project?
- Are the users still committed to the project?
- Is the IT department still committed to the project?
- Can we adequately resource the project?

Critical success factors when evaluating and approving the business case are:

- Do we need the benefits?
- Can we achieve the benefits?
- What are the risks?

Critical success factors when preparing the operational requirement are:

- Does the project team have the correct balance of skills and available resources to define the detailed requirements?
- Is the scope of the project, as defined in the summary of requirements, still correct?
- Is the operational requirement a forward-looking document?
- Will the operational requirements be checked for consistency (especially important for a large document)?
- Are all requirements designated either mandatory or desirable?
- Is a quality review part of the preparatory procedures?

Table 3.2 cont.

Critical success factors	Tick-list

Critical success factors when preparing the invitation to tender are:

- Have we selected the best short-list of suppliers to issue the invitation to tender?
- Does the invitation to tender adequately reflect our requirements?

Critical success factors in producing the final short-list of suppliers are:

- Have the most likely suppliers responded to the invitation to tender?
- Do we understand our key selection criteria well enough to differentiate between suppliers?
- Will our evaluation model and procedures produce the best final short-list?
- Are we addressing the fourth of the fundamental decision-making criteria (*Are we achieving the benefits at optimum cost?*)

Critical success factors when making and approving the recommendation are:

- Have we considered the organizational impact of the project?
- Have we considered the personnel and training ramifications of the project?
- What change management issues does the project raise?
- Have we considered all the risks?
- Did we select the best suppliers for the final short-list?
- Did the evaluation model help us identify the issues and differentiate between the suppliers?
- Have we identified all the costs?
- How accurate are the costs?
- Is the recommended supplier committed to the project?
- Does the supplier understand our business objectives?
- Have we selected the optimum cost solution?

Critical success factors when preparing, approving and authorizing the capital request are:

- Do we need the benefits?
- Can we achieve the benefits?
- What is the risk?
- Are we achieving the benefits at optimum cost?

Critical success factors when negotiating and finalizing supply agreements are:

- Do we understand the strengths and weaknesses of our position?
- Do we understand the strengths and weaknesses of the supplier's position?
- Do we have the necessary technical, purchasing and legal skills?

Table 3.2 cont.

Critical success factors	Tick-list
■ Are we approaching the negotiations to conclude a win/win agreement with the supplier?	
Critical success factors when implementing the solution are:	
■ Define what success is! ■ Review and redefine the roles, responsibilities and terms of reference of the project team ■ Review and redefine the roles, responsibilities and terms of reference of the steering committee ■ Manage the internal levels of expectation and commitment ■ Manage the supplier ■ Manage the benefits	
The critical success factors for post-implementation reviews are:	
■ Create an environment where the objectives and benefits of the post-implementation reviews are understood by all concerned so that the reviews are conducted in a positive atmosphere ■ Give clear terms of reference for the reviews ■ Conduct the post-implementation reviews independently and impartially ■ Act on the results of the post-implementation reviews	

Once the key factors are taken into account it should be possible to construct an outline plan. The process described in this book will identify the tasks to be performed in a typical selection. It is not possible to quantify how long each step or task will take as this will depend on the size of organization and size, scope and complexity of the project. Figure 3.1 is an outline project plan for a medium-sized organization selecting a new accounting and distribution system; Figure 3.2 is an outline project plan for a systems software selection; and Figure 3.3 is an outline project plan for an outsourcing/facilities management selection.

An analysis on the case studies researched for this book gives the average elapsed selection time between the start of the feasibility phase of the project and the signing of a supply agreement as follows:

Applications software	6–7 months
Systems software	4–5 months
Facilities management/outsourcing	9 months (including three months to negotiate the agreement)

When the outline project plan is agreed with its critical success factors each step can be further divided into a number of tasks and subtasks as

		January				February				March				April					May				June			
ID	Task Name	01	08	15	22	29	05	12	19	26	05	12	19	26	02	09	16	23	30	07	14	21	28	04	11	18	25	02
1	**Feasibility phase**																											
2	Planning																											
3	Project team training																											
4	Define business needs																											
5	Agree benefits																											
6	Summary of requirements																											
7	Quality review																											
8	Request for proposal																											
9	Short-list options																											
10	Short-list suppliers																											
11	Prepare business case																											
12	Evaluate business case																											
13	Approve business case																											

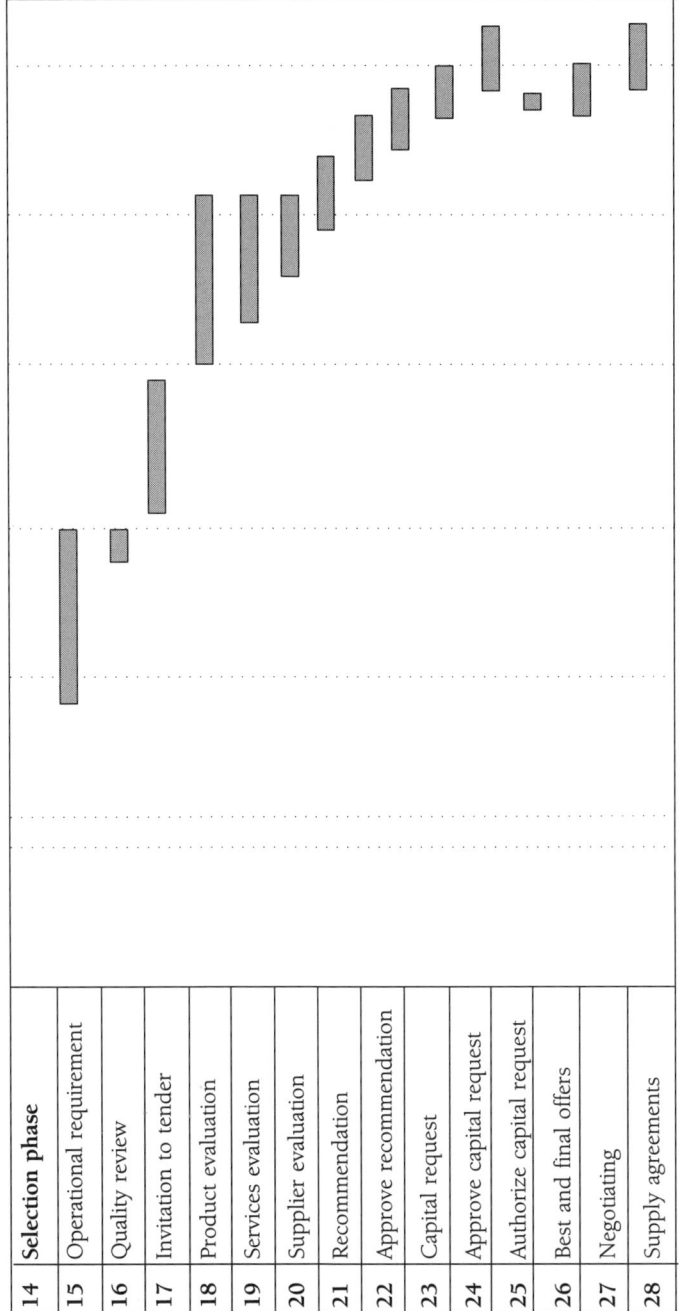

Figure 3.1 *Outline project selection plan: application software.*

ID	Task Name	January				February				March				April					May		
		01	08	15	22	29	05	12	19	26	05	12	19	26	02	09	16	23	30	07	14	21
1	Feasibility phase																					
2	Planning																					
3	Project team training																					
4	Define business needs																					
5	Agree benefits																					
6	Summary of requirements																					
7	Quality review																					
8	Request for proposal																					
9	Short-list options																					
10	Short-list suppliers																					
11	Prepare business case																					
12	Evaluate business case																					
13	Approve business case																					

Figure 3.2 *Outline project selection plan: systems software.*

ID	Task Name	January				February				March				April				May				June				July				August				September		
		01	08	15	22	29	05	12	19	26	05	12	19	26	02	09	16	23	30	07	14	21	28	04	11	18	25	02	09	16	23	30	06	13	20	27	03	10	17	24
1	**Feasibility phase**																																							
2	Planning																																							
3	Project team training																																							
4	Define business needs																																							
5	Agree benefits																																							
6	Summary of requirements																																							
7	Quality review																																							
8	Request for proposal																																							
9	Short-list options																																							
10	Short-list suppliers																																							
11	Prepare business case																																							
12	Evaluate business case																																							
13	Approve business case																																							

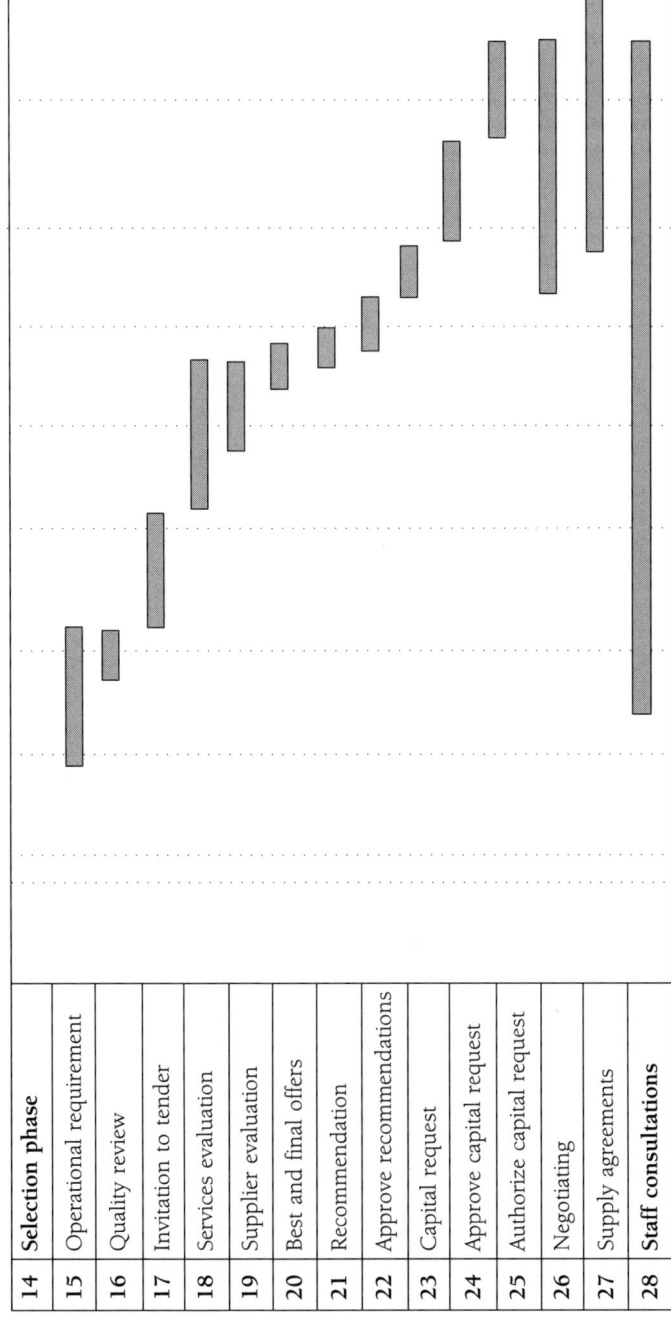

Figure 3.3 *Outline project selection plan: facilities management/outsourcing.*

described further in the book. Depending on the size of project and the number of people involved, it might be appropriate to document each task or subtask with a job sheet stating the objective, guidelines as to how the job is to be accomplished, start/end dates, estimated actual time, responsibility and reporting (see Figure 3.4). It is recommended that a formal project planning tool is used to assist in the planning, monitoring and management of large projects. For small projects a simple manual project bar chart and project responsibility matrix will suffice (see Figures 3.5 and 3.6).

PLANNING FOR SUCCESS 41

PROJECT	SELECT NEW DISTRIBUTION SYSTEM	Issued by: Richard Philips Date: 8 Sept. 1994
STEP	Short-list options and suppliers	Issued to: David Henry
TASK	Issue request for proposal	Start date: 19 Sept. 1994 Finish date: 30 Sept. 1994
SUBTASK	Answer suppliers' technical questions	Commitment: Part-time

OBJECTIVE
Answer suppliers' reasonable technical questions arising from the request for proposal as quickly as possible.

GUIDELINES
Do not be drawn into commercial questions, refer these to the project manager.

ADDITIONAL NOTES

REPORT RESULTS TO: Richard Philips   BY: 3 Oct. 1994

REFER TO FOR ADVICE: Martin Appleby

Figure 3.4   Example project job sheet.

42 GOOD BUYS IN IT

STEP/TASK/SUBTASK		Weeks					
STEP 4: SHORT-LIST OPTIONS and SUPPLIERS		8	9	10	11	12	13
4.1	Agree critical success factors	X					
4.2	Determine supply options	X					
4.3	Identify suppliers for long-list	←——→					
4.4	Issue request for proposal			X			
4.4.1	Answer technical questions				←——→		
4.4.2	Answer commercial questions				←——→		
4.4.3	Receive suppliers' proposals					X	
4.5	Build evaluation models			←——→			
4.6	Evaluate suppliers' proposals						←——→

Figure 3.5   *Example project bar chart.*

STEP/TASK/SUBTASK		Responsibility					
STEP 4: SHORT-LIST OPTIONS and SUPPLIERS		AB	NJ	RP	DH	JL	DR
4.1	Agree critical success factors	X		Q			
4.2	Determine supply options	X					
4.3	Identify suppliers for long-list	X	X				
4.4	Issue request for proposal					X	
4.4.1	Answer technical questions				X		
4.4.2	Answer commercial questions			X			
4.4.3	Receive suppliers' proposals					X	
4.5	Build evaluation models		X	X			
4.6	Evaluate suppliers' proposals	X	X	X	X	X	X

Where   D = Decide   R = Review
         Q = Quality review   X = Perform

Figure 3.6   *Example project responsibility matrix.*

Quality

CHAPTER 4

Why do many projects fail to deliver projected benefits? Why do some projects fail altogether? There are many reasons: unmatched expectations between the parties involved; lack of proper procedures by the parties involved; communication difficulties between the parties; changes in business circumstance; underestimation of the technical difficulties involved; underestimation of the difficulties in managing the change process.

All the above are probably contributing factors. Three of the fault-lines which are particular to IT are first, an over-concentration by IT professionals on technical issues and the possible benefits of new technology; second, lack of focus by project teams in meeting business needs; and third, IT solution providers being too remote from the users, who in turn have been insufficiently involved in IT projects. One of the recent and growing trends that illustrate these points is users wanting to take ownership of IT, believing that they will achieve better results if they manage their investment in IT themselves.

Recognizing that well-thought-out quality programmes will help them to deliver the right product or service consistently to the customer on time, some IT solution providers have already gained TICK IT/BS 5750/ISO 9000 accreditation. However, it takes two to tango! It is equally important that users also adopt quality programmes.

The definition of quality and the objectives of organizations initiating quality programmes varies greatly. In this book quality is defined as a set of processes and procedures to achieve a consistent result. It follows, therefore, that well-thought-out processes and procedures will achieve consistently high levels of results but poor processes and procedures will consistently produce a low level. The emphasis is on the word *consistently*, as the objective of any quality programme is to achieve the defined result! Put another way, quality is the result of good practice.

The process described in this book has been developed based on experience of the author and research specifically conducted for this book. The objective is to define a process to select IT solutions that is relevant to the needs of the business today. The book should be viewed as a generic quality manual that can be adapted and used by each organization as part of its own quality programme.

The use of a defined process together with the associated monitoring and management functions enables expectation levels and anticipated results to be quantified and therefore success measured. Further, the use of a defined process enables the use and success of the process itself to be measured. This in turn means that the process can be continually improved and adapted to the benefit of future projects.

An analysis of the case studies researched for this book shows the following:

- No quality assurance plans for the selection (43 per cent)
- Self-checking quality assurance built into the project plan (57 per cent)
- Self-checking quality assurance built into the project plan and external consultants used to advise on quality assurance and independently check the quality plan (36 per cent).

Within the process described in this book quality is a consistent theme. At each critical step the work of the project team is independently checked and the responsibility for achieving the review clearly stated (see Figure 4.1).

QUALITY 45

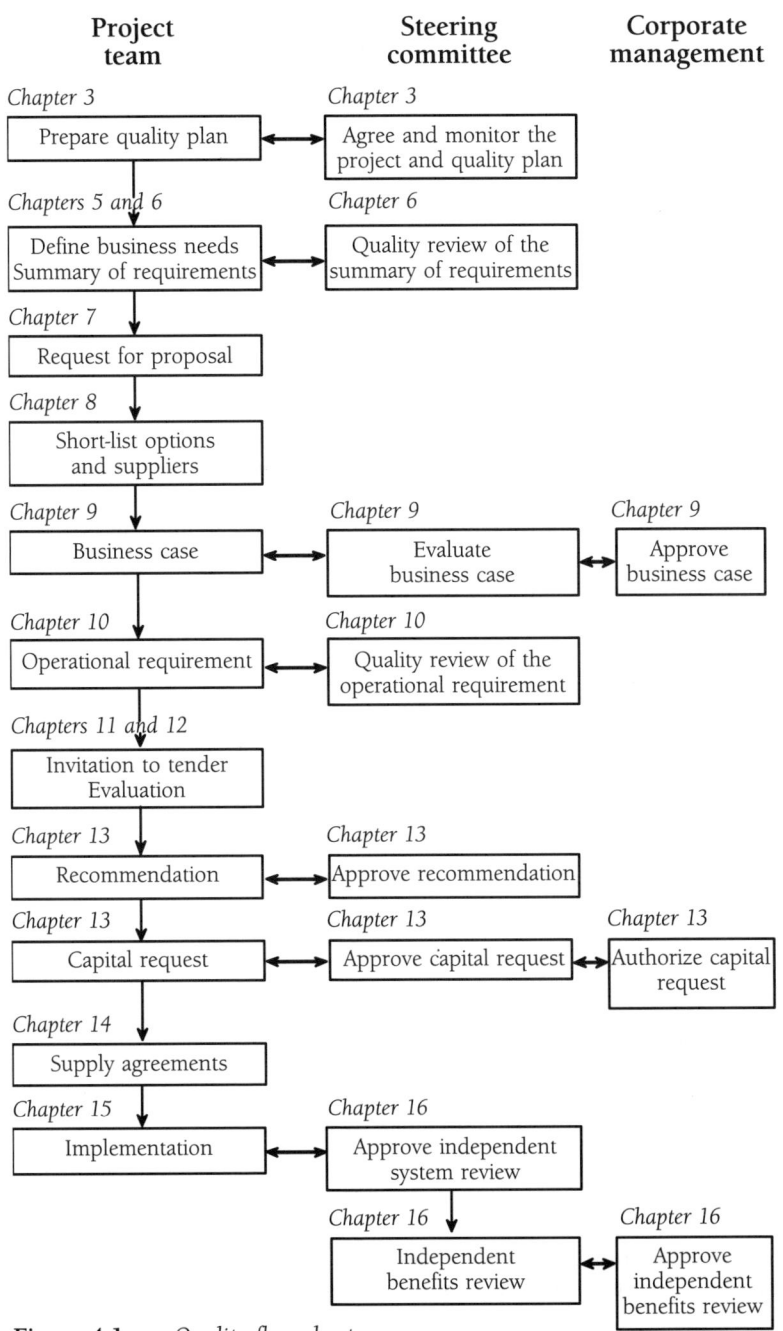

Figure 4.1 *Quality flow chart*

CHAPTER 5

Business needs and benefits

Feasibility phase

The feasibility phase of the evaluation, selection, purchasing and implementation cycle is described here and in Chapters 6-9. This phase encompasses defining business needs, identifying business benefits, specifying the summary of requirements, short-listing supply options, estimating costs and preparing, reviewing and approving the business case. The objective of the feasibility phase is to take a preliminary and decisive view, when the business case is reviewed, of the first three of the fundamental decision-making questions:

- Do we need the benefits?
- Can we achieve the benefits?
- What is the risk?

During the subsequent selection phase these three questions will be re-addressed as well as the fourth of the fundamental decision-making questions:

- Are we achieving the benefits at optimum cost?

The feasibility phase is illustrated in Figure 5.1. The objectives of each step are defined below.

Define needs (Chapter 5)

The objective of this step is for the project team to define and agree the business needs with users and management.

Identify benefits (Chapter 5)

The objective of this step is for the project team to identify and quantify business benefits with their *owning* users and management.

BUSINESS NEEDS AND BENEFITS

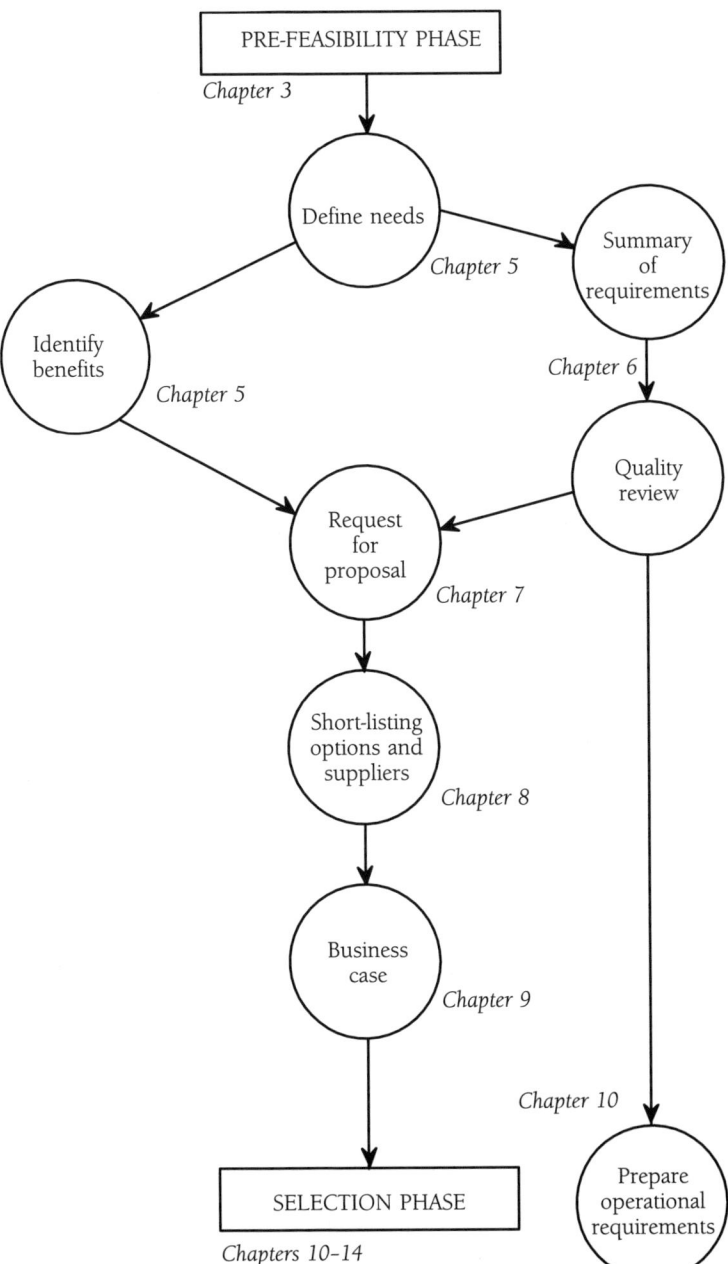

Figure 5.1 Feasibility phase.

Summary of requirements (Chapter 6)

The objective of this step is for the project team to specify the outline requirements to meet the business need as well as how and when the requirements will be implemented.

Request for proposal (Chapter 7)

The objective of this step is for the project team to prepare a short and concise request for proposal that is issued to potential suppliers, as part of the next step of the process, inviting short responses.

Short-listing options and suppliers (Chapter 8)

The objective of this step is for the project team to consider the viable options, prepare a long-list of suppliers to whom to issue the request for proposal, evaluate the suppliers' responses, prepare an initial short-list of suppliers and gather estimated costs.

Business case (Chapter 9)

The objective of this step is for the project team to prepare the business case for submission and presentation to the steering committee.

Approve business case (Chapter 9)

The objective of this step is for the steering committee to evaluate the business case and gain approval from corporate management to proceed.

Critical success factors

Critical success factors in defining business needs and identifying benefits are:

- Are the business needs relevant to current business objectives and corporate priorities?
- Have the benefits been agreed by the *owning* users and management?
- Do we understand the assumptions made in calculating the benefits?
- Are the benefits achievable?
- Are the benefits measurable?

Business needs

Definition of business needs

A business need is an objective to move an organization forward.

Types of business needs

Cost-driven

These are changes that are necessary to reduce costs, contain costs or achieve cost leadership.

BOLTON METRO **CASE STUDY**
Bolton Metro is a local authority in the North-west of England. It employs 12 000 staff and has a revenue budget of £200 million. It had a central IT unit of 70 staff managed as a business unit within the finance department. Bolton Metro is politically stable, has a strong tradition of openness and consensus management and a policy to devolve authority away from the centre to the operating departments. By 1993 Bolton Metro found itself with the central IT unit offering traditional services, based on an ICL mainframe, and departments with their own IT staff developing their own new systems and controlling their use of PCs and workstations. The total IT budget is about £6 million with about two-thirds accounted for by the central IT unit and one-third by the departments. Paradoxically, whereas the new systems are being built as departmental systems, demand on the existing mainframe systems is growing.

During the 1980s Bolton Metro had tried to develop an IT strategy, without much success. In 1991–2 a chief officer group, chaired by the finance director, reviewed IT strategy and considered three options:

1. Centralize all IT activities into one unit run as a direct service organization
2. Decentralize IT, make each department totally responsible for its own IT, with a small central standards and coordinating team
3. Continue with status quo.

The decision was to continue with the status quo. However, by spring 1993 this decision was reconsidered in the light of the government's compulsory competitive tendering regulations due to take effect in 1996. Coopers & Lybrand were invited to undertake a short ten-day study of the competitiveness of the central IT unit. Their report confirmed that the central IT unit offered a good-quality service but was at risk under compulsory competitive tendering. This created a situation that was potentially difficult for the council members of Bolton Metro, as their policy is one of no compulsory privatization. Soundings of members and staff were taken and a decision reached to explore the potential benefits of facilities management. The staff were assured that during this process they would have the right to veto and stop the process at key check points. At this stage facilities management was defined as transferring the staff and the delivery of the service, but not the assets; the scope of the services to be transferred was left open.

The evaluation of the in-house prospects indicated:

- A high operating cost of the mainframe computer compared to a facilities management supplier
- Difficulty in matching the flexibility of processing and development requirements of the users in the future
- Likely staff reductions, to match staffing to the workload in the future, might make the unit too small and therefore not viable, and in any case, might not still be enough to win a competitive tender in 1996 due to anticipated intense competitive pressure.

Infrastructure improvement

These are changes that are necessary to improve the overall efficiency and working of an organization, i.e.:

- Improving management information
- Improving planning cycles
- Speeding up and shortening lines of communication by investing in computing power, communications facilities and office automation.

CASE STUDY

PRUDENTIAL ASSURANCE

The sales department of the Home Service Division of the Prudential employs 7000 representatives, the traditional front line of the Prudential, knocking on doors and, until recently, collecting money. They generate more than 50 per cent of the Prudential's premium income and are organized into five regions and 180 branches. They were supported by standalone PCs in each branch that were used to produce quotations and reconcile cash. In order to use a PC each salesperson had to come into the office and wait their turn. In practice, of course, this did not happen. The PCs were not connected to any of the back-office systems and they were not significantly adding to the overall sales effort.

There was recognition in the IT department that in order to take advantage of point-of-sale technology an infrastructure creating a new branch platform needed to be built. This would offer the potential of each representative having a portable PC capable of producing instant and accurate quotations linked to the back-office systems. This recognition coincided with proposals to re-engineer the back-office systems from a product to a customer focus. In the past each individual product was supported by its own system. This meant that if a customer had more than one product it was difficult for a representative to get a complete picture of the customer's account without knowing all the products their customer had purchased and their reference numbers. The re-engineering of the product systems enables a complete picture of a customer to be built up quickly and easily.

All this created the potential of building a customer information system (CIS) that could support the representatives. The project, with a total budget of £15 million, is viewed as an infrastructure investment replacing the PCs in the branch offices.

Key business ratios

Changes necessary to improve key business ratios involve:

- Working capital
- Stock turn
- Debtors' days
- Service levels
- Turnover per employee
- Profitability per employee

CASE STUDY

SMITHKLINE BEECHAM
The Chemical Division of SmithKline Beecham has five major production sites around the world and a number of smaller sites, all working continuously. These sites were using a mixture of in-house-developed applications and packages for their maintenance management systems. However, they all faced the same issues of compliance with regulatory bodies; interfacing their maintenance management systems with condition base monitoring systems, financial systems and other systems; as well the introduction of total productive maintenance. In 1989 a worldwide project team was set up to decide an overall approach to engineering systems.

In parallel with this project a Divisional team was also looking ahead and applying business process re-engineering techniques. One of the areas being considered was the relationship between the operators of the plant and the tradesman and craftsman maintaining it. A number of the management team had visited Japan and were struck by the sense of ownership by the Japanese operators of their equipment. The Japanese operators took a wider view of their job and consequently were more efficient as they could quickly sort out many of the jobs that in the UK required a craftsman. This was in stark contrast to the traditional way of working in the UK plants, that had a strong demarcation between the duties of the operators and tradesman. The project team concluded that by multi-skilling the operators, providing them with the necessary training and tools, then a lot of the work previously carried out exclusively by craftsmen could be done by the operators with big productivity gains.

The Irvine site has been one of the plants subject to an independent efficiency audit as part of its continuous monitoring and improvement programme. During the life of this project the rating has improved from 47 per cent in 1989, which was then viewed as slightly above average, to 89 per cent in 1992.

Market driven

These are changes that are necessary to react to or anticipate market trends, competitor activity or enter a new market.

CASE STUDY

BRITISH TELECOM

Managed Network Services is responsible for the business-to-business data networking and messaging products of BT. Managed Network Services is the market leader in the UK, with a turnover of around £150 million and 600 employees. The sector is now very competitive with new products and suppliers entering the market as a result of the competition policy of the UK government. The Managed Network Services accounting system was an old, heavily modified package that was dependent on downloading information to PC spreadsheets to produce meaningful reports. More importantly, the system was inflexible and had become incapable of producing the range of management information needed to run the business.

In order to react to, and anticipate, competitive pressures Managed Network Services needed to reduce its cost structure and build new management information systems. These systems had to be flexible and capable of delivering information directly to the line managers to enable them to react quickly in a fast-changing marketplace.

In parallel with the financial systems project a business process re-engineering exercise is being managed by the deputy director. Business process re-engineering identified the four main processes of the business as win business; provide service; provide after-service; and bill and collect. The early results of the business process re-engineering exercise were already demanding a fourth dimension to the general ledger coding system to capture process (or activity) costs as well as a requirement to focus the whole organization more on the customer.

Organizational

These are the changes that are needed to systems, processes and procedures of an organization resulting from:

- Take-overs and mergers
- Legislation
- Regulatory authority's directives
- Change in status
- Security of data.

BUSINESS NEEDS AND BENEFITS   53

CASE STUDY

TRENT REGIONAL HEALTH AUTHORITY
The year 1988 saw the start of the changes in the National Health Service initiated by the government. Until then the regional computer centre (RCC) had been funded by the regional health authority (RHA) offering a computing, system development and communication service to the RHA, district health authorities (DHAs) and hospitals. The RCC turnover was about £4 million per annum. The service included a number of packages that had been developed on a consortia basis by the RCC for use within the region (e.g. accounting, payroll, supplies, patient administration). A situation was building up where, on the one hand, the RHA was reluctant to invest in the RCC because it was no longer considered a core activity and, on the other, the RCC customers wanted to take ownership of their own IT and some of them were beginning to build up their own local IT expertise. The RCC was experiencing problems in retaining junior staff and was also being encouraged to compete for its work within the RHA. It was being hindered by not having the flexibility to change pay structures, nor being allowed to compete for work outside of the region and a lack of investment.

The regional general manager decided to investigate alternative funding arrangements for the RCC as the RHA was not prepared to invest any more money in it.

Risk management

Changes that are necessary to avoid a high-risk situation developing by:

- Anticipating changes in business circumstance
- Replacing old systems which are becoming unreliable, expensive to maintain or dependent on a declining skill base.

CASE STUDY

CASTLE CEMENT
Castle Cement Ltd is Britain's second largest cement producer with over 25 per cent of the market, 1200 employees and a capacity of over 3 million tonnes per year. Castle Cement was originally formed in 1982 as RTZ Cement through the acquisition of three cement companies. The new company was renamed Castle Cement in 1986 and then purchased in 1988 by Scancem Group Ltd, a 50:50 joint venture company between Aker a.s. of Norway and Euroc AB of Sweden.

In 1989 the company had five major sites, seven sales ledgers, seven purchase ledgers and nine general ledgers running on a ten-year-old accounting system at two data centres. The maintenance of these systems was dependent on two external contract programmers as the company no longer had any internal expertise. The financial director decided to replace the old systems and recruit an accountant to manage the selection and implementation.

Volume driven

These are changes that are needed to accommodate the processing of higher volumes.

Benefits

Definition

The benefits associated with a business need are the realizable advantages together with the time scales over which they will be achieved. Tangible benefits can be quantified and their impact on the organization measured. On the other hand, intangible benefits cannot be easily quantified but their impact on the organization can be just as great. It is normal that associated with any business need will be a mixture of both tangible and intangible benefits. Benefits are seen differently by different users within the organization, depending on how they see the changes and how they affect them.

> **EXAMPLE**
>
> The benefits of reducing stock locations, and therefore stock holdings, could be seen by the finance director as reducing working capital, the accountant as reducing stock provisions, the stores manager as improving efficiency and the distribution manager as improving customer service.

Types of tangible benefits

The following are some examples of different types of tangible benefits.

Capital

Quantifiable improvements in working capital.

> **CASE STUDY**
>
> YULE CATTO
>
> Yule Catto Building Products Division has a turnover of about £100 million and is part of Yule Catto. The Building Products Division was built up by acquisition and consists of seven companies in three European countries. These companies had a diverse range of systems running on eight different computers. The larger Speciality Chemical Division of Yule Catto had built up a strong tradition of using standard systems and senior management had appreciated the benefits in terms of both cost saving and the availability of consistent management information.
>
> The accounting, sales order processing, stock control, purchasing and costing systems of seven companies within the Building Products Division each

had their own local IT staff thus proving expensive to run and maintain. By 1990 it was clear to the Building Products Division that it would benefit from using standard systems and moving away from a hardware- to a software-led approach. It was decided to standardize on a package for supply chain management and to run the payroll on either a local PC or a local bureau.

The tangible benefit of replacing the eight different systems with one package was a significant cost saving. The new system could be supported by a small central team and there would no longer be any requirement for local IT staff. Further, the introduction of an integrated sales order processing and stock control system should realize significant stock reductions.

The intangible benefits of standardizing were consistent reporting to senior management; the knowledge that once a report had been produced by one company it could quickly and easily be produced by another; and the opportunity to understand better the cost structure of the Division to enable senior management to optimize manufacturing throughout Europe.

Compliance

Complying with required changes.

Costs

Measurable and quantifiable savings in labour, materials and/or overheads resulting in cost containment, cost reduction or productivity improvements.

BOLTON METRO — CASE STUDY
The business need was to anticipate the consequences of compulsory competitive tendering. The tangible benefits were to protect the interests of the staff and to *make significant revenue savings* for Bolton Metro.

Profitability

Quantifiable improvements in profitability as a result of, say, the ability to process higher volumes or increasing market share or reducing unit costs.

PEPE JEANS — CASE STUDY
The business need was to reduce significantly the operational costs of running the company by restructuring and implementing new integrated systems. The tangible benefits of implementing an integrated system and changing the way people work are to reduce the operational costs by eliminating the labour effort necessary to maintain system interfaces, and to eliminate the role of the information provider by providing management information directly to the end-users. The intentions were to halve the size of the accounting department and completely do away with the IT department, as it is not core to Pepe Jeans' business.

The project has been very successful to date. The size of the accounting department has reduced from 100 to 45, the IT department from 16 to two and the company is back in profit.

Service levels

Measurable improvements in service levels.

CASE STUDY

BIRMINGHAM CITY COUNCIL

In 1988 Birmingham City Council found itself with a large central IT unit of 200 staff and significant concern among the senior management team of the City Council about its performance. Birmingham City Council is one of the largest authorities in the UK and the largest individual city authority. Already the larger departments in the City had their own IT unit and had always been responsible for their own PCs and workstations. In order to achieve greater flexibility the city treasurer, with the support of the council members, decided to outsource the computer operations, communications network and the central development operations of the City. The intangible benefits were to:

- Anticipate the government's intentions to introduce compulsory competitive tendering throughout the public sector
- Improve the level of service to the user departments within the City, particularly for systems development
- Create a situation whereby the City could begin to divest from its old COBOL-based mainframe systems and utilize newer technologies, down-size applications where appropriate, and to use more packages
- Devolve the responsibility for IT to the user departments
- Reduce management time in running a large and complicated technical department.

At the end of the first year most of the anticipated benefits had been realized. Operational cost savings had been achieved and the development service had improved considerably.

Types of intangible benefits

By their very nature, intangible benefits are difficult to quantify but in many cases seem obvious. For example what are the benefits of improving customer service levels by 10 per cent? There could be a number of intangible benefits such as less time spent on dealing with customer queries and complaints, higher customer satisfaction, more new business recommendations from satisfied customers. However, whereas all these are beneficial, it is very difficult to quantify their impact on the bottom line. The following are some examples of different types of intangible benefits.

External

How an organization is viewed externally by the market, media, competitors, customers, shareholders and suppliers will affect sales, customer loyalty and recruitment. The potential external impact of a new project needs to be considered. Projects that are helping the organization to achieve technical excellence or cost leadership or improving service levels should have an obvious benefit. However, consideration should also be given to the potential down side. For example, if stocking points are being rationalized to reduce stock levels and increase customer service this might be seen by some customers, especially those close to a stocking point that is due to be closed, as a negative.

> **BOLTON METRO** — **CASE STUDY**
> The intangible benefits were to achieve more flexibility in the delivery of IT and to gain advantage from being the first authority in the North West to set up a facilities management arrangement.
>
> According to Peter Horrocks, IT manager of Bolton Metro and now manager of the new client support unit: 'We believe that we will benefit by being the first authority in the North West to commit to a facilities management arrangement as CFM are basing their new northern regional office in Bolton.'

Internal

Equally important is how an organization is viewed internally. How will the project be viewed? Will it improve internal service levels? Will it improve employee retention and morale? Will there be unquantifiable benefits from reduced paper flow, quicker access to information? Or will the impact be negative, downgrading jobs and career prospects?

> **BOLTON METRO** — **CASE STUDY**
> The business need was to anticipate the consequences of compulsory competitive tendering. The tangible benefits were to *protect the interests of the staff* and make significant revenue savings for Bolton Metro.

Management

The organization can be managed more effectively by:

- Improving management information
- Speeding up the flow of information
- Providing timely and consistent data which reconciles across systems eliminating arguments as to whose data is correct

- Decentralizing decision making
- Improving planning and budgeting cycles
- Introducing flexible systems that are able to respond to the changing needs of the organization and market pressures.

> **CASE STUDY**
>
> LEICESTER CITY COUNCIL
> In 1989 Leicester City Council found themselves in a situation with their three key financial applications, general ledger, accounts payable and accounts receivable running on three different computer platforms. Data was taking lots of effort to put in and even more effort to get out in a useful format. A six-month financial management information system study was commissioned from KPMG Peat Marwick that reported in late 1991. This report was accepted and it was decided that a new integrated system was needed to meet the needs of the Council in the 1990s.
>
> The primary need of the Council was to invest in a new management information system to increase overall efficiency and to devolve more financial management responsibility to individual departments.

Strategic

Long-term investments that are required resulting in:

- Speeding up to time to get a new product to market
- Improved market positioning
- Infrastructure investments in computer power, communications, office automation on the principle *get it right now, the savings will come later.*

> **CASE STUDY**
>
> PRUDENTIAL ASSURANCE
> The intangible benefits are first, moving the Prudential into a position to use point-of-sale technology and achieve efficiency benefits by linking the branch and back-office computer systems, and second, increasing sales by providing the representatives with much-improved customer account information leading to more effective prospecting. These conclusions were reached as a result of a prototype CIS tested in the field. The field trial also concluded that a CIS type system was an essential tool for a representative to do their job properly.

Business process re-engineering

Business process re-engineering is not the subject of this book. However, some IT projects will be as a direct result of business process re-engineering, and even if they are not, it is useful to take into account some of the business process re-engineering messages and techniques when identifying business needs and assessing benefits.

The essential message from business process re-engineering is that in order to achieve significant productivity improvements organizations must be viewed as a series of processes. Historically, most organizations are departmental with each department staffed by like people who perform roughly the same task that has been made as simple as possible. The result of all these individual tasks put together is complex and requires significant effort to manage. The final result of all the departments' efforts put together is very complex. By the very nature of the operation, many of these tasks are consecutive and therefore the result takes a long time to achieve, and normally no one person is responsible for achieving a complete task.

Taking a top-down approach, business process re-engineering redraws the organization as a series of processes (as against the traditional departmental structure). It then redesigns the systems and procedures around the processes trying to make each individual process as simple as possible (see Figure 5.2). Needless to say this approach is opposite to the traditional approach of most organizations that are trying to incrementally improve inter- and intra-departmental systems.

Benefits claimed by business process re-engineering are:

- Significant productivity improvements

- Creating parallel processes to accommodate standard and non-standard transactions making it easier to design systems and, more importantly, allowing simultaneous working to speed up the time taken to complete both standard and non-standard transactions

- Elimination of many departmental barriers

- Flattening the organization and making individuals accountable for their actions as each process is more results-oriented

- Changing the management and supervisory roles as day-to-day decision making is devolved to the teams and groups responsible for each process who are empowered to make decisions.

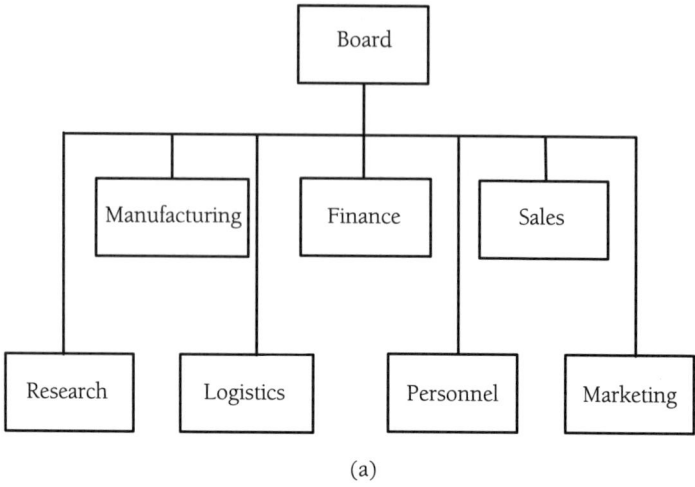

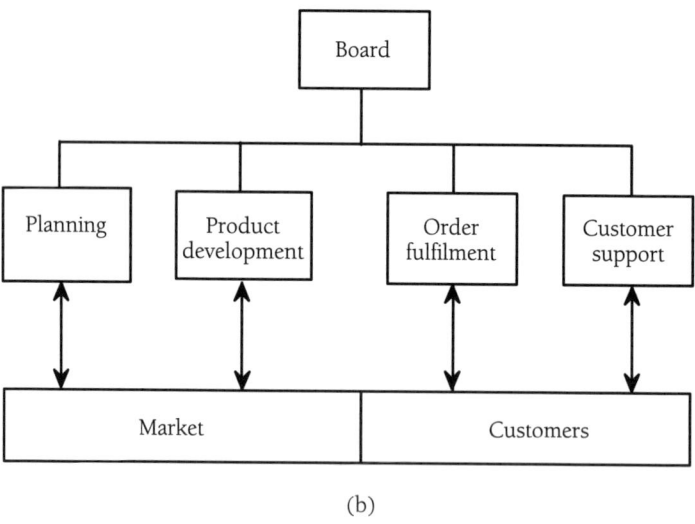

Figure 5.2 *(a) Traditional departmental organization. (b) Structure after business process re-engineering.*

SMITHKLINE BEECHAM **CASE STUDY**

The Chemical Division of SmithKline Beecham has five major production sites around the world and a number of smaller sites all working continuously. These sites were using a mixture of in-house-developed applications and packages for their maintenance management systems. However, they all faced the same issues of compliance with regulatory bodies; interfacing their maintenance management systems with condition base monitoring systems, financial systems and other systems; as well the introduction of total productive maintenance. In 1989 a worldwide project team was set up to decide an overall approach to engineering systems.

In parallel with this project a Divisional team was also looking ahead and applying business process re-engineering techniques. One of the areas being considered was the relationship between the operators of the plant and the tradesman and craftsman maintaining it. A number of the management team had visited Japan and were struck by the sense of ownership by the Japanese operators of their equipment. The Japanese operators took a wider view of their job and consequently were more efficient, as they could quickly sort out many of the jobs that in the UK required a craftsman. This was in stark contrast to the traditional way of working in the UK plants, that had a strong demarcation between the duties of the operators and tradesman. The project team concluded that by multi-skilling the operators, providing them with the necessary training and tools, a lot of the work previously carried out exclusively by craftsman could be done by the operators with big productivity gains.

The decision to change the method of working of the plant operators and craftsmen at the Irvine site needed careful planning to train the operators in their wider roles. Critically it was essential to win the cooperation of the craftsmen, who currently had all the skills, to help with the skills transfer. This was achieved by team working and the realization that their craft skills would also be enhanced as part of the initiative. Once the right atmosphere had been created the craftsmen relaxed and cooperated with helping to produce the multi-video tools necessary to train and help the operators in their wider role.

Another ramification of the business process re-engineering was the need to upgrade the IT systems with the resultant increase in IT staff. At the Irvine site the central IT *cell* of eight is responsible for strategy and coordination and competes with external suppliers for departmental business. Two of the key outcomes of the business process re-engineering are to flatten the organization and to devolve routine decision making to empowered workers. Fundamental to achieving these are information systems that can deliver the necessary information directly to the empowered worker, bringing only exceptions to the attention of management.

An interesting side effect of this is that management are not normally included in the information flow for the simple reason that the decision making has been devolved downwards and they did not need the information. It is essential therefore to implement a change management programme for management to adjust to the new way of working and the very different management responsibilities.

Identifying business needs and benefits

The sponsor, during the pre-feasibility phase, will have reached agreement as to the broad parameters within which the project will be working. The objective of the project team now is to define the business need in detail and identify benefits. This step is normally an interactive process between senior management and users coordinated by the project team.

The processes used to achieve the definition of business needs and identification of benefits are normally interviews with senior management and planning workshops.

Interviews

Properly prepared and structured interviews with relevant senior management and line managers are an effective method of direct communication. To set up the interview the interviewer should:

- Prepare questions in advance
- Notify the interviewee in advance of the time, place and duration of meetings, the purpose of the meeting, areas of discussion and likely questions
- Record the interview
- Send a minute of the interview to the interviewee for comments and agreement.

Typical questions are:

- What are your current areas of concern?
- What do you anticipate will be your areas of concern in the future?
- What are the key differences between now and what you see in the future?
- What changes do you need to satisfy your areas of concern?
- How do these changes fit into current business objectives and corporate priorities?
- How do you envisage achieving these changes?
- What are the short-term consequences?
- What are the long-term consequences?
- What do you anticipate are the critical success factors in achieving these changes?

- What are the tangible benefits of achieving these changes?
- Can you quantify them?
- What are the intangible benefits of achieving these changes?
- What is the impact if these changes are not achieved?

Planning workshops

Planning workshops can be a useful follow-on from direct interviews as more people can participate and a consensus formed as to the definition of the business needs and the benefits. For a workshop to be successful it must be prepared for carefully.

Preparation by project team

- Notify attendees in advance stating the time, place and duration of the meeting (typically all day); objectives of the workshop; agenda; preparation required by each attendee for the workshop (i.e. information requirements, research, pre-prepared presentation material)
- Consolidate information gathered from the interviews and distribute it in advance of the workshops to the attendees
- Decide on the techniques to be used during the workshop. A simple but effective technique to get things going and create a *brainstorming* atmosphere is SWOT (strengths, weaknesses, opportunities and threats). It enables each issue or situation to be analysed and discussed constructively by consecutively looking at its strengths, then its weaknesses, then the opportunities it creates and lastly the threats it presents. By highlighting the points raised a complete picture can quickly be built
- Decide on the technique to be used during the workshop to make decisions. How are the needs and benefits to be agreed? If SWOT is used then a lot of ideas will be raised, some good, some bad and some completely irrelevant. Once the brainstorming has run out of steam and the ideas, issues and points raised consolidated the final job is to prioritize them. A very successful way of doing this is to give each delegate a fixed number of votes that are allocated by the delegate to the consolidated list. The normal result is that the important points are quickly identified, the less important points will attract very few votes as will pet hobbyhorses and the workshop will achieve the necessary consensus. This technique, apart from achieving a consensus, encourages ideas and, of equal importance, allows them to be discussed and prioritized without the promoter of the idea losing face.

During the workshop

- Start the workshop with an overview of the current situation, analysis of interviews to date and a background briefing of any other relevant factors
- Continue with why the organization needs to change and where it needs to be in the future
- Create a conducive environment by having the necessary presentation aids available
- Be sure to have a good chairperson.

After the workshop (project team)

- Define the scope of the business needs
- List and quantify tangible benefits identified with their *owning* line management stating the assumptions made
- List intangible benefits identified
- List critical success factors
- Circulate the above to attendees for comment and approval
- Follow up on action points.

Summary of requirements (SOR)

CHAPTER 6

Critical success factors

When the business needs are agreed the next step is to define the outline requirements to meet these needs. The objective is to specify the scope and key functional requirements in straightforward business language. When the summary of requirements is agreed it is developed into a request for proposal that is used to short-list suppliers.

Critical success factors when preparing the summary of requirements are:

- Does the project team have the correct balance of skills to define the application, technical and management requirements?

- Is the scope of the project defined correctly?

CASE STUDY

The importance of defining the scope of the project as early as possible is more than adequately illustrated in Chapter 17 by the comparison between case study A and case study B. Case study A produced a short one-page document that was agreed by the users, set the correct level of expectation and led to a successful project. Case study B did not produce an agreed scope or requirements document and as a direct result did not set user expectations. This led to an on-going implementation with neither the users or the IT department knowing when the project was finished.

- Do the requirements accurately reflect our business needs?

EXAMPLE

For many years a major concern of the IT industry has been programmer productivity and still is in many large organizations that are dependent on bespoke systems. There are now many tools on the market that will increase programmer productivity. Following this line of requirement should result in an efficient system development department but does it meet the business need? The scenario assumes that programmers are required and that all that is necessary is to make them as productive as possible. Applying basic business process re-engineering might challenge these assumptions. It is very unlikely that the business need is to raise programmer productivity. Alternative requirements might therefore be application packages or tools that can be used by end users eliminating or reducing the use of programmers.

- Do the technical requirements fit in with our IT strategy?

> **CASE STUDY**
>
> CASTLE CEMENT
> The Castle Cement IT strategy is based on a Digital VAX platform. Sales order processing is viewed as a core system capable of delivering competitive advantage and therefore is an in-house bespoke-developed application. The advantage of this to Castle Cement is that first, the sales order processing meets their exact requirements, and second, as it is under their control it is capable of being enhanced quickly to meet new business opportunities. The financial systems, on the other hand, do not offer such obvious competitive advantage, and not wanting to re-invent the wheel, Castle Cement decided to evaluate packages.

- Is a quality review part of the preparatory procedures?

Summary of requirements

Definition

The summary of requirements is a short statement of key requirements to achieve the business need that is quickly and easily developed into a request for proposal.

Format

1 Introduction

The introduction is brief and to the point. It refers to business needs and anticipated benefits, outlines the purpose of the summary of requirements and covers the background (see Figure 6.1).

2 Scope

The scope defines the breadth of the requirement and usage.

> **CASE STUDY**
>
> YULE CATTO
> It was decided to standardize on a package for supply chain management and to run the payroll on either a local PC or a local bureau for the ten companies in Europe of the Building Products Division.

SUMMARY OF REQUIREMENTS 67

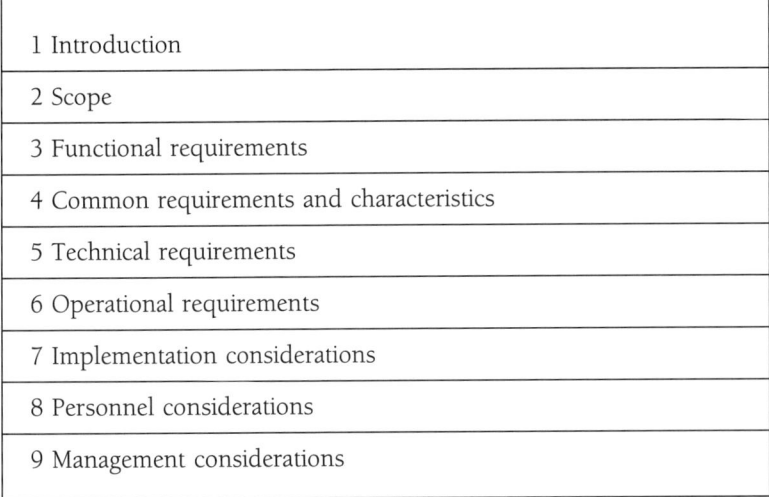

Figure 6.1 *Summary of requirements format.*

If the business need is for management information to be available at departmental level and the benefit better control of operating costs, then the requirement might be a general ledger system with a flexible chart of charts and an integrated budgeting and cost-allocation module. However, very quickly, on investigating the potential of general ledger packages and the implementation ramifications, decisions will have to be made on subsystems such as project costing, cash book and employee expenses. These decisions will significantly affect the scope of the project and its time scales and need to be managed carefully by the steering committee.

EXAMPLE

3 Functional requirements

This section is the core of the document. Requirements are grouped into functional areas describing each *key* requirement in non-technical user terms.

4 Common requirements and characteristics

This section states requirements that are common to all the functional requirements expressed in non-technical terms. In the case of software this section will contain requirements with respect to security options, report writer flexibility, screen painting and formatting, on-line access to data, drill down and zoom, electronic data interchange (EDI), integration with spreadsheets, workgroup applications, etc.

5 Technical requirements

This section states relevant technical requirements. In the case of a solutions-oriented summary of requirements then the technical requirements will be normally minimal as they will act as a restraint when the summary of requirements is developed into the request for proposal and issued to suppliers. If appropriate, then requirements for operating systems, database management systems, 4GL and back-up procedures are stated. In the case of a facilities management/outsourcing summary of requirements then the technical requirements specifies the hardware and software.

6 Operational requirements

This section states the operational requirements, i.e. number of users, transaction volumes, performance and service levels. Critically, it also states the flexibility required in the future.

7 Implementation considerations

This section outlines how and when the requirements will be implemented and interface/integration requirements with other systems as well as support required from suppliers both during and after the implementation.

8 Personnel considerations

This section addresses the personnel issues that will need to be addressed. Depending on the requirements, this will include project team training, user training, employment of new staff, redeployment of existing staff, redundancies or the transfer of staff. This section is not normally carried forward as part of the request for proposal.

9 Management considerations

This section identifies the management issues that will need to be addressed and is not normally carried forward as part of the request for proposal.

Preparing the summary of requirements

Researching the summary of requirements

Prior to setting up the project team it is likely that during the pre-feasibility phase a lot of informal research will take place. Typically, this will be a mixture of reviewing existing applications and looking outside the organization for ideas. It should be possible to form a view of current trends and available solutions by availing oneself of the multiple sources of information:

- Discussing ideas with suppliers at trade shows and suppliers' seminars
- Attending conferences and subject oriented workshops
- Visiting known reference sites
- Articles in the national, technical and trade press
- Advice from consultants
- Competitor activity.

Preparing the summary of requirements

The project team should now have sufficient information to prepare a first draft summary of requirements based on the definition of the business need, preliminary research and the knowledge inherent in the project team. When preparing the summary of requirements the key factors are:

- Only define key requirements (detailed requirements are prepared later in the process and issued only to short-listed suppliers)
- Describe key requirements in straightforward non-technical terms
- Focus on the business need, use imagination to look forward to where the organization will be or should be when the solution is implemented, do not simply restate existing systems and procedures
- The summary of requirements can be as short as one page but more likely will be two or three pages.

When preparing the first draft any gaps in the knowledge of the project team will quickly become apparent. These are normally filled by either interviews with users and management or roundtable discussions with the relevant parties. Occasionally, for a large project or in a large organization, surveys are appropriate. However, surveys are generally better suited to assist in specifying detailed requirements and are covered more thoroughly in Chapter 10.

Before the draft summary of requirements is finalized it is important to test out the project team's view of the requirements and achieve the necessary consensus of users and management to proceed. A good method of achieving this is to run a conference room pilot.

Conference room pilot

This is a structured work-through of the requirements. Like the workshop, for it to be successful it must be prepared for carefully.

Preparation by project team

- Notify attendees (users, management and the project team) in advance stating the time, place and duration of the meeting (typically 1-2 days); the objective of the conference room pilot; and the agenda
- Prepare schematics of the requirements broadly following the format and content of the summary of requirements.

During the conference room pilot

- Start the conference room pilot by giving an overview of the business needs and projected tangible and intangible benefits
- Define the purpose of the conference room pilot and the roles of the attendees, namely to review, test, comment on and agree the summary of requirements
- Create a conducive environment by having the necessary presentation aids available
- Structure the conference room pilot in five sessions:
    1. Introduction
    2. Key requirements
    3. Technical and operational requirements
    4. Implementation considerations
    5. Personnel, management and training issues.

After the conference room pilot (project team)

- Follow up on action points
- Reissue the summary of requirements for final agreement
- Review critical success factors.

Conference room pilots are normally successful and can play a key role in correctly identifying requirements and thinking through any ramifications. An advantage of a conference room pilot is that as a result of the preparatory work by the project team, that might well include building small prototypes, the abstract nature of software is made more tangible, allowing users and managers to decide more quickly on their requirements.

Quality review of the summary of requirements

The summary of requirements is the foundation document of the evaluation and selection process. The scope of the requirement, application and technical requirements and implementation considerations will control and influence the selection of options and the detail work to follow. It is therefore essential, that, as far as possible, this document accurately reflects the requirements of the organization. An error at this stage, or a change in the scope of a key requirement later in the process or, worse still, after the implementation has started, is expensive to correct. It is therefore advisable to commission an independent review to check that the project is on track before proceeding to the subsequent steps of formally contacting potential suppliers and building a business case.

Terms of reference for the quality review are to confirm that:

- The project team is following its own quality plan, is adequately resourced and is maintaining good internal communications
- The summary of requirements complies with standards and procedures
- The business needs are relevant to current business objectives and corporate priorities
- The benefits are agreed by *owning* users and management
- The scope of the project is defined
- The key requirements are defined and relevant to the business needs
- The risks have been properly assessed.

The importance of this quality review cannot be overstated. Projects with poorly defined benefits will probably not be and should not be approved. Those with poorly defined requirements and an ambiguous scope will prove to be very difficult to manage. This is because the boundaries of the proposed solution are vague and levels of expectation for users and management not clearly set and therefore open to interpretation.

CHAPTER 7

Request for proposal (RFP)

Critical success factors

The major part of the request for proposal is brought forward from the summary of requirements. The success of the request for proposal is therefore dependent on the successful completion of the summary of requirements and the additional work necessary to create the request for proposal. Critical success factors when preparing the request for proposal are:

- Does the request for proposal effectively convey our business requirements to potential suppliers enabling them to respond quickly and efficiently?

- Does the suppliers section of the request for proposal clearly state our requirements from suppliers?

Request for proposal

Definition

The request for proposal is a concise document that is issued to potential suppliers outlining the organization's requirements to enable potential suppliers to respond quickly and efficiently.

Objective

The objective of the request for proposal is to collect budgetary costs and enable the organization to select an initial short-list of suppliers based on their responses to the request for proposal.

Format

1 Introduction

The introduction is based on the original introduction to the internal summary of requirements enhanced so that it is clear to an external supplier. It introduces your organization to a potential supplier, gives essential background information and the reason for the procurement, outlines the purpose and structure of the request for proposal and states what comes next (see Figure 7.1).

1	Introduction
2	Scope
3	Functional requirements
4	Common requirements and characteristics
5	Technical requirements
6	Operational requirements
7	Implementation considerations
8	Supplier requirements

9	Instructions to suppliers
	  9.1 Terms and conditions (t&cs)
	  9.2 Timetable
	  9.3 User and technical contacts and procedures
	  9.4 Evaluation criteria
	  9.5 Format of suppliers' response
	      9.5.1 Management summary
	      9.5.2 Products and services proposed
	      9.5.3 Schedule of costs and suppliers' response on t&cs
	      9.5.4 Detailed response
	      9.5.5 Company overview and financial statement
	      9.5.6 Product overviews
	      9.5.7 Company experiences
	      Suppliers' appendices

Figure 7.1 *Request for proposal format.*

2 Scope

(Note: This section is carried forward from the summary of requirements.) The scope defines the breadth of the requirement and usage.

3 Functional requirements

(Note: This section is carried forward from the summary of requirements.) This section is the core of the document. Requirements are grouped into functional areas describing each *key* requirement in non-technical user terms.

4 Common requirements and characteristics

(Note: This section is carried forward from the summary of requirements.) This section states requirements that are common to all the functional requirements expressed in non-technical terms. In the case of software this section will contain requirements with respect to security options, report writer flexibility, screen painting and formatting, on-line access to data, drill down and zoom, electronic data interchange (EDI), integration with spreadsheets, workgroup applications, etc.

5 Technical requirements

(Note: This section is carried forward from the summary of requirements.) This section states relevant technical requirements. In the case of a solutions-oriented request for proposal then the technical requirements will be normally minimal as they will act as a restraint. If appropriate then requirements for operating systems, database management systems, 4GL and back-up procedures are stated. In the case of a facilities management/ outsourcing request for proposal then the technical requirements specifies the hardware and software.

6 Operational requirements

(Note: This section is carried forward from the summary of requirements.) This section states the operational requirements, i.e. number of users, transaction volumes, performance and service levels. Critically, it also states the flexibility required in the future.

7 Implementation considerations

(Note: This section is carried forward from the summary of requirements.) This section outlines how and when the requirements will be implemented and interface/integration requirements with other systems as well as support required from suppliers both during and after the implementation.

8 Supplier requirements

This section contains questions about the supplier that are not included in the summary of requirements, i.e.

- Suppliers' organization
- Personnel policies
- Compliance with BS 5750 and other relevant standards
- Implementation capability
- Service levels achieved.

9 Instructions to suppliers

9.1 Terms and conditions (t&cs)
This section indicates the terms and conditions that will probably apply to any subsequent procurement. They could be special terms and conditions for this procurement (particularly important for facilities management and outsourcing selections); standard terms and conditions; relevant terms and conditions from the Chartered Institute of Purchasing & Supply (available from the CIPS Book Shop, Easton House, Easton on the Hill, Stamford PE9 3NZ, telephone 01780 56777); or it could be the intention to use suppliers' terms and conditions. Other items to include in this section are:

- Any constraints on suppliers
- Any preference for particular types of bids and whether partial bids are acceptable
- Any mandatory requirements not covered or not obvious in previous sections
- A disclaimer not to be liable for any suppliers' costs prior to contract
- A confidentiality clause to cover information released to potential suppliers during the evaluation and selection process.

9.2 Timetable
This section states the summary timetable for the procurement with clear instructions as to the procedures and date by when suppliers' proposals must be received and how many copies are required.

9.3 User and technical contacts and procedures
This section states the user and technical contacts that are to be used while

the suppliers are preparing their proposals as well as any requirements for presentations and demonstrations.

9.4 Evaluation criteria

This section outlines how the suppliers' proposals will be evaluated, i.e.

- Quality of proposal
- Functional fit
- Financial stability and track record
- Product range
- Support organization, resources and skill levels.

9.5 Format of suppliers' response

9.5.1 Management summary

This section summarizes key aspects of the suppliers' proposal.

9.5.2 Products and services proposed

This section contains an outline specification of all products and services proposed and a schedule of all software proposed.

9.5.3 Schedule of cost and suppliers' response on terms and conditions

A schedule of costs that can be quantified at this stage highlighting areas of costs that are difficult to estimate, e.g. software amendments, implementation.

One-off costs

- Computer hardware
- Communication equipment
- Software licences
- Software modifications
- Implementation and training
- Project management
- Services

On-going costs

- Computer hardware support and maintenance
- Communication equipment support and maintenance
- Software licences
- Software support and maintenance
- Project management

- Services

Standard discounts available for multiple purchases.

This section must also contain the suppliers' response to the terms and conditions and any special requirements and/or conditions of the suppliers' proposal, e.g. environmental needs (air-conditioned computer room, networking infrastructure), pre-loaded software (database management system, 4GLs).

9.5.4 Detailed response

This section must include a detailed response to Sections 3-7 of the request for proposal.

9.5.5 Company overview and financial statement

This section includes an overview of the company together with appropriate financial statements.

9.5.6 Product overviews

This section contains a paragraph giving an overview of each product or service proposed.

9.5.7 Company experiences

This section contains details of the suppliers' previous experience in similar industries or market sectors, similar projects, numbers of users and reference sites.

Appendices.

This section contains relevant brochures, product literature, software licences and suppliers' standard terms and conditions.

Preparing the request for proposal

Planning the request for proposal

The use of the request for proposal can vary. In the process described in this book it is assumed that the request for proposal is a pre-selection document that enables the project team to produce the initial short-list. The request for proposal is then followed by the invitation to tender that is issued to the suppliers on the initial short-list. If the invitation to tender is fulfilling a different function then the objective of the request for proposal needs to be reconsidered.

Preparing the request for proposal

The major part of the request for proposal is brought forward from the summary of requirements. The differences are the introduction, supplier requirements and supplier instructions. Preparing these should be a straightforward task for the project team, perhaps assisted by the purchasing department. Bearing in mind that one of the key objectives of the request for proposal is to enable suppliers to respond quickly then it is advisable to keep the request for proposal as informal as possible, perhaps to the extent of omitting altogether the instructions to suppliers section.

Short-listing options and suppliers

CHAPTER 8

Introduction

The selection of options and suppliers is a three-step process (see Figure 8.1). The first step is to decide which type of solution is being sought. Frequently this decision is so obvious that it is not a consideration. The supply options when looking for an IT solution are broadly:

- Internal
- Software houses/software authors/software publishers
- Hardware manufacturers
- Distributors or dealers
- Value-added resellers
- Systems integrators
- Facilities management/outsourcing suppliers
- Third-party maintenance companies
- Consultants.

It is reasonable to consider one or more types of supply when looking for a solution especially as some of the suppliers can easily be categorized more than once.

EXAMPLE

A small government department looking for a turnkey stock control system approached its traditional computer hardware suppliers with their requirement. Needless to say, the suppliers were keen to help and initiated a series of meetings and introductions. After six months the department came to the conclusion that it was getting nowhere. It retained a consultant to review the situation who immediately put them in touch with the leading software houses in this field. A normal evaluation and procurement followed with a satisfactory conclusion. However, the department had lost six months by not selecting the right option in the first place from which to look for a solution.

80 GOOD BUYS IN IT

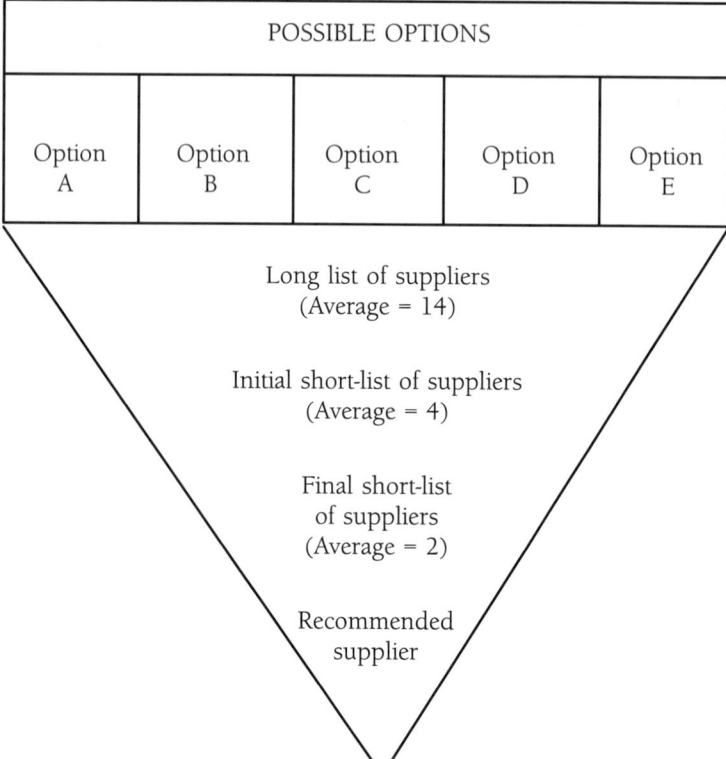

Figure 8.1 *Selecting options and suppliers.*

The products and services available are:

- Application software packages (e.g. accounts packages, word processing)
- System software products (e.g. operating systems, database management systems, 4GLs)
- Turnkey solutions
- Computers and peripherals
- Communications equipment
- Services to develop new bespoke systems or to re-engineer old ones
- Services to integrate complex requirements
- Facilities management services for data centres, communications networks, helpdesks, systems and program maintenance

- Outsourcing of business process (this differs from facilities management in so much as the outsourcer also takes ownership of the assets involved)
- Hardware services to maintain computers, peripherals and communications equipment.

Re-engineering of computer systems is not the same as business process re-engineering. Re-engineering is rebuilding the application, frequently automatically, in a new environment that probably has a lower cost of ownership. The advantage of re-engineering is that the system retains the same look and feel so that it can continue to be used without any end-user retraining. The disadvantage is that it does not move the organization forward, other than saving operating costs, and potentially creates a problem for the future as the re-engineered system might be difficult and expensive to maintain.

The second step is to issue the request for proposal to the suppliers on the long-list, evaluate their responses and to produce the initial short-list of viable suppliers.

The third step is to issue detailed requirements, probably in the form of an invitation to tender, to the suppliers on the initial short-list inviting detailed and considered responses for final evaluation and recommendation (see Chapters 10-14).

The reason for this structured approach is to optimize the time of both the project team and the suppliers. The request for proposal enables suppliers to be pre-selected and for the project team to concentrate on the suppliers most likely to deliver the best solution. The request for proposal also prepares the ground for the suppliers. Suppliers are traditionally wary of unexpected and unsolicited invitation to tenders that demand a lot of work in a short period of time, suspecting that the selection is predetermined and that they are just making up the numbers!

Critical success factors

Critical success factors in short-listing options and suppliers are:

- Have we selected the right options?
- Have we long-listed the right potential suppliers to issue the request for proposal?
- Have we followed the correct procedures when we issued the request for proposal (particularly important to the public sector and some parts of industry who are subject to EU and GATT regulations)?
- Have the most likely suppliers responded to the request for proposal?

- Do we understand our key requirements well enough to differentiate between suppliers?
- Will our evaluation model and procedures produce the best initial short-list?

Supply options

The first step, prior to building a list of potential suppliers for the long-list, is to decide what type of suppliers to send the request for proposal. It is not necessary or desirable to decide on only one option at this early stage. In a solutions-oriented approach it is essential not to eliminate potential options. If the selection of the options is not obvious then it is up to the judgement of the project team and the steering committee which are the most suitable.

Suppliers can broadly be categorized as follows. (However, it must be noted that some of the larger suppliers fall into more than one category.)

Internal

Internal suppliers are, by definition, part of the same organization that is looking for an IT solution. They could be a local IT department or a corporate IT department probably supplying system development and computer processing services. The difference between insourcing and outsourcing is that when insourcing, the user is responsible for the delivery and the supplier provides the necessary tools and people; when outsourcing the supplier is responsible for the delivery and the user responsible for the specification. When considering facilities management and outsourcing then internal options include management buy-outs and buy-ins.

Software houses

Software houses can be categorized into application software package authors, systems software authors and software services companies that develop bespoke applications and re-engineer old ones. Most application package authors sell directly to the end user, but some also distribute their products on a non-exclusive basis via value-added resellers, system integrators and manufacturers. They will also supply a turnkey solution consisting of their software and services plus the necessary additional software and hardware to provide a total solution to the customer.

System software authors distribute their products by all channels. Key factors, to the software house, when deciding the best distribution channel are the selling price of the product, the amount of effort required to sell it and the amount of post-sale support required. Software services companies deal directly with their customers and frequently act as system integrators.

Software publishers

Software publishers distribute their products by all channels. Frequently they are supplied automatically with a new computer, or incorporated by software houses and value-added resellers in their products. Their products are available via distributors or dealers.

Hardware manufacturers

Hardware manufacturers design and manufacturer computers, peripherals such as printers and disk drives and communications equipment. They distribute their products directly and via distributors, dealers and value-added resellers. Broadly, the higher the value of the product, the more likely it is to be supplied by the manufacturer, a systems integrator, or a value-added reseller. Hardware manufacturers also act as systems integrators and turnkey solution providers.

Distributors and dealers

Distributors and dealers sell hardware, application software and systems software that does not require significant pre- or post-sales support to both end users and value-added resellers.

Value-added resellers

As the name implies, value-added resellers add value to the products that they are selling. This frequently takes the form of expertise in vertical markets supported by additional software products for those markets. The value-added reseller is frequently the delivery point of contact with the customer, supplying hardware, licensed software from software authors and the expertise to make it work.

Systems integrators

Systems integrators specialize in high-value complex deals. The function of the integrator is to ensure that the solution works. This normally means that the systems integrator is the prime contractor with all the other suppliers subcontracting to the systems integrator. The systems integrator does not have to supply any product, their role is to manage the project on behalf of the user and to take the risk. Alternatively, the systems integrator can act only in a project management role, in which case the customer will contract directly with the suppliers and the systems integrator paid an agreed fee to manage the project.

Facilities management/outsourcing suppliers

Facilities management suppliers manage hardware facilities and systems development and maintenance resources on behalf of their clients. This does not include acquiring the hardware but will normally involve the facilities management company employing the relevant staff. Facilities management agreements are normally for a fixed period of time and can be either on- or off-site. There are arguments both for and against on- and off-site. Factors to take into account are future flexibility, cost, staff considerations, service levels, user requirements and the availability of accommodation.

Outsourcing suppliers provide a range of IT and other services for their clients, frequently initiated by the outsourcing company acquiring the hardware facilities and employing the staff of their client. In this respect the only difference between facilities management and outsourcing is that the outsourcing supplier owns the hardware. When the outsourcing suppliers owns the hardware and the software and is therefore providing a service in which the customer has no proprietary interests, then this type of service is frequently referred to as transaction processing or managed services. Examples outside the IT industry of transaction processing and managed services are security, distribution and cleaning; an example of facilities management is industrial catering.

Third-party maintenance companies (TPMs)

Third-party maintenance companies maintain hardware they do not manufacture. There are two types of third-party maintenance companies: independent companies who do not manufacture anything and who might specialize in either one manufacturer's equipment or in one type of hardware (e.g. PCs and desktops) and manufacturers who offer multi-vendor services maintaining their own and other manufacturers' hardware.

Consultants

Consultants are normally independent of any of the suppliers and offer a range of services covering consultancy, planning, business process re-engineering, quality assurance, project management, selection, systems development and implementation.

Table 8.1 is a simple guide as to which supply options to take depending on the nature of the requirement. The options to consider will vary from project by project. The two case studies below illustrate the point.

Table 8.1

Requirement	Supply options
Application software packages	
Multi-user	Package authors
	Value-added resellers
	Computer manufacturers
Shrink wrapped	If not supplied with the computer, then distributors or dealers
Systems software products	If not supplied with the computer or solution then the package authors, or distributors or dealers
Turnkey solutions	Software authors
	Value-added resellers
	Hardware manufacturers
	System integrators if large and complex
Computers and peripherals	Original supplier, manufacturers, distributors, or dealers
Communications equipment/ network services	Original supplier, manufacturers, distributors, or dealers
Bespoke application development	Internal
	Software houses
	Systems integrators
	Computer manufacturers
Re-engineer old systems	Internal
	Software houses
	Systems integrators
	Computer manufacturers
Integrate complex requirements	Internal
	Systems integrators
	Computer manufacturers
Facilities management/outsourcing	Facilities management and outsourcing suppliers
Hardware maintenance	Manufacturers
	Third-party maintenance companies

CASE STUDY

PRUDENTIAL ASSURANCE

A detailed requirements' specification was prepared. The requirements included:

- Specification of the standard packages required and bespoke developments to build the CIS system
- Specification of system software to build the new client/server branch platform consisting of PC WINDOWS clients and UNIX servers in each branch connected to the back-office IBM mainframe computer
- Specification of the PC clients and UNIX server computers
- Specification of the development tools to build the bespoke application software
- Specification of the system software to manage the new branch platform environment (ensuring that no technical skill was needed in the branch and that the new environment could be managed remotely by the central IT department).

Of the various options available, the Prudential decided to:

- Build a bespoke system based on the earlier prototype for the account management, portfolio management and prospecting components of the CIS
- Evaluate packages for the word processing and spreadsheet components of the CIS
- Build and integrate the system management software as it had already been determined that there was not yet a suitable comprehensive package available
- Evaluate and select the database software, tools and hardware necessary to create the new branch platform
- Manage the project in-house and not use a system integrator.

CASE STUDY

TRENT REGIONAL HEALTH AUTHORITY

During the last few months of 1988 various options were explored and considerable effort was put into finding a partner. However, these came to nothing as the RHA was not prepared to share the risks and rewards nor was it empowered to set up a joint company. It was therefore decided to sell (or outsource) the computer operations and systems development of the RCC to a suitably qualified purchaser but to retain ownership of the data communications network. Consideration was given to a management buy-out. However, this option was rejected as it was felt the new company would need strong management, marketing and sales skills to survive, which were not present in the RCC.

Identifying suppliers

Once the options have been agreed by the project team and steering committee a list of potential suppliers can be made up from a wide number of sources:

- Suppliers' responses to notices in official journals
- Hardware, software and services directories like *The Software Users Year Book* and *The Computer Users Year Book* from VNU Business Publications, 32-34 Broadwick Street, London, W1A 2HG, telephone 0171 439 4242 and International Computer Programs, Inc., 823 East Westfield Boulevard, Indianapolis, IN 46220, USA, telephone (001) 317 251 7727 or from their UK distributor, Engineering Information Services, 63 Edendale Road, Melton Mowbray, LE13 0EW, telephone 01664 60951
- Software directories that are published by major computer hardware manufacturers and database management and 4GL suppliers listing the application packages available on their platform
- Supplier advertisements in trade magazines and journals
- Trade exhibitions
- Consultants' advice
- Previous experience of project team members
- Information from independent research organizations like the Gartner Group UK Limited, Parkside House, 33-39 Sheet Street, Windsor, Berkshire, SL4 1BY, telephone 01753 831122
- Professional institutions like the Institute of Chartered Accountants, PO Box 433, Chartered Accountants Hall, Moorgate Place, London, EC2P 2BJ, telephone 0171 628 7060, who publish a list of recommended products and functional checklists
- The Dennis Keeling Partnership, Templestowe, Longbottom Lane, Sear Green, Beaconsfield, Buckingham, HP9 2UL, telephone 01494 680907 who publish *profiles* of business and accounting packages
- Specialized guides like the *UNIX Software Directory* from Pinpoint Response Ltd, Farrier House, 223 High Street, Henley-in-Arden, Solihull, B95 5BG, telephone 01564 795046
- It is also probable that computer-assisted short-listing systems will be available during 1995.

An analysis of the case studies researched for this book indicate that most organizations (62 per cent) prepared the long-list of potential suppliers themselves using a mixture of the sources above without seeking external advice The minority of organizations (38 per cent) took professional advice or went out to public tender. The average number of suppliers on the long-list is 14.

Issue request for proposal to suppliers

When the long-list is decided, whether by public notice as is necessary for organizations subject to EU and GATT regulations, or simply determined by the project team, the request for proposal is issued to suppliers. It is reasonable to allow five to ten working days for the suppliers to respond, providing, of course, that the request for proposal is short. In some circumstances the task of issuing the request for proposal and receiving the responses is handled by the purchasing department, but as often as not it is done by the project team. Be prepared to answer suppliers' questions arising from the request for proposal.

Evaluation models

Prior to issuing the request for proposal to the suppliers on the long-list it is essential that the project team agree the short-listing criteria with the steering committee. Once this has been done the necessary models are quickly built. The overall balance of the request for proposal suppliers' evaluation model is critical and must reflect the business needs and requirements. The objective is to use the criteria to reduce the long-list of suppliers to an initial short-list. An analysis of the case studies researched for this book show that the average long-list of 14 is reduced to an initial short-list of four potential suppliers at this stage.

The following is a list of criteria to consider when preparing for this step of the selection process. The starting point for determining the criteria is the request for proposal which has in turn been prepared from the summary of requirements that should reflect the business needs and requirements.

Functional requirements

What are your key functional requirements that will help you to differentiate between one supplier's products and services and those of another? The difficulty and different methods of selecting an initial short-list of application software suppliers is illustrated between the two case studies of Yule Catto and British Telecom. In the case of Yule Catto the requirements to meet the needs of the business were very clear, making short-listing relatively easy. In British Telecom, requiring a more horizontal solution, the short-listing was more difficult and necessitated a functional checklisting approach.

SHORT-LISTING OPTIONS AND SUPPLIERS

YULE CATTO

The 20-page invitation to tender detailed the functional requirements of the various modules required. However, in order to meet the business need the following key requirements were all important:

- An international package that could meet the varying requirements of the European operating companies
- A modern package that will continue to meet the requirements of the Division in the future
- A UNIX-based solution that could run on Hewlett-Packard, the preferred computer hardware supplier
- A black-box solution, without any bespoke changes, that could be run at each operating company without the need for any local IT staff and backed by a supplier who could support each operating company directly
- A package that could meet the key functional requirements of the building industry in configuring products to customers' specifications
- Flexible software pricing to reflect the differing sizes of the operating companies, i.e. from an eight- to a 64-user licence.

CASE STUDY

The options had been pre-selected in that an international package was required from a software house with Hewlett-Packard as the preferred computer hardware manufacturer.

A long-list of potential software suppliers was drawn up by inviting each operating company's financial director to suggest possible suppliers based on their local research. The long-list was reviewed by the head office project team who quickly produced an initial short-list of three software houses based on the key requirements above.

BRITISH TELECOM

A 20-page statement of requirements was developed on a consensus basis with the user departments. The statement of requirements mainly took the form of a functional checklist.

The old system was running in a Hewlett-Packard UNIX environment and the decision was taken to continue in this environment with ORACLE as the BT standard database management system. The evaluation process was therefore to select an application package, running in this environment, to be implemented by the project team in conjunction with the successful supplier.

A long-list of twelve potential suppliers was drawn up based on the personal knowledge of the project team members, analysis of *The Software Users Year Book*, independent research and advice from the external consultant. These twelve suppliers were issued the invitation to tender and given three weeks to reply.

In parallel with issuing the invitation to tender an evaluation model was prepared to score the responses. Each item on the invitation to tender was allocated a weighting that was scored between 0 and 10 depending on the functionally match and its availability, i.e. 7–10 available in the current release, 2–5 due in the next release, 0 not available. The total scores for each section were then reduced to fit into the overall model:

CASE STUDY

Common requirements	13%	
Technical requirements	10%	
Reporting requirements	16%	
Security requirements	5%	44%
General ledger	12.5%	
Accounts receivable	12%	
Accounts payable	9%	
Fixed assets	7.5%	
Cash book	5%	
Project management	10%	56%
Total		100%

The mechanical scoring of the responses to the invitation to tender produced an initial short-list of four.

Common requirements and characteristics

What are your key common requirements and characteristics that will help you to differentiate between one supplier's products and services and those of another (e.g. report writer, integration with spreadsheets, electronic data interchange)?

Technical requirements

What are your key technical requirements that will help you to differentiate between one supplier's products and services and those of another (e.g. future flexibility; preference for a particular operating platform, database management system or 4GL)?

Operational requirements

What are your key operational requirements that will help you to differentiate between one supplier's products and services and those of another (e.g. standby arrangements, service levels)?

Implementation considerations

What are your key implementation considerations that will help you to differentiate between one supplier's products and services and those of another (e.g. previous experience in similar implementations, capacity and flexibility of resources, multinational support)?

Supplier requirements

What are your key supplier requirements that will help you to differentiate between one supplier and another (e.g. stability, track record, position of the supplier's products or services within their natural life cycle, product range, future flexibility, compliance with terms and conditions, personnel policies)?

When the criteria have been established the next step is to decide the relative importance of each individual criterion to the total, risk factors and the rules for applying the criterion. Relative importance and risk factors are taken into account in the evaluation model below. The critical decision is the balance of the request for proposal supplier's evaluation model. Rules and guidelines are required for the following when evaluating the supplier's response to the request for proposal:

- Guidelines to ensure consistent scoring
- How to react to non-compliance of mandatory requirements
- When selecting products in particular deciding where you want to be in the products' natural life cycle. At the beginning and potentially gaining competitive advantage and a long usage but at the risk of sorting out early teething problems? In the middle, when any early problems have been sorted out? Or at the end, when the functionality of the product is high, the price coming down and the technology ageing?

Whether a formal evaluation model is required depends entirely on the nature of the project and how difficult it is to produce the initial short-list of suppliers. The three individual models illustrated in Tables 8.2–8.4 comprise the total model. The lowest model in the hierarchy is matrix at functional item level by supplier. This model feeds into a supplier model, reducing where necessary the functional scores on a pro rata basis to the score allowed in the overall model. This supplier model then feeds into a supplier summary model to give the final comparative positions. At this stage the evaluation model places little emphasis on costs. The objective is to short-list viable solutions and, at the same time, gather the necessary cost estimates for the preparation of the business case. Costs are taken into account during the business case preparation and evaluation.

Evaluate suppliers' responses

The type of project will generally determine how the suppliers' responses are evaluated. The quickest method is to evaluate the responses without any supplier contact and then invite those suppliers on the provisional initial short-list to present their solution. This should answer any questions

92 GOOD BUYS IN IT

Table 8.2 Request for proposal functional item evaluation model

RFP cross-ref.	Requirement	Max. score	Supplier scores					
			A	B	C	D	E	etc.
3.3.1	Multi-currency sales ledger	5	2	5	5	0	4	
3.3.2 etc.	Cash flow forecasting	5	0	4	5	3	2	
3.	Functional requirements Subtotal	200	110	164	180	88	123	
	Multiply by 250/200=1.25 to carry forward to supplier's model	250	138	205	225	110	154	

Notes

1. The maximum score in this example is 5, with marking rules of 5 for good response, 4 for satisfactory response, 2 for a requirement that can be satisfied in the future, 1 for requirement that requires a modification and 0 for non-compliance.
2. It is probable that the subtotals, corresponding to the criteria in the supplier's model, will not agree, in which case the subtotal is factored accordingly. The advantage of this scoring system is that any number of functional items can be added with the result that the subtotal in this model can be either very large or very small. This does not necessarily reflect its importance which is taken into account by the factor used to carry the total through to the supplier's model. For example a functional section with many items, but of minor importance, might have a high score in this model but be reduced when carried forward to the supplier's model, whereas a small section, of major importance, will be increased. In the table the functional score of 164 scored by supplier B is multiplied by the factor of 1.25, giving a total of 205 to be carried forward to the supplier's model.

SHORT-LISTING OPTIONS AND SUPPLIERS 93

Table 8.3 Request for proposal supplier's evaluation model (supplier B)

Criteria	Max. Score	Risk (Note 1)	Weighted score	Evaluation score	Notes
Functional requirements	250	0.8	205	164	2
Common requirements and characteristics	150	0.8	131	105	2
Technical and operational requirements	100	0.9	72	65	2
Implementation considerations	50	0.9	41	37	2
Supplier requirements	50	1.0	45	45	3
Product range and flexibility	100	0.7	80	56	4
Supplier stability	150	1.0	135	135	3
Supplier track record	100	1.0	90	90	3
Compliance to terms and conditions and cost of proposal	50	1.0	42	42	3
Totals	1000			739	

Notes
1. Risk is a subjective factor decided by the project team for each of the criteria in the supplier's model. The risk factor range in this example is 0-1, with the assessment rules of 1.0 for a very low risk, ranging to 0.5 for a high-risk criterion.
2. A new product with good functional specification but with obvious concern over its reliability and ease of implementation.
3. A major supplier with a good track record and no concern about stability.
4. The product range looks good on paper but as it is not yet complete there is some concern over when it will be available.

Table 8.4 Request for proposal summary evaluation model

Criteria	Max. score	Suppliers A	B	C	D	E	etc.
Functional requirements	250		164				
Common requirements and characteristics	150		105				
Technical and operational requirements	100		65				
Implementation considerations	50		37				
Supplier requirements	50		45				
Product range and flexibility	100		56				
Supplier stability	150		135				
Supplier track record	100		90				
Compliance to terms and conditions and cost of proposal	50		42				
Totals	1000		739				

from the suppliers' responses and enable the suppliers to be confirmed on the initial short-list. The objective of this step is to produce the initial short-list of suppliers and collect budgetary costs for the business case. The detailed evaluation of product, services or suppliers comes later. The key guidelines for dealing with suppliers at this stage are:

- Ensure that everyone within your organization who is likely to have any dealings with the suppliers is fully briefed

- Be consistent between suppliers

- Confirm any presentations or demonstrations required, clearly stating their objective, who is attending and how much time has been allocated

- Remind suppliers of any mandatory requirements that must be satisfied

- Ensure that any information exchanged with suppliers is treated as confidential by them

- Notify suppliers as soon as possible of your decision.

CASE STUDY

LEICESTER CITY COUNCIL
The statement of requirement was incorporated within an invitation to tender which was advertised in the *EU Journal*. Twenty-eight suppliers responded to the advertisement in the *EU Journal*, 28 invitations to tender were issued and 22 responses received. These responses were evaluated without any contact with the suppliers. Potential suppliers were evaluated based on their size, credibility and track record. The detailed responses to the functional requirements were scored against the checklist model. As a result of this process a long-list of ten suppliers was produced.

When selecting software products or turnkey solutions the situation can appear very confused. It is possible to identify two or three suppliers for the same product, i.e. the author, a systems integrator and a computer manufacturer. Selecting the best suppliers to go forward onto the initial short-list can be difficult. There is no necessity to eliminate any of them at this stage provided that they are offering a viable solution and are adding value. The trend in the market is to deal directly with the software author where possible. Circumstances when this does not apply are when the total solution is large and complex and a systems integrator role is necessary. If this is the case then the added value, responsibilities and risks of the systems integrator are clear and can be quantified.

Lastly, what happens if you cannot put together a viable short-list? First, review the original supply options considered and decisions taken. Second, review your requirements document. If it is still not possible to produce a viable short-list then perhaps there is not a solution available.

Business case

CHAPTER 9

Introduction

The culmination of the project team's effort during the feasibility phase is the business case. The objective of the project team in preparing the business case is to receive authority to proceed from the steering committee and corporate management. In order to achieve this authority the business case must answer the first three of the fundamental decision-making questions:

- Do we need the benefits?
- Can we achieve the benefits?
- What is the risk?

During the selection phase these questions are re-addressed as well as the fourth and last of the fundamental decision-making questions:

- Are we achieving the benefits at optimum cost?

The decision-making process is illustrated in Figure 9.1. Organizations that authorize projects on receipt of the initial business case, such that projects are not then subject to a final capital approval step, will need to adapt this process by bringing forward to this phase some of the steps in Chapter 13.

It is assumed that most organizations will already have a standard business case pro forma. The objective therefore of the steps of the feasibility phase described in this book is to ensure that the project team collects all the necessary data to build the business case.

Critical success factors

Critical success factors in preparing the business case are:

- Are the business needs still relevant to current business objectives and corporate priorities?
- Have the benefits been agreed by the *owning* users and management?
- Are the benefits achievable?

96 GOOD BUYS IN IT

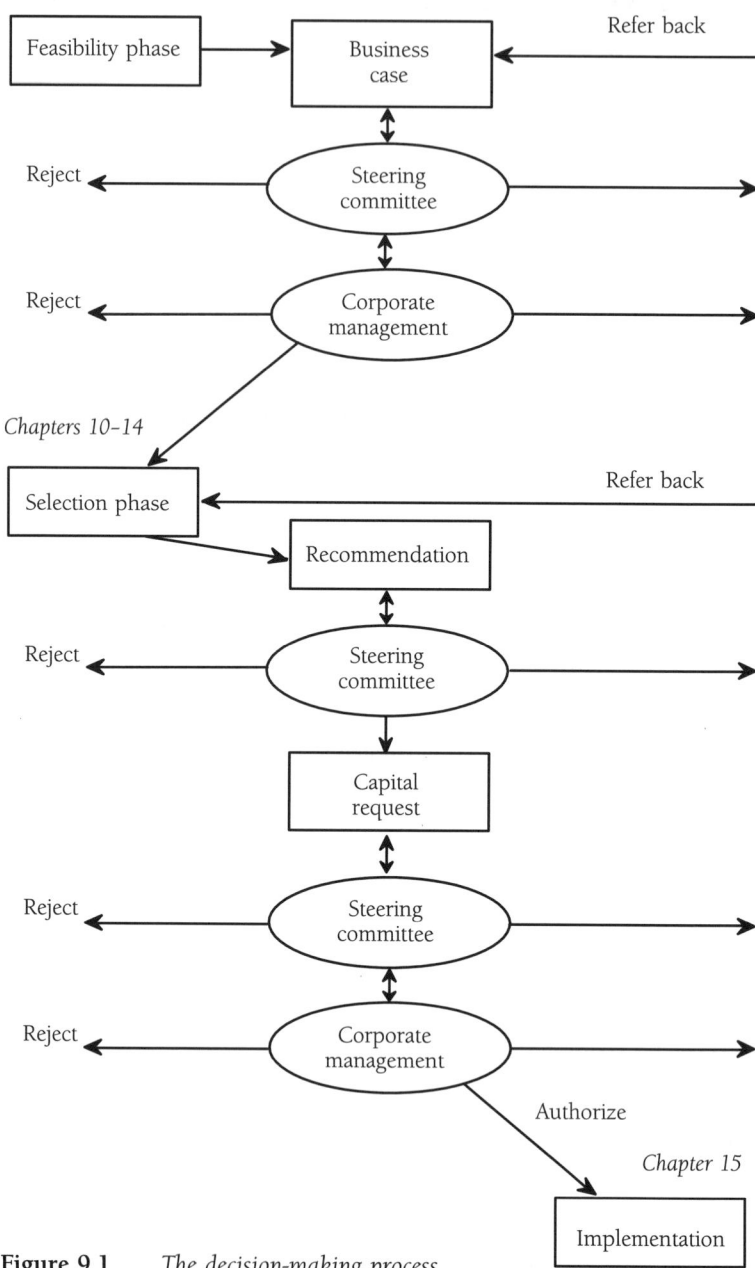

Figure 9.1 *The decision-making process.*

- Is the scope of the project defined correctly?
- Do the requirements accurately reflect our business needs?

EXAMPLE

A car body repair garage convinced itself that it needed a new integrated computer system developed for the motor industry for estimating, stock control, purchasing, and accounts. The benefit seemed to be a significant efficiency improvement, enabling the one administrator to handle more volume. However, an analysis of the key documents showed that they were all variations of each other and that the number of documents processed per day was very low. This indicated that a complex computer system was probably unsuitable, as each document was not going to be processed often enough for the administrator to become familiar with it. The solution was to implement a PC-based word processing and accounts package that allows for a large number of documents to be stored, and for these documents to be quickly recalled and updated whenever necessary (i.e. recall customer estimates, print parts lists, print invoices). The solution was quickly implemented, required little skill to use, realized all the anticipated time savings and was significantly cheaper than the more complex integrated solution.

- Do the technical requirements fit in with our IT strategy?
- Have we selected the right supply options?
- Have we followed the correct procedures when we issued the request for proposal (particularly important to the public sector and some parts of industry who are subject to EU and GATT regulations)?
- Have we selected the best suppliers for the initial short-list?
- Have we considered the organizational impact of the project?
- Have we considered the personnel and training ramifications of the project?
- What management issues does the project raise?
- What change management issues does the project raise?
- Have we considered all the risks?
- Is the level of expectation set correctly for management?
- Is the level of expectation set correctly for users?
- Are management still committed to the project?
- Are the users still committed to the project?
- Is the IT department still committed to the project?
- Can we adequately resource the project?

Business case

Definition

The business case is an internal proposal that is submitted to management for a decision. This decision will normally be to proceed to the selection phase and complete the selection, defer or refer the business case for further consideration, or reject the business case. The business case includes seven key elements:

1. Management summary
2. Statement of the business need
3. Summary of requirements
4. Supply options
5. Costs
6. Benefits
7. Risk analysis.

Objective

The business case serves many purposes. From the project team's point of view the objective in submitting the business case is to receive authority to proceed from the steering committee and corporate management; establish terms of reference and lines of communication; agree time scales, budgets and project life cycle for evaluation purposes; and understand the final decision-making process.

From a wider perspective the business case is the method by which projects compete for the resources of the organization by showing benefits. It is during this process that the project must gain the commitment of the management team, the users and the IT department to the project; and, crucially, set the correct level of expectation for the management team and users.

From the viewpoint of the steering committee and corporate management the business case is a way of initially prioritizing and comparing projects, managing them during selection and implementation and reviewing them after implementation. These management processes are made much easier if a standard business format is used as well as standard selection, implementation and review processes.

Format

1 Management summary

The management summary introducing the business case states the nature of the decision required from the steering committee and corporate management, the timetable and the management issues arising from the proposal.

2 Statement of the business need (see Chapter 5)

In this section the business need is clearly stated and categorized accordingly, i.e.

- Cost driven
- Infrastructure improvement
- Key business ratios
- Market driven
- Organizational
- Risk management
- Volume driven.

3 Summary of requirements (see Chapter 6)

- Scope
- Functional requirements
- Common requirements and characteristics
- Technical requirements
- Operational requirements
- Implementation considerations
- Personnel considerations
- Management considerations
- Supplier requirements (see Chapter 7).

4 Supply options (see Chapter 8)

This section states the supply options considered and the suppliers on the initial short-list.

5 Costs (see Chapter 8)

A schedule of estimated supply costs:

- One-off costs
  - Computer hardware
  - Communication equipment
  - Software licences
  - Software modification
  - Implementation and training
  - Project management
  - Supplier services
  - Consulting fees
  - Legal fees
- Recurring costs
  - Computer hardware support and maintenance
  - Communication equipment support and maintenance
  - Software licences
  - Software support and maintenance
  - Project management
  - Services.

Plus an indication of other costs:

- Personnel and training
- Internal IT services
- Change management
- Organizational impact
- Environmental, i.e. buildings, infrastructure, air conditioning
- Project management
- Contingency.

6 Benefits (see Chapter 5)

This section schedules the tangible and intangible benefits and *owning* users and management. It is normal to quantify tangible benefits, but in doing so the assumptions used to calculate the benefits must be stated. It is not normal to quantify intangible benefits.

7 Risk analysis (see below)

An assessment of the risks, impact and consequences associated with the proposal.

Preparing the business case

Introduction

The preparation of most of the material needed for the business case by the project team is covered in earlier chapters, i.e.

- Statement of the business need (Chapter 5)
- Summary of requirements (Chapter 6)
- Supply options (Chapter 8)
- Costs (Chapter 8)
- Benefits (Chapter 5).

The two additional areas for the project team to complete are:

1. The impact of the project on the organization
2. Risk analysis.

The impact of the project on the organization

The project can impact the organization in many different ways. It can impact employees and the way they work; it can impact and make demands on the infrastructure of the organization; it can impact previous decisions; it can impact and make demands on the environment of the organization; and it can raise management issues.

Employees

How will the project impact the employees of the organization? What personnel, training and change management policies need to be developed?

> **YULE CATTO** — *CASE STUDY*
> The new system could be supported by a small central team and there would no longer be any requirement for local IT staff.

> **PRUDENTIAL ASSURANCE** — *CASE STUDY*
> The critical issue was not training the representatives how to use the system, but how to change their way of working so that they exploited and benefited from the system. This was always recognized as being a slow process. *How to* training and usability laboratories were used to build up individual skills. Best practice was then sought and individuals who had quickly appreciated the

potential of the new system were encouraged to tell others how it had benefited them.

> **CASE STUDY**
>
> PEPE JEANS
>
> The tangible benefits of implementing an integrated system and changing the way people work are to reduce the operational costs by eliminating the labour effort necessary to maintain system interfaces, and by eliminating the role of the information provider by providing management information directly to the end users.

Infrastructure

How will the project impact the infrastructure of the organization? What are the demands on current computing facilities, communications capabilities, internal IT resources, management time?

Previous decisions

Does the project impact or compromise previous decisions? What are the accounting ramifications if this project supersedes a previous project?

Environment

What are the environmental needs of the project? Are there any special requirements?

Management issues

What management issues does the project raise? How will management ensure the success of the project? How will the project team be motivated? How will *owners* of benefits be encouraged to achieve them?

Risk analysis

Analysing the risks associated with the project is an essential part of the business case preparation. Each risk must be considered and, if necessary, costed or allowed for in the time and costs contingencies. If the risk is significant it is included in the management summary.

Scope

The original decisions on the scope of the project will impact the project's success as much as any other decision. The scope directly impacts the costs of the project and the time scales. It also helps to limit and set levels of

BUSINESS CASE 103

expectation. When reviewing the scope of the project for the business case apply the following three criteria. First, does the scope of the project reflect the business need? Second, is the scope of the project clearly defined? And third, what is the down side?

When specifying the scope of an outsourcing requirement the options are broadly: **EXAMPLE**

- Outsourcing or facilities management
- On- or off-site
- Data centre management
- Computer operations
- Data preparation
- Communications network management
- Helpdesk
- Application systems development
- Application systems maintenance.

Which options are specified in the scope can only be dependent on the business need and the achievable benefits, taking into account the downside of implementing the proposed project. The possible down sides to outsourcing and facilities management are loss of control, cost containment over the life of the contract and the high cost and disruption associated with retendering. Not all these down sides will be applicable to every option. Balancing the down sides against the benefits per option is the only way to determine the scope.

Supply options?

When reviewing the supply options the key criterion is common sense. Have we short-listed credible suppliers who can do the job? At this early stage in the selection process it is not always possible to judge the suitability of proposed supplier solutions. An area to consider carefully is when to select an application package and when to select a bespoke-developed solution. If in doubt, at this stage, include both a package supplier and a services supplier on the short-list to compare solutions and costs during the detailed evaluation. However, a key factor in this decision is which comes first, the package or the user? If the package fit is greater than 85 per cent then normally a package is the better solution. However, what happens if the package is less than 85 per cent? The options are to modify the package with resultant on-going support and upgrade problems, change the user's way of working to fit the package, or build a bespoke solution. These are potentially key decisions. To manage the risk associated with them, leave the options open until the detailed evaluation and build in quality procedures to ensure that the options are considered carefully. The danger is that the project team will slowly get committed to a preferred solution and end up recommending it without being able to see the wood for the trees.

EXAMPLE A pharmaceuticals company when selecting a supply chain management system quickly identified a preferred package solution. During the detailed evaluation, supplier workshops and conference room pilots the users specified a series of *small* amendments that were documented and quoted for by the supplier. At the end of the evaluation the package was duly selected. However, no-one had reflected on the total impact of all the *small* amendments. The combined effect of them was to make the package very difficult for the supplier to support and impossible to upgrade, losing two of the key advantages of selecting a package in the first place.

Expectation levels?

The expectation levels of management, users and the IT department can only be set and *managed* by continual effort by the project team and steering committee. As success is ultimately judged against expectation levels the risk associated with not setting and managing expectation levels correctly is *failure*; no matter how well the project actually seemed to go to the project team and the steering committee! Judging expectation levels is a subjective process. If there is any doubt in the mind of the project team that expectation levels are unrealistically high (or low) or management and users do not fully comprehend the amount of effort and pain involved with the project then an education programme needs to be initiated.

Commitment?

The commitment to the project by management, users and the IT department is essential to the project's success. Commitment is initially tested by the business case process itself, as the commitment of the users to the project will be one of the decision-making criteria used by the steering committee. If that commitment is in doubt then potentially the whole feasibility phase will need to be recycled. On an on-going basis the commitment of the management, users and the IT department will need to be retested to ensure their continual support and, if necessary, the project will have to be *resold* or reviewed to ensure that support.

CASE STUDY PRUDENTIAL ASSURANCE
The biggest problem was retaining the interest and support of senior management in the project. The project was all about building for the future and as such offered few (if any) tangible short-term benefits. The cost of not going ahead with the project, on the other hand, was potentially very high in loss of competitive position. The lesson learnt is that to successfully manage this type of project requires, first, the commitment of a senior management sponsor, and second, for that commitment to be tested and reinforced regularly.

BUSINESS CASE

Change management?

What are the risks associated with the proposed changes to the organization, its employees and their working practices? How will it be viewed externally?

Technical?

Are there any technical risks associated with hardware or software? Are we using tried and tested solutions, or are we proposing to use new technology that it is not yet fully tried and tested but might offer long-term or competitive advantage? Do the technical requirements fit in with our IT strategy?

Project risk

What are the project risks? How large is the project? How difficult will it be to manage? Is the project too big? Can it be subdivided? Can the implementations be phased? Is it necessary to commit to the total solution? Can each phase be made dependent on the success of the previous phase? Can we resource the project with the right skill levels? Have we allowed enough time for the project?

Costing

How accurate are the costings? What is the margin of error?

Achieve benefits

How achievable are the benefits? What is the definition of success of the project? How committed are the *owners* of the benefits to achieving them? How predictable are the benefits?

CASE STUDY

BIRMINGHAM CITY COUNCIL
In 1988 Birmingham City Council found itself with a large central IT unit of 200 staff and significant concern among the senior management team of the City Council about its performance. Birmingham City Council is one of the largest authorities in the UK and the largest individual city authority. Already the larger departments in the City had their own IT unit and had always been responsible for their own PCs and workstations. In order to achieve greater flexibility the city treasurer, with the support of the council members, decided to outsource the computer operations, communications network and the central development operations of the City.

 The tangible benefits to the City of this decision were to reduce the on-going running costs of these services and receive a capital injection for the sale of the assets. The intangible benefits were to:

106 GOOD BUYS IN IT

- Anticipate the government's intentions to introduce compulsory competitive tendering throughout the public sector
- Improve the level of service to the user departments within the City, particularly for systems development
- Create a situation whereby the City could begin to divest from its old COBOL-based mainframe systems and utilize newer technologies, downsize applications where appropriate, and use more packages
- Devolve the responsibility for IT to the user departments
- Reduce management time in running a large and complicated technical department.

At the end of the first year most of the anticipated benefits had been realized. Operational cost savings had been achieved and the development service had improved considerably. In subsequent years the City believe that it is still receiving a value for money service. This is despite the fact that demands for mainframe services has gone up, and not down as had been expected, with a resultant increase in costs.

Do nothing!

What is the risk to the organization of doing nothing?

Calculating costs

Supplier costs are prepared during the short-listing step. Additional internal costs will also need to be taken into account and will be produced as a bi-product of considering the impact of the project on the organization. These will include both financial costs and time as well as:

- Personnel and training
- Internal IT services
- Change management
- Organizational impact
- Environmental, i.e. buildings, infrastructure, air conditioning
- Project management (10-15 per cent)
- Contingency (10-25 per cent).

When calculating internal costs a clear view needs to be taken on how overhead recovery and infrastructure running costs are charged. Overhead recovery includes national insurance, pension contributions, health insurance, company cars, other staff benefits, rent, rates, telephone and management charges. Infrastructure running costs include communications and computing.

Charge-out rates need to take into account non-productive time and either over- or undercapacity. In practice, when calculating daily staff costs it is reasonable to work on 150-200 productive days per year. When calculating infrastructure running costs the two biggest problems are, first, calculating the true costs of running the service, and second, calculating a unit cost. This applies to both communications and computing, as at any point in time the service is likely to be either under- or overloaded.

Business case evaluation and approval

Introduction

The approach of the project team when preparing the business case is essentially qualitative. The approach of the steering committee when evaluating the business case is both qualitative and quantitative. The approach of corporate management is essentially quantitative.

The review of the business case by both the steering committee and corporate management is rational and dispassionate. The options are to refer the business case back for further work, approve it or reject it. The last option is a realistic possibility in organizations that are constantly exploring new ideas. Some of these ideas will be successful and realize significant benefits to the organization. On the other hand, some will fail. If they are going to fail then it is far better for them to fail at this step rather than later and after the investment of further resources. It must be assumed that most project teams are committed to *their* project and therefore will present a good business case. Quite reasonably, they will also be very disappointed if *their* business case fails. However it does not mean that they have done a bad job—a point to consider when business cases are rejected.

In order to get a dispassionate view of business case proposals it is becoming more common for organizations to subcontract this step to external consultants.

CASE STUDY

PRUDENTIAL ASSURANCE
The business case prepared by the project team was first approved by the delivery board and then taken by the sponsor, in this case the sales director, to the Home Service divisional board. The project, because of its size, then needed to go to head office for approval. This involved an independent quality review by Andersen Consulting before being submitted to the chief executive for signature.

Evaluating the business case

The options available to the steering committee when evaluating the business case are to forward it to corporate management for approval, to refer it back to the project team for further work, or to reject it altogether. When evaluating the business case the steering committee applies the first three of the fundamental decision-making criteria:

- Do we need the benefits?
- Can we achieve the benefits?
- What are the risks?

The decision factors associated with each question are:

Do we need the benefits?

- Are the business needs still relevant to our current business objectives and corporate priorities?
- Do we need the benefits?
- Does the business case move the organization forward? Are the underlying assumptions radical enough? Do we need to apply business process re-engineering before going any further?
- What happens if we do nothing?

Can we achieve the benefits?

- Have the benefits been agreed by the *owning* users and management? Are they achievable? How accurate is the costing? What is the margin of error?
- Are the benefits measurable?
- What is the commitment to the project? Is management committed? Are the users committed? Is the IT department committed? Is the project team committed?
- What is the level of expectation? Is it achievable? Is it set correctly for management and users?

What are the risks?

- Project management:
  - Is the scope of the project defined correctly?
  - Do the requirements accurately reflect our business needs?
  - Have we selected the right supply options and suppliers?

- Do we understand the technical risks associated with any hardware or software?
- Do we understand the risks associated with the project, i.e. size, complexity, duration, phasing, difficulty?
- Does the project have a viable plan?
- Is the project on time?
- Is the project following its quality plan?
- Is the project on budget?
- Can we adequately resource the project?

- Has the project team fully considered the organizational impact of the project? Personnel and training ramifications? Change management issues? Management issues?

- Have we considered all the risks? Has anything changed that affects risk?

If this step is used to approve the project for the first time then the steering committee will also:

- Decide on the membership of the project team and their training requirements

- Agree terms of reference with the project team

- Agree reporting arrangements with the project team

- Agree critical success factors with the project team

- Agree the project plan with the project team

- Agree time scales, budgets and project life cycle for evaluation purposes

- Agree the selection processes, procedures and techniques to be used by the project team

- Agree the final decision-making process with the project team.

Approving the business case

The options available to corporate management when evaluating the business case are to approve it, refer it back, or reject it altogether. When evaluating the business case corporate management primarily applies the first of the fundamental decision-making criteria *Do we need the benefits?* The decision factors associated with it are:

- Are the business needs relevant to our current business objectives and corporate priorities?

EXAMPLE

The board of a private limited company received a straightforward business case proposal from a subsidiary company. However, unknown to the subsidiary company the limited company was in preliminary take-over talks with another company that would radically change the shape and size of its subsidiary company. Much to the anxiety of the subsidiary company, the board of the limited company *sat* on the business case proposal until the take-over was sorted out.

- Do the benefits represent a reasonable return on investment?

CASE STUDY

The tangible benefit of downsizing the marketing system from the IBM to an open solution was a one-year return on investment.

- How will the project be viewed externally? By our competitors? By our customers? By our investors? By the government?

CASE STUDY

TRENT REGIONAL HEALTH AUTHORITY

In 1988 the total number of staff in the region was about 100 000 of which about 1500 were employed directly by the RHA. The government had signalled its intentions to radically change the structure of the National Health Service and core to that was the concept of purchaser and provider. Trent RHA took the view that running the RCC as a service for the benefit of the DHAs and hospitals was not part of its core responsibilities.

The initial review after one month concentrated on identifying outstanding issues and ensuring that they were followed up by management. This was followed six months later by a benefits/business review. A strict cost comparison between the old and the new is no longer possible, as it would not be comparing like with like. However, on a broader front the 14 regional health authorities that existed in 1988 are now being reduced to eight and are being phased out altogether in 1996. From that strategic viewpoint the project has achieved its objectives.

- What happens if we do nothing?

Operational requirement (OR)

CHAPTER 10

Selection phase

The selection phase of the evaluation, selection, purchasing and implementation cycle is described here and in Chapters 11-14. This phase encompasses preparing the operational requirement; issuing the invitation to tenders to suppliers on the initial short-list; evaluating the suppliers' responses to produce the final short-list; recommending a solution; gaining internal approval; and negotiating, preparing and executing supply agreements. The selection phase is illustrated diagrammatically in Figure 10.1.

Operational requirement (this chapter)

The objective of this step is for the project team to prepare a detailed operational requirement that can quickly and easily be developed into an invitation to tender.

Invitation to tender (Chapter 11)

The objective of this step is for the project team to prepare an invitation to tender that is issued to the suppliers on the initial short-list and for their responses to form the starting point of the evaluation.

Evaluation (Chapter 12)

The objective of this step is for the project team to evaluate the suppliers' responses to the invitation to tender and produce a final short-list.

Decision making (Chapter 13)

The objective of this step is for the project team to decide on a recommended solution and gain acceptance internally.

112 GOOD BUYS IN IT

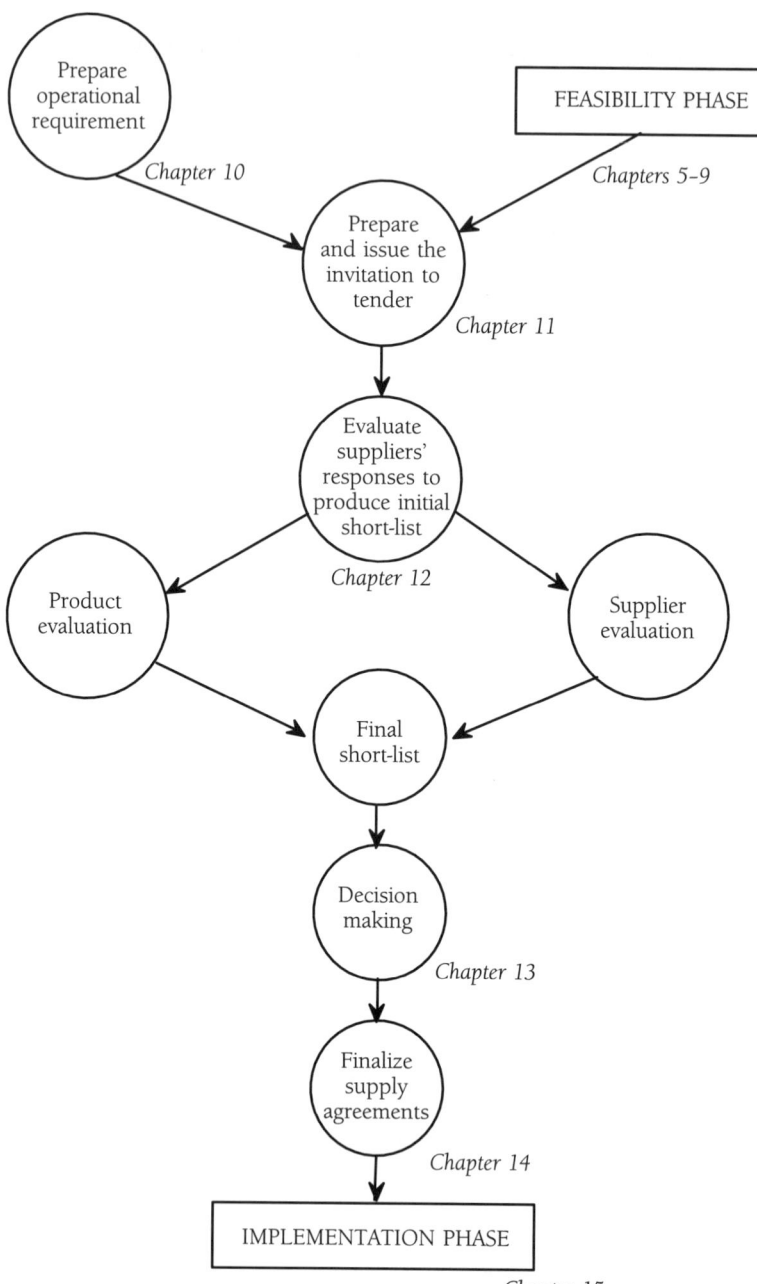

Figure 10.1 *The selection phase.*

Supply agreements (Chapter 14)

The objective of this step is to finalize supply agreements.

Critical success factors

The operational requirement is potentially a large document that can take a long time to prepare. If this is the case then work can start on preparing the operational requirement as soon as the summary of requirements has completed its quality review. This work is in parallel with the preparation and issuing of the request for proposal and the business case. Obviously, if the business case is either rejected or referred back to the project team, then work on the operational requirement ceases.

Critical success factors when preparing the operational requirement are:

- Does the project team have the correct balance of skills and available resources to define the detailed requirements?
- Is the scope of the project, as defined in the summary of requirements, still correct?
- Is the operational requirement a forward-looking document (and not just a restatement of the current system or a checklist of fancied features)?
- Will the operational requirement be checked for consistency (especially important for a large document)?
- Are all requirements designated either mandatory or desirable?
- Is a quality review part of the preparatory procedures?

Operational requirement

Definition

The operational requirement is a detailed statement of requirements, developed from the original summary of requirements, that is quickly and easily developed into an invitation to tender and is supported as necessary by specifications of existing systems.

Format

(Note: The format of the operational requirement is similar to the summary of requirements (see Figure 10.2).)

1	Introduction
2	Scope
3	Functional requirements
4	Common requirements and characteristics
5	Technical requirements
6	Operational requirements
7	Implementation considerations
8	Personnel considerations
	Appendices

Figure 10.2 *Operational requirement format.*

1 Introduction

The introduction states the background to the operational requirement, its purpose and the terms of reference of the project team.

2 Scope

The scope defines the breadth of the requirement and usage.

3 Functional requirements

This section is the core of the operational requirement. Requirements should be grouped into functional areas describing each requirement in non-technical user terms.

OPERATIONAL REQUIREMENT 115

4 Common requirements and characteristics

This section states requirements that are common to all the functional requirements expressed in non-technical terms. In the case of software this section will contain requirements with respect to security options, report writer flexibility, screen painting and formatting, on-line access to data, drill down and zoom, EDI, integration with spreadsheets, workgroup applications, etc.

5 Technical requirements

This section states relevant technical requirements. In the case of a solutions-oriented operational requirement then the technical requirements will be normally minimal as they will act as a restraint when the invitation to tender is issued to suppliers. If appropriate then requirements for operating systems, database management systems, 4GL and back-up procedures are stated. In a facilities management/outsourcing operational requirement the technical requirements will specify the hardware and software.

6 Operational requirements

This section states the operational requirements, i.e. number of users, transaction volumes, helpdesk arrangements, back-up and standby procedures, performance and service levels. Critically, it also states the flexibility required in the future. In the case of maintenance requirements this section states the service levels required (which might be different for different types of hardware, i.e. on-site 4-hour response for file servers and 24-hour back to base for screens, terminals and non-critical workstations).

7 Implementation considerations

This section states how and when the requirements will be implemented and interface/integration requirements with other systems as well as support required from suppliers both during and after the implementation.

8 Personnel considerations

This section covers the personnel issues that will need to be addressed. Depending on requirement, this could include project team training, user training, employment of new staff, redeployment of existing staff, redundancies or the transfer of staff. This section is not normally carried forward as part of the invitation to tender.

Appendices

The appendices will contain details of supporting information, i.e. specification and comments on existing systems: inputs, outputs, processes, file formats, interfaces with other systems; leases; software licences.

Preparing the operational requirement

Planning

The original summary of requirements is normally prepared quickly by the project team and then reviewed with a wider audience for comments using techniques such as a conference room pilot. The operational requirement will require a greater effort and frequently involve setting up subproject teams. These teams are normally led by the appropriate departmental manager, reporting to the project team, and responsible for defining the departments' requirements. The IT department will normally document existing systems, interface requirements and any other technical requirements.

During the planning stage the summary of requirements is analysed in detail and the task of preparing the operational requirement broken down into its constituent parts.

CASE STUDY

PEPE JEANS

The core project team was European and multi-lingual, consisting of a Dutchman, an Englishman, a German and a Scot. The project team was supported by five subproject teams defining functional requirements, i.e. sales order processing, warehousing, sales administration, procurement, finance and accounting. Each subproject team had two or three active members out of a total of five or six. The subproject teams were made up of representatives from the European operating companies.

Preparation

To help the project and subproject teams it is advisable to issue guidelines as to how requirements are to be determined, what techniques will be used to collect and define requirements and the format of the operational requirement. The level of detail will depend on the nature of the project. Where possible, focus on defining requirements (and not the detailed solution) as it will be then incumbent on the suppliers to propose solutions. In many cases the detail can then be sorted out during the implementation. It must also be remembered not to overlook basic detailed functional requirements. Preprepared functional checklists are available from professional associations, trade organizations and consultants.

For a large project, and particularly when it is difficult for users to meet, surveys are an effective method of gathering requirements.

CASE STUDY

SMITHKLINE BEECHAM
A functional checklist of about 100 items for the core maintenance management systems was prepared and distributed to each site. This document served two purposes. First, to form a consensus as to the worldwide requirement and second, to find out which of these functional items were available in the local in-house systems.

Review

When the draft operational requirement is available it is essential that the project team thoroughly reviews the requirements, some of which will have been prepared by the project team and some prepared by remote subproject teams, to ensure that:

- There is consistency in functional requirements
- Requirements specified reflect the business need and are forward-looking and are not a wish-list of fancied features or simply a restatement of the existing system
- Requirements are prioritized into mandatory or desirable
- Requirements are formatted consistently. This will make life much easier for the project team when analysing the suppliers' responses to the invitation to tender.

At this stage consider running an in-house conference room pilot to achieve a consensus on the consolidated requirements.

Preparation by project team

- Notify attendees (users, management and the project team) in advance stating the time, place and duration of the meeting (typically, 1-2 days); the objective of the conference room pilot; and the agenda
- Prepare schematics of the requirements broadly following the format and content of the operational requirement
- Consider building prototype models of the requirements.

During the conference room pilot

- Start the conference room pilot by reviewing the project to date and the tangible and intangible benefits being sought

- Define the purpose of the conference room pilot and the roles of the attendees:
  - To finalize the operational requirement
  - To decide the suppliers' requirements for inclusion in the invitation to tender
  - To consider the risks associated with the project to ensure the optimum procurement and implementation plan

- Structure the conference room pilot into seven sessions:
  - Introduction
  - Key requirements
  - Technical and operational requirements
  - Implementation considerations
  - Suppliers' requirements
  - Personnel, management and training issues
  - Risk analysis:
    - Is the scope of the project accurate and clearly defined?
    - How accurate are the requirements?
    - What are the technical risks?
    - Is the project too big?
    - Is the project too long?
    - Should the project be sub-divided?

After the conference room pilot (project team)

- Follow up on action points

- Reissue the operational requirement for final agreement

- Review critical success factors.

Quality review of the operational requirement

The operational requirement is the core document of the invitation to tender. The danger is that in its preparation the project team loses sight of the business needs and requirements and overcomplicates, changes or compromises the original intention. Terms of reference for the quality review are to confirm that:

- The project team is following its own quality plan, is adequately resourced and is maintaining good internal communications

- The operational requirement complies with standards and procedures
- The scope of the project is defined
- The requirements are defined and reflect the outline in the original summary of requirements
- The risks have been properly assessed.

CHAPTER 11

Invitation to tender (ITT)

Critical success factors

The major part of the invitation to tender is brought forward from the operational requirement. The success of the invitation to tender is therefore dependent on the successful completion of the operational requirement and the additional work necessary to create the invitation to tender. Critical success factors when preparing the invitation to tender are:

- Have we selected the best initial short-list of suppliers to issue the invitation to tender?
- Does the invitation to tender adequately reflect our requirements?

Invitation to tender

Definition

The invitation to tender is a formal document that is issued to potential suppliers. It specifies the organization's requirements with appropriate terms and conditions inviting suppliers to respond within a specified time period.

Objective

The objective in issuing the invitation to tender is to select a supplier based on the evaluation criteria stated and to include the supplier's responses to it in any subsequent agreement to define the supplier's obligations.

Format

(Note: The format of the invitation to tender is similar to the request for proposal (see Figure 11.1).)

INVITATION TO TENDER 121

1   Introduction
2   Scope
3   Functional requirements
4   Common requirements and characteristics
5   Technical requirements
6   Operational requirements
7   Implementation considerations
8   Supplier requirements

9   Instructions to suppliers
    9.1   Terms and conditions (t&cs)
    9.2   Timetable
    9.3   User and technical contacts and procedures
    9.4   Evaluation criteria
    9.5   Format of suppliers' response
          9.5.1 Management summary
          9.5.2 Products and services bid
          9.5.3 Schedule of costs
          9.5.4 Suppliers' response on t&cs
          9.5.5 Detailed response
          9.5.6 Company overview and financial statement
          9.5.7 Product overviews
          9.5.8 Company experiences
          Suppliers' appendices

Appendices

Figure 11.1   *Invitation to tender format.*

1 Introduction

The introduction is based on the original introduction to the internal operational requirement, enhanced so that it is clear to an external supplier. It introduces your organization to a potential supplier, gives essential background information and the reason for the procurement and outlines the purpose and structure of the invitation to tender.

*2 Scope**

The scope defines the breadth of the requirement and usage.

*3 Functional requirements**

This section is the core of the document. Requirements should be grouped into functional areas describing each requirement in non-technical user terms.

*4 Common requirements and characteristics**

This section states requirements that are common to all the functional requirements expressed in non-technical terms. In the case of software this section will contain requirements with respect to security options, report writer flexibility, screen painting and formatting, on-line access to data, drill down and zoom, EDI, integration with spreadsheets, workgroup applications, etc.

*5 Technical requirements**

This section states relevant technical requirements. In the case of a solutions-oriented invitation to tender then the technical requirements will be normally minimal as they will act as a restraint. If appropriate then requirements for operating systems, database management systems, 4GL and back-up procedures are stated. In the case of a facilities management/ outsourcing invitation to tender the technical requirements will specify the hardware and software.

---

* These sections are carried forward from the operational requirement. The best way to present them in an invitation to tender is in a landscape table, creating a turnaround document, defining on the left-hand side the requirement and leaving sufficient room on the right-hand side for the supplier to respond to the questions. Sometimes it is helpful also to issue a word processed floppy disk to be returned with the questions answered.

6 Operational requirements*

This section states the operational requirements, i.e. number of users, transaction volumes, helpdesk arrangements, back-up and standby procedures, performance and service levels. Critically, it also states the flexibility required in the future. In the case of maintenance requirements this section states the service levels required (which may be different for different types of hardware, i.e. on-site 4-hour response for file servers and 24-hour back to base for screens, terminals and non-critical workstations).

7 Implementation considerations*

This section states how and when the requirements will be implemented and interface/integration requirements with other systems as well as support required from suppliers both during and after the implementation.

8 Supplier requirements

This section contains questions about the supplier that will probably not have be included in an operational requirement, i.e.

- Supplier's organization
- Personnel policies
- Compliance with BS 5750 and other relevant standards
- Skill levels and number of staff available to support proposed products and services
- Standby arrangements
- Helpdesk arrangements
- Hot-line support
- Spare part stocking policy, how spare parts are procured and actual service levels achieved in the field.

9 Instructions to suppliers

9.1 Terms and conditions (t&cs)

This section indicates the terms and conditions that will probably apply to any subsequent procurement. They could be special terms and conditions for this procurement (particularly important for facilities management and outsourcing selections); standard terms and conditions; relevant terms and conditions from the Chartered Institute of Purchasing & Supply (available from the CIPS Book Shop, Easton House, Easton on the Hill, Stamford PE9

3NZ, telephone 01780 56777); or it could be the intention to use the supplier's terms and conditions.

The use of the invitation to tender has been very casual in the IT industry for many years. It is now common for suppliers not to read the terms and conditions in the invitation to tender, simply responding to the invitation to tender attaching their own terms and conditions, and leaving negotiations to the end. If it is your intention to use the terms and conditions included in the invitation to tender, and this is not negotiable, then state this very clearly, otherwise it will not be believed by the suppliers.

CASE STUDY

BOLTON METRO

These five suppliers were then issued with the invitation to tender. The invitation to tender included a draft facilities management agreement from a private firm of solicitors that formed the basis of the final agreement. Four responses were received.

Other items to include in this section are:

- Any constraints on suppliers, i.e. single tender only, subcontracting arrangements, turnkey bids, partial bids

- Any mandatory requirements not covered or not obvious in previous sections

- A disclaimer not to be liable for any of the supplier's costs prior to contract

- A confidentiality clause to cover information released to potential suppliers in the course of the evaluation and the selection process.

9.2 Timetable

This section states the summary timetable for the procurement with clear instructions as to the procedures and date by when suppliers' responses to the invitation to tender must be received and how many copies are required.

9.3 User and technical contacts and procedures

This section states the user and technical contacts that are to be used while the suppliers are preparing their responses as well as requirements for presentations, demonstrations and workshops.

9.4 Evaluation criteria

This section outlines how the suppliers' responses will be evaluated, i.e.

- Quality of proposal

- Functional fit

- Financial stability and track record

- Product range
- Support organization, resources and skill levels.

9.5 Format of suppliers' response

9.5.1 Management summary
This section summarizes key aspects of the supplier's response.

9.5.2 Products and services bid
This section contains an outline specification of all products and services bid and a schedule of all software stating current version numbers, availability of source code, author and distribution arrangements.

9.5.3 Schedule of costs
A schedule of all costs including software amendments and implementation.

- One-off costs
  - Computer hardware
  - Communication equipment
  - Software licences (with and without source)
  - Software modification
  - Implementation and training
  - Project management
  - Services

- On-going costs
  - Computer hardware support and maintenance
  - Communication equipment support and maintenance
  - Software licences
  - Software support and maintenance
  - Project management
  - Services.

9.5.4 Suppliers' response on terms and conditions
This section must state the suppliers' compliance with the terms and conditions of the invitation to tender, any conditions on which the response is based, and the obligations and duties of the customer.

9.5.5 Detailed response
This section must include a detailed response to Sections 3-7 of the invitation to tender (probably) on the turnaround pro forma documents supplied. Each question must be answered:

F for fully compliant
P for partially compliant with a comment, i.e. subject to future release, requires a modification
N for non-compliant.

9.5.6 Company overview and financial statement

This section includes an overview of the company together with appropriate financial statements.

9.5.7 Product overviews

This section contains a paragraph giving an overview of each product or service proposed.

9.5.8 Company experiences

This section contains details of the suppliers' previous experience in similar industries or market sectors, similar projects, numbers of users and full details of reference sites.

Appendices

This section contains relevant brochures, product literature, software licences and suppliers' terms and conditions if applicable.

Preparing the invitation to tender

Planning

The use of the invitation to tender can vary. In the process described in this book it is assumed that the invitation to tender follows the request for proposal and is issued to suppliers on the initial short-list. The advantages of this approach are first, it limits the circulation of the invitation to tender to qualified suppliers only, and second, the suppliers' responses can then be used to start the evaluation. Case study examples of this are Bolton Metro and Yule Catto.

CASE STUDY

BOLTON METRO

The 24 suppliers responding to the advertisement in the *EU Journal* were issued a pre-tender questionnaire. The responses to the pre-tender questionnaire were evaluated by the evaluation panel using a 30-line model of requirements. The intention of the model was to produce an initial short-list of facilities management suppliers who were well established and had the necessary local government and technical experience. The evaluation was completed without any contact with the suppliers and produced an initial short-list of five suppliers. These five suppliers were then issued with the invitation to tender. The invitation to tender included a draft facilities management agreement from a private firm of solicitors that formed the basis of the final agreement. Four responses were received.

CASE STUDY

YULE CATTO

A long-list of potential software suppliers was drawn up by inviting each operating company financial director to suggest possible suppliers based on their local research. The long-list was reviewed by the head-office project team who quickly produced an initial short-list of three software houses based on the key requirements.

The 20-page invitation to tender detailed the functional requirements of the various modules required and was then sent to the suppliers on the initial short-list.

However, this approach is not the most appropriate for all situations. The invitation to tender can be issued to suppliers on the long-list, the final short-list or only to the recommended supplier.

Issuing the invitation to tender to the suppliers on the long-list is more common when it is more difficult to short-list suppliers. This may be because of the horizontal nature of a requirement or because of public sector operating procedures. Two case study examples of this are Leicester City Council and British Telecom.

CASE STUDY

LEICESTER CITY COUNCIL
The statement of requirement was incorporated within an invitation to tender which was advertised in the *EU Journal*. Twenty-eight suppliers responded to the advertisement in the *EU Journal*, 28 invitations to tender were issued and 22 responses were received.

CASE STUDY

BRITISH TELECOM
A long-list of 12 potential suppliers was drawn up based on the personal knowledge of the project team members, analysis of *The Software Users Year Book*, independent research data and advice from external consultants. These 12 suppliers were sent the invitation to tender and given three weeks to reply.

Issuing the invitation to tender to the suppliers on the final short-list is less common. In the case of Trent Regional Health Authority the very nature of the selection was iterative and it was only towards the end of the selection process when the final two suppliers had been selected that the invitation to tender was issued.

CASE STUDY

TRENT REGIONAL HEALTH AUTHORITY
February 1989: agree a long-list of eight potential suppliers. March 1989: invite proposals from suppliers on the long-list. April 1989: agree final short-list of two suppliers. May 1989: staff meet with the final two short-listed suppliers; issue invitation to tender.

The project was particularly difficult to plan as this was an unprecedented step in the National Health Service. The first phase of the project was simply exploring the options available and to ascertain the positioning of the outsourcing suppliers as to what and what not they were prepared to offer. Consequently the planning was iterative, with each next step very dependent on the outcome of the previous one. The overall structure of the project was, however, clearly defined. The selection process encompassed three parallel actions: a commercial selection process that would produce a short-list of recommended suppliers; staff meetings with the short-listed suppliers to take soundings; and finally meetings between the preferred supplier and RCC customers.

Issuing the ITT to preferred suppliers only is unusual. However, a good example is the BP Oil case study. The project team selected the preferred solution of hardware and software and then purchasing issued the invitation to tender to secure the best supplier.

CASE STUDY

BP OIL

Once the recommendation had been accepted by the executive management team a formal invitation to tender was issued to four value-added resellers for the recommended solution. Responses were then evaluated by purchasing using a price-sensitive model.

Preparation

The major part of the invitation to tender is brought forward from the summary of requirements. The differences are the introduction, supplier requirements, and supplier instructions. The critical area is the supplier requirements as once the products and services have been evaluated and the final short-list decided then the results of the supplier evaluation will be a major influencing factor on the final recommendation.

Issue invitation to tender to suppliers

When the initial short-list is decided the invitation to tender is issued to the suppliers on it. It is reasonable to allow 20 working days to respond. In many cases the task of issuing the invitation to tender and receiving the responses to the invitation to tender is handled by the purchasing department, otherwise it is done by the project team. Be prepared to answer suppliers' questions while they are preparing their responses to the invitation to tender.

Evaluation

CHAPTER

12

Introduction

The evaluation step of the process is essentially qualitative. Its objective is to produce the final short-list of suppliers. An analysis of the case studies researched for this book show that the average initial short-list of four is reduced to a final short-list of two potential suppliers at this stage. The next chapter starts with building a financial model to complete the comparison between the suppliers on the final short-list. It is during this financial comparison that, say, balancing a high-cost solution, with greater flexibility, with a limited low-cost option is considered.

Critical success factors

Critical success factors in producing the final short-list of suppliers are:

- Have the most likely suppliers responded to the invitation to tender?
- Do we understand our key selection criteria well enough to differentiate between suppliers?
- Will our evaluation model and procedures produce the best final short-list?
- Are we addressing the fourth of the fundamental decision-making criteria.

   Are we achieving the benefits at optimum cost?

Evaluation planning

The evaluation strategy and plan will be influenced by the type and nature of the selection. Application software selection traditionally follows a presentation, demonstration, workshop and prototyping route. The software is not normally tried out prior to contract. This is because the number of people involved in a typical application software implementation is too large to contemplate a live test in a pre-contract competitive situation.

On the other hand, with systems software it is easier to test the software in a live situation. This is because the number of people involved with technical products is smaller and the products can be satisfactorily tested in a live, or pseudo-live, situation prior to contract.

Large-scale services like systems integration, facilities management and outsourcing cannot really be tested prior to contract. This places a heavy reliance on:

- The project team to define requirements
- Suppliers to demonstrate their understanding of the requirements
- The suppliers' credibility
- Reference checking by the project team
- Both sides to prepare a sound agreement.

The strategy and plan for each selection will be different. Table 12.1 is a list of items typically undertaken during an evaluation. Tables 12.2, 12.3 and 12.4 are example timetables for application software, system software and facilities management/outsourcing evaluation, respectively, for suppliers on the initial short-list. The target dates for the selection will be notified to the suppliers in the invitation to tender. It is advisable to agree a detailed evaluation timetable with the suppliers on the initial short-list as soon as possible to ensure that the project runs to schedule.

Table 12.1 List of items typically undertaken during an evaluation

Item	Time
Prepare and agree detailed working plan, evaluation models and procedures	1-5 days
Initial scoring of invitation to tender response	1 day
Prepare for supplier presentation	Half a day
Supplier presentation or demonstration	1 day
Prepare for supplier workshop	1 day
Supplier workshop	1-2 days
Debrief supplier workshop	Half a day
Prepare for conference room pilot	Half a day
Suppliers' conference room pilot	1-5 days
Prototype build	2-10 days
Stress tests	1-5 days
Live trial	5-20 days
Build an implementation plan	1 day
Ad-hoc technical meetings	Half a day each
Supplier evaluation	1-2 days
Supplier references	1-3 days

Table 12.2 Typical application software evaluation timetable

Item	Ave. qty	Actual days	Elapsed days	Cumulative elapsed days
Prepare and agree detailed plan, evaluation models and procedures while waiting for invitation to tender responses	1	1–5	5	5
Receive invitation to tender responses			20	20
Initial scoring of invitation to tender responses and preparing for suppliers' presentations and demonstrations	4	4	5	25
Supplier presentations and demonstrations	4	4	5	30
Debrief above and decide on final short-list of suppliers		1	0	30
Prepare data for workshops	2	2	2	32
Supplier workshops	2	4	10	42
Ad-hoc technical meetings	6	3	0	42
Prepare for conference room pilot	2	2	3	45
Suppliers' conference room pilot	2	4	8	53
Build an implementation plan	2	2	2	55
Supplier evaluation	2	2	5	60
Supplier references	2	4	10	70
Complete evaluation and write report	1	5	5	75

Table 12.3 Typical system software evaluation timetable

Item	Ave. qty	Actual days	Elapsed days	Cumulative elapsed days
Prepare and agree detailed plan, evaluation models and procedures	1	1	1	1
Prepare for suppliers' presentations and demonstrations	4	1	1	2
Supplier presentations and demonstrations	4	4	7	9
Debrief above and decide on final short-list of suppliers		1	1	10
Prepare data for workshops	2	2	2	12
Supplier workshops	2	2	5	17
Ad-hoc technical meetings	6	3	1	18
Prototype build	2	10	10	28
Stress tests or live running	2	6	10	38
Supplier evaluation	2	2	2	40
Supplier references	2	4	5	45
Complete evaluation and write report	1	5	5	50

Table 12.4 Typical facilities management/outsourcing evaluation timetable

Item	Ave. qty	Actual days	Elapsed days	Cumulative elapsed days
Prepare and agree detailed evaluation strategy, plan, models and procedures while waiting for invitation to tender responses	1	1-5	5	5
Receive invitation to tender responses			20	20
Initial scoring of invitation to tender responses and preparing for suppliers' presentations	4	4	10	30
Supplier presentations	8	8	20	50
Ad-hoc meetings	8	8	5	55
Debrief above and decide on final short-list of suppliers		1	5	60
Final commercial presentations	2	2	5	65
Final staff presentations	2	2	5	70
Presentations to users	2	2	5	75
Final discussions with management, staff and users	10	5	5	80
Supplier evaluation	2	4	5	85
Supplier references	2	6	10	95
Complete evaluation and write report	1	5	5	100

Evaluation models

The time allowed for suppliers to respond to the invitation to tender is the time to update the original evaluation model that was used to produce the initial short-list of suppliers. The objective of the new model is to help the project team decide the final short-list of suppliers. The timing of when this is done is important, as many organizations require the decision-making models to be lodged with an independent body prior to receiving the suppliers' responses to the invitation to tender.

As with the earlier model, the new model consists of three individual models illustrated in Tables 12.5, 12.6 and 12.7. The lowest model in the hierarchy is a matrix at functional item level by supplier. This model feeds into a supplier model, reducing where necessary the functional scores on a prorata basis to the score allowed in the overall model. This supplier

Table 12.5 Invitation to tender functional item evaluation model

ITT cross-ref.	Requirement	Weight (note 1)	Max. score (note 2)	Supplier A Actual score (note 3)	Supplier A Weighted score (note 4)	Supplier B Actual score (note 3)	Supplier B Weighted score (note 4)	Etc.
4.1.1	User-driven report writer	5	25	4	20	3	15	
4.1.2	Screen formatter	2	10	2	4	4	8	
etc.								
4.	Common requirements and characteristics	Subtotal	250		174		192	
	Multiply by 125/250 = 0.5 to carry forward to suppliers' model	0.5	125		87		96	

Notes:
1. The weightings in this example are in the range 1–5, with allocation rules of 4–5 for mandatory items and 1–2 for desirable items.
2. The maximum score is the weight times five. Five is the maximum score for an individual item, giving a result in the range 1–25.
3. The maximum actual score in this example is 5, with marking rules of 5 for good response, 4 for satisfactory response, 2 for a requirement that is satisfied in the future, 1 for a requirement that requires a modification and 0 for non-compliance.
4. The weighted score is the actual score times the weighting for that item.
5. It is probable that the subtotals, corresponding to the criteria in the supplier's model, will not agree, in which case the subtotal is factored accordingly. The advantage of this scoring system is that any number of functional items can be added, with the result that the subtotal in this model can be either very large or very small. This does not reflect its importance. This is taken into account by the factor used to carry the total through to the suppliers' model. For example, a functional section with many items, but of minor importance, may have a high score in this model but be reduced when carried forward to the suppliers' model, whereas a small section, of major importance, will be increased. In the example above the functional score of 174 scored by supplier A is multiplied by the factor of 0.5, giving a total of 87 to be carried forward to the suppliers' model.

model then feeds into a supplier summary model to give the final comparative position. The critical decision when constructing the models is the balance of the invitation to tender suppliers' evaluation model.

The invitation to tender functional item evaluation model reflects the invitation to tender with each item of the invitation to tender represented as a line on the model and weighted according to its importance.

The invitation to tender suppliers' evaluation model follows a similar structure to the earlier one. However, this time less emphasis is placed on supplier credibility, as this is considered when the initial short-list is produced, and more emphasis is placed on the cost. The balance of the model is critical and must reflect the overall business needs and requirements. Not included in Table 12.6 is Miscellaneous. This is often included in the suppliers' evaluation model to cover such items as the subjective views of the project team on the attitude, professionalism and friendliness of the suppliers' staff.

Table 12.6 Invitation to tender suppliers' evaluation model (supplier A)

Criteria	Max. score	Risk (note 1)	Weighted score	Evaluation score	Notes
Functional requirements	200	0.9	170	153	2
Common requirements and characteristics	125	0.8	87	70	3
Technical and operational requirements	125	0.9	72	65	2
Implementation considerations	100	1.0	82	82	2
Supplier requirements	75	1.0	45	45	2
Future options	50	0.6	40	24	4
Product range	75	0.7	60	42	4
Supplier stability	50	0.9	50	45	2
Supplier track record	50	1.0	40	40	5
Cost of proposals	150	0.9	130	117	6
Totals	1000			683	

Notes:
1. Risk is a subjective factor decided by the project team for each of the criteria in the suppliers' model. The risk factor range in this example is 0-1, with the assessment rules of 1.0 for a very low risk, ranging to 0.5 for a high-risk criterion.
2. An established product from a reputable supplier.
3. Common characteristics of the product are functionally rich but ageing.
4. Product is mid-way through its natural life cycle with some uncertainty about future development.
5. The product and supplier have a well-established track record in our industry.
6. Risk associated with the suppliers' costing is minimal as the supplier costing is based on previous experience in similar circumstances.

Table 12.7 Invitation to tender summary evaluation model

Criteria	Max. score	Suppliers					
		A	B	C	D	E	Etc.
Functional requirements	200	153					
Common requirements and characteristics	125	70					
Technical and operational requirements	125	65					
Implementation considerations	100	82					
Supplier requirements	75	45					
Future options	50	24					
Product range	75	42					
Supplier stability	50	45					
Supplier track record	50	40					
Cost of proposal	150	117					
Totals	1000	683					

Evaluation procedures

Before starting the evaluation, agree the procedures and terminology that is to be used during the evaluation. It is also advisable to notify suppliers of these where appropriate. The suppliers are competing to win the evaluation, and setting the ground rules as early as possible will make life easier for everyone.

- For all meetings between the project team and the suppliers, or anyone else in the organization, distribute an agenda in advance, agree who will attend, the purpose of the meeting, notify questions in advance if possible and use pre-formatted note pads for making notes

- Make a note of all important telephone calls

- Use an effective internal communications system to keep all members of the project team up to date with progress

- Agree all the necessary contact points with suppliers

- Agree procedures if suppliers wish to meet management outside of the project team

- Summarize and agree after each meeting what has been accomplished, issues arising and what needs to be done next. After a few meetings it is very easy to confuse suppliers and their products and services. This can be simply done by printing pre-formatted note pads from the invitation to tender, or relevant parts of it, with plenty of space for making notes and scoring suppliers' responses to questions

- Review the short-list progressively and be prepared to eliminate a supplier at any time

- Be clear as to the purpose of every meeting with a supplier:
  Meeting: To find out information? To address an issue?
  Presentation: Gives the supplier the opportunity to present and discuss products and services
  Demonstration: Gives the supplier the opportunity to demonstrate how products work
  Workshop: Gives the evaluation team and *real* users the opportunity to gain hands-on experience in using the products and test the products with user-prepared data
  Benchmark: A benchmark is usually a joint exercise between the supplier and the project team to quantify the amount of resources required to process transactions. Subsequently, results may be included in an agreement to help to define performance criteria
  Stress testing: Using simulators, normally developed by the hardware manufacturers, it is possible to simulate a mix of transactions and users to test to destruction the capacity of a system. Stress testing is useful if there is concern about the impact on performance of the volume and mix of transactions to be processed
  (Note: Both benchmarking and stress testing require a high level of technical expertise to perform, understand the results and tune the system. Very different results can be achieved depending on how the system is configured.)
  Conference room pilot: In this context a supplier-led exercise to map requirements against product and build a pilot implementation. This is sometimes chargeable by the suppliers

- Be consistent with the information given to suppliers. Decide in advance what information is released, i.e. project budget, the names of the other suppliers competing and competitive quotations. The arguments against releasing unnecessary information to suppliers are a buyer's understandable position of not wanting to divulge information that may undermine a future negotiating position, ethical guidelines from the Chartered Institute of Purchasing & Supply and frequently the simple fact that the budget has not been set due to insufficient information. The argument in favour is to make as much information available to suppliers as possible to receive feedback, to allow the suppliers to qualify out of the bid if they wish or to cut their cloth accordingly.

Evaluate invitation to tender responses

The first task is to review the responses to the invitation to tender and score the results on the invitation to tender functional item evaluation model. This is much easier if the suppliers have followed the instructions in the invitation to tender and prepared their response as requested, i.e.

1. Management summary

2. Products and services bid

3. Schedule of costs

4. Suppliers' response on terms and conditions

5. Detailed response
    - Functional requirements
    - Common requirements and characteristics
    - Technical requirements
    - Operational requirements
    - Implementation considerations
    - Supplier requirements

6. Company overview and financial statement

7. Product overviews

8. Company experiences

Appendices

When planning for the initial review and scoring of the responses to the invitation to tender the simplest method is to allocate the workload to the member of the project team, or the subproject team, responsible for preparing the questions. When the project team is checking and reviewing the initial scoring for consistency it may be possible to further short-list suppliers. However, it is more likely that final short-listing will not take place until after the suppliers' presentations and workshops, unless, of course, a major non-compliance becomes apparent on a mandatory item. The other objective of the initial review and scoring of the invitation to tender responses is to plan and prepare for the suppliers' presentations and demonstrations.

Product evaluation

The operational requirement, invitation to tender and the suppliers' responses are the starting point for the product evaluation. If, after the invitation to tender responses are scored, all the products on the initial short-list seem to meet the requirement then a good product-evaluation strategy is as follows. First, concentrate on the differences between the products and decide how important these differences are to you. Second, if appropriate, use rapid prototyping techniques to test the products and build tangible solutions.

Functional requirements

Depending on the number of functional modules, it may be necessary to set up a number of subproject teams so that key areas can be evaluated in parallel. The relative importance of each functional area and item is stated in the evaluation model and suppliers are aware of the mandatory and desirable items. Agree with suppliers the structure of each meeting and be clear as to its objective. After the presentations and demonstrations scan the evaluation model and make notes of items that require further attention or give cause for concern.

Now prepare for the workshops and ensure that items identified at the presentations or demonstrations are dealt with adequately, prepare data in advance for the workshop and insist on keying the data yourself. Do this for critical transactions, especially high-volume ones, as well as following up on items already identified where you want to be absolutely clear as to how they work. Co-opt *hands-on* users for this task who are familiar with the current procedures and who will be responsible for processing the items in the new system. During the workshop stage it is essential not only that you understand the software but that the supplier also understands your requirements, especially if you are identifying any modifications. Each item in the operational requirement should be confirmed as fully, partial or non-compliant.

For the partially compliant items subdivide into *futures* and *amendments*. For the *futures*, review them again when looking at the supplier's development plans and track record of releasing new versions. For the *amendments*, specify with the supplier the requirement and ask the supplier to quote. For both *futures* and *amendments* timing is critical as they can significantly affect product acceptance and implementation plans. Whereas it is essential to quantify the costs of amendments it is probably better not to finalize your position as to whether they are required or not until the conference room pilot. The conference room pilot, if not part of the evaluation, is typically one of the first implementation tasks and is the best time to finalize what amendments are required.

Common requirements and characteristics

Common requirements and characteristics are normally divided into three. The first group is normally addressed at the beginning of the supplier's presentation and demonstration. It includes the common areas of the software like screen painters and report writers that are necessary to understand in order to evaluate the application functionality. The second group are functional items to be evaluated in their own right and will, of course, include the items in the first group, i.e.

- Screen painters
- Report writers
- Security
- Drill down and zoom
- Electronic data interchange
- Integration with spreadsheets
- Client/server relationship.

The third group is made up of items that will arise during the course of the evaluation, such as product integration, amendment development and release procedures, future releases and product upgrade procedures.

Key areas to look at when evaluating the common areas of the software, apart from its functionality, are the skill level required and how it works. Skill levels are particularly important when using report writers and 4GL. The best way of determining the capability of the product is to ask the suppliers to produce a report or programme. The best method of determining the skill level required is to use it in a workshop environment or a live trial.

How it works is particularly relevant to client/server relationships, procedures for releasing new releases and package integration. Client/server is currently more of an idea than a standard. If the requirement is for a client/server type solution first define it. Then test the supplier's definition against yours to make sure that you are both on the same wavelength. Procedures for accepting new releases and software amendments can be very complicated. Who is responsible? How is it tested? Will it affect other modules? What happens to any previous modifications? How long will it take? Do new releases come out on schedule? What are the release procedures? Which environment is released first? What are the quality controls on new releases? Does the supplier have established beta sites that take new releases first before they are put on general release? Integration can be achieved in many different ways—batch, real time or a combination of the two. The effects and consequences of how integration is achieved will impact functionality, processing overhead and ease of use.

> **EXAMPLE** A functional requirement might be to see an up-to-date situation anywhere in the system. When goods are received should the system update stock, purchase ordering, commitments and general ledger accruals? The more modules that are updated, the higher the processing overhead and potentially the longer the transaction will take to process. If a purchase invoice or payroll transaction is processed should it automatically update the general ledger? Perhaps not, because in a high-volume situation it quickly becomes very difficult to control and reconcile the modules.

Technical requirements

Frequently, the starting point for this part of the evaluation is the supplier's response to the invitation to tender. This is especially true in a solutions-oriented invitation to tender where the emphasis is on stating the requirement and not the solution. The first objective is therefore to understand the supplier's response. This can be divided into three: hardware, software and others:

- Hardware
    - Computer configuration
    - Communications
    - Environmental requirements
    - Hardware upgrade options

- Software
    - Operating system
    - Database platform
    - 4GL
    - Development language
    - Application software

- Others
    - Interfacing and integration with external systems
    - Compliance with standards
    - All documentation.

In a solutions-driven evaluation the hardware is normally subservient to the software decisions. The more likely sequence for the technical evaluation is therefore software, hardware and others.

Key questions and areas to concentrate on when evaluating software are:

- The compatibility between the operating system, database management system, 4GL or development environment and the application package. It is not always valid to assume that you can mix and match software. It is advisable to check that the configuration being considered is tried and tested

- How easy is it to implement a new release?

- What happens if only one of the components is upgraded?

- What is the development environment of the application package? Is this its native environment? How is the application software ported from one environment to another? How does this affect operational efficiency? What version numbers of the software are being proposed? Are they the latest versions?

CASE STUDY

LEICESTER CITY COUNCIL
On reflection, the project team now believe that they took too much on trust from the suppliers. A particular problem they found was that it was not possible to verify all the statements of the suppliers with respect to the various environments that they supported, which version numbers of products were available in which environment, when new versions would be available, what features were in what release and the quality control procedures for each new release. This was compounded by the habit of nearly all suppliers to demonstrate the latest version of their product, not necessarily in the environment that is being evaluated or finally chosen.

- As a double-check ensure that all software evaluated is included in the supplier's response to the invitation to tender, e.g. operating system, database management system, 4GL, development tools, utility programs and application software

- At the end of an application software product evaluation it is important to reflect on overall product fit. If the product fit is below 85 per cent then is it the right product for you? If in order to achieve an acceptable level of fit to the requirement amendments have been specified or there is a reliance on future releases consider their long-term impact. Software amendments will impact the initial acceptance procedures and each new release of the software. As a result, too many amendments can significantly affect both risk and cost calculations.

The two key criteria with respect to the hardware are initial sizing and configuring, and flexibility in the future. Hardware products are normally in overlapping ranges. The effect of this is that a configuration at the top of one range might be cheaper than a configuration at the bottom of the next range. However, the cost of upgrading from the top of a range is normally high, as it involves a box swap; whereas the cost of upgrading from the bottom of a range is less, as it is normally a field upgrade. It is therefore important to understand the product ranges, their pricing and match this to future requirements.

Other items will come to the surface during the course of the software and hardware evaluations. Items to evaluate are interfacing and integration

EVALUATION

with external systems, compliance with relevant standards and the quality of all documentation.

Operational requirements

Key items to consider are:

- Level of expertise required to administer and manage the system

> **CASE STUDY**
>
> **PEPE JEANS**
> The requirements stated '... a standard off-the-shelf package operating in a computing and communications environment that could be facility managed'. Once the software supplier had been selected a very quick hardware evaluation selected NCR with AT&T as the facility's manager for the computer and communications network.

- Backup procedures and how long they will take
- Standby arrangements
- Resilience of the hardware and software to degradation
- Allowances for growth for the future
- Sizing and performance guarantees are notoriously difficult to extract from suppliers because of the complexities involved. One way round this is to include stress test and benchmark results in the agreement as a way of indicating performance. In practice, this is only realistic for large and complex systems or when there is genuine concern over the response time of critical transactions, i.e. sales order processing. Sizing and performance can also be significantly affected by how the software is used. It is therefore advisable to delay the final sizing calculations, if possible, until after the conference pilot when the use of the software will be reasonably well defined. Factors that can affect performance and sizing are the communications environment, the amount of data required to be available on-line, the profile of typical on-line enquiries, module integration and the options selected for critical high-volume transactions. When planning for the future it is safer to assume that as more functionality is added, and software made easier to use, each new release of the software will demand more computing resources.

Services evaluation

Services are people and people need training, management and experience. The following is a checklist to evaluate suppliers' services.

Experience

Do the supplier's staff have the necessary experience? Is this experience relevant to our needs? Is this experience relevant to our industry?

Implementation capability

Does the supplier have the capability to implement our solution? A good way to test capability is to build a detailed implementation plan with the final short-listed suppliers during the evaluation. Using the experience gained from the evaluation to date, build implementation plans bearing in mind the suppliers' capability, their products and services, and your assessment of the risk. Typical questions arising are will the implementation involve third parties? How do the suppliers react to this? What are the responsibilities and duties of the supplier and the customer? How does this affect the agreement?

A typical implementation plan for a turnkey solution will clearly indicate project team, user and suppliers' responsibilities and includes:

- Final implementation planning and quality procedures
- Project team training
- Hardware delivery and acceptance
- Software delivery and acceptance
- Conference room pilot
- Final agreement on changes or amendments resulting from the conference room pilot
- Design of forms and stationery
- Developing user procedures, manuals and training courses
- Delivery and acceptance of modifications
- Technical manuals
- Systems testing
- User training
- Data take-on
- Pilot or parallel running
- Hand-over
- Live
- Procedures for future changes.

EVALUATION 145

BRITISH TELECOM **CASE STUDY**
The [implementation] plan is for each individual department within finance to own its part of the implementation. This plan was agreed with Oracle during the evaluation and a factor in the decision-making process.

Management

Is the supplier's management team committed to our solution?

Personnel

What are the suppliers' personnel policies? Are they compatible with ours? Do we want to agree not to poach each other's staff?

Project management

Does the supplier have the necessary project management skills and experience to manage our project? Have they managed a similar project? Is our project larger or smaller than their average project?

Service levels

How many staff does the supplier employ? Are subcontractors used? What is the supplier's organizational structure? How many staff are actually available to support our project? How many other projects is the supplier supporting? What is the ratio of customers to helpdesks? What is the average response time from the helpdesk? How are helpdesk calls prioritized? Are service level statistics available for inspection? Does the supplier have standard service level agreements?

Technical competence

Do the supplier's staff have the necessary technical competence to support our project?

Training

What are the supplier's training programmes to keep their staff up to date?

Supplier evaluation

Supplier evaluation is a key part of the initial short-listing criteria and is then traditionally not revisited until the end of the selection phase. Certainly not everyone agrees with this!

> **CASE STUDY**
>
> PEPE JEANS
> Rob de Meij also believes that preparing the invitation to tender should have taken only two months and that the evaluation would have been quicker and easier had they taken up references earlier.

Financial viability

Review the supplier's most recent accounts and request a full list of all new business won in the last year. Within the IT industry suppliers are continually waxing and waning, try to position where the supplier's products and services are within their natural life cycle. Also try to position how the products or services on offer fit into the supplier's overall business plan. Two situations to beware of are older products, probably rich in functionality, but viewed by the supplier as a cash cow and receiving little investment; and products or services that are peripheral to the supplier's main line of business and therefore liable to be either ignored by senior management or divested.

Research and development

Try to take a balanced view of each supplier's future and direction. How will they respond to changes in the market that will happen during the projected life cycle of the new system? What is their track record for delivering new products and releases on time?

> **CASE STUDY**
>
> PRUDENTIAL ASSURANCE
> The product evaluation was managed by the specialist IT procurement group. Each short-listed system software product was benchmarked against each short-listed hardware product using the CIS prototype as a model to simulate the technical requirements. The results of this technical evaluation were then compared with the research and development plans of the suppliers, their track record of delivering new releases on time, quality of new releases, product life cycle expectations, price performance and an overall supplier appraisal.

Internal procedures

Ask to see the supplier's quality manual, visit the supplier and check that the procedures are actually being followed.

User references

User references are normally carried out late in the evaluation process. Their purpose is to confirm views already formed by the project team. The selection of references is largely dependent on the suppliers and you should expect supplier-supplied references to be good. In order to get as accurate a picture as possible, discuss the selection of references in detail with the suppliers. The objective of a reference might severely restrict the choice of possible sites. Broadly, objectives are credibility that is best gained by talking to as many references as possible; confirming implementation plans that is best achieved by talking to sites of a similar size and in the same industry; and confirming technical points that is best achieved by talking to sites using the proposed configuration and processing similar volumes. Sometimes all the above objectives can be achieved from two or three references. If this is not possible, proceed in parallel with your different objectives, talk to as many references as is required. As far as possible, try to stay in control of the selection of the reference sites and do not leave it to the supplier whose objectives are not necessarily in line with yours.

To make each reference visit or telephone call as productive as possible plan carefully:

- Identify areas for discussion

- Decide who will attend (the fewer, the better)

- Ask the suppliers to supply details of references, i.e.
  - Contact
  - When products installed or service started
  - Version numbers of software
  - Status, i.e. live or implementing
  - Use of products
  - Number of users
  - Size of project team
  - Scope of implementation
  - Length of implementation.

Send or fax in advance to the planned user references the background of your evaluation and list of areas that you would like to discuss. When talking to references take into account where they have come from and what they have achieved. By careful selection and preparation it is possible to check via references:

- Supplier service levels

- Implementation ability of supplier

- Technical ability of the supplier

- Ease of implementation
- Product functionality
- Product ease of use
- Technical efficiency of the product in the proposed environment.

Lastly, major products and service organizations normally have user groups. Sometimes it is possible to attend user group meetings, but in any case it should be possible to talk to representatives of the user group. A large user group will also have subgroups for each major product and service.

Final short-list

The objective of this step is to produce a final short-list of between one and three suppliers for detailed financial analysis. The average of case studies researched for this book is two.

Decision making

CHAPTER
13

Introduction

The two steps of the decision-making process are first, the recommendation and second, the capital request. The recommendation is the selection by the project team of the best solution to meet the business needs and requirements. The project team recommendation is presented to the steering committee for approval and followed by the capital request. The capital request is an updated business case with its benefits to justify proceeding with the recommendation. It is presented to the steering committee for approval and to corporate management for authority to proceed. The total decision-making process is illustrated in Figure 9.1.

Organizations that authorize projects on receipt of the initial business case, such that projects are not then subject to a final capital approval step, will need to complete only the first part of this step as the second part is unnecessary.

Recommendation

Critical success factors

Critical success factors when making and approving the recommendation are:

- Have we considered the organizational impact of the project?
- Have we considered the personnel and training ramifications of the project?
- What change management issues does the project raise?
- Have we considered all the risks?
- Did we select the best suppliers for the final short-list?
- Did the evaluation model help us identify the issues and differentiate between the suppliers?

- Have we identified all the costs?
- How accurate are the costs?
- Is the recommended supplier committed to the project?
- Does the supplier understand our business objectives?
- Have we recommended the optimum cost solution?

Format of the recommendation

The recommendation consists of an introduction, details of the final short-listed suppliers and the recommended solution with its supporting arguments.

Introduction

The introduction includes details of the project team, their responsibilities and terms of reference as well as key dates and activities. It also outlines the key selection criteria stating the number of suppliers on the long-list that were issued the request for proposal, the number of suppliers on the initial short-list that were issued the invitation to tender, the number of suppliers responding to the invitation to tender and the number of suppliers on the final short-list.

Final short-listed suppliers

For each supplier on the final short-list include the invitation to tender supplier's evaluation model (see Chapter 12) and the suppliers' financial evaluation model (see below) together with a short assessment covering:

- Functional requirements
- Common requirements and characteristics
- Technical and operational requirements
- Implementation considerations
- Suppliers' requirements
- Further options
- Supplier track record
- Cost of proposals
- Compliance with terms and conditions.

Recommendation and reasons

(See below.)

Suppliers' financial evaluation model

The suppliers' evaluation model consists of an individual model per supplier. Each individual model contains all the costs associated with that supplier's proposal. These costs include all the direct costs from the suppliers' response to the invitation to tender as updated by the evaluation process or as a result of a post-invitation to tender best and final offer bid. The costs are obviously more accurate if an agreement has been negotiated as part of the evaluation process. The costs also include all the costs of implementing the solution, e.g. initial environmental costs of preparing a computer room, implementation costs, on-going running and management costs. The model is built either for the life cycle of the project or whatever time period is used to evaluate projects.

One major area is hidden costs. This is particularly relevant when comparing mainframe, distributed and workstation/PC-based solutions. There is currently considerable debate as to the real costs of running the latter two solutions. This is because the costs are distributed, i.e. hardware, software, support, management time and communications, and because the technology is new and still evolving. Mainframe costs are easier to quantify simply because mainframes have been around for a long period of time and are therefore well understood.

The underlying assumption at this stage is that all the suppliers on the final short-list can supply a satisfactory solution. The evaluation to date has been essentially qualitative and the merits of each final short-listed supplier scored in the invitation to tender summary evaluation summary (see Chapter 12). To complete the evaluation a quantitative financial analysis of the competing solutions is prepared as the last step in the evaluation process (see Table 13.1). The last line in the example model is contingency. This is used both as a contingency and as a risk factor. If within the costs there are areas of risk or uncertainty then add either a fixed amount to the costs of the proposal or a percentage in line with the risk.

Table 13.1 Suppliers' financial evaluation model (£000)

Supplier's name ....

Years	1	2	3	4	5	6	7	etc.
INITIAL SUPPLIER COSTS								
Computer hardware								
Communication equipment								
Software licences								
Software modification								
Implementation and training								
Fixed price								
Variable price								
Project management								
Services								
ON-GOING SUPPLIER COSTS								
Computer hardware support and maintenance								
Communication equipment support and maintenance								
Software licences								
Software support and maintenance								
Project management								
Services								
INITIAL OTHER COSTS								
Environment								
In-house implementation								
ON-GOING OTHER COSTS								
Telecommunications								
Staff support costs								
Consumables								
Environment								
CONTINGENCY								
TOTALS								

Making the recommendation

The culmination of the project team's effort at the end of the selection phase is the recommendation. The objective of the project team in preparing the recommendation is to select the best solution.

The two key decision factors associated with this are first, does the invitation to tender suppliers' evaluation model accurately reflect our requirements and our qualitative assessment of the suppliers' responses? Second, does the suppliers' financial evaluation model accurately reflect our quantitative analysis of the proposed solutions?

These two documents are the prime input to the decision-making process. The systematic approach used to prepare them will ensure that the project team has been thorough. The invitation to tender suppliers' evaluation model is built up step by step. Supply options are carefully considered in line with the business requirements and the qualitative assessment of each short-listed supplier is based on the operational requirements of the organization and should accurately reflect the overall quality of each supplier's solution. The suppliers' financial evaluation model includes all the direct costs and the indirect costs associated with the solution. Once the project team is satisfied that these two documents are complete and that all the suppliers on the final short-list can supply a satisfactory solution then the final evaluation takes place. Frequently the decision is straightforward. If one solution wins both the qualitative and quantitative models then the decision is obvious. If, however, the answer is not clear-cut then the right balance has to be struck between the qualitative and the quantitative. One simple solution is to select the lowest-cost option. Another is to assume that all costs within a pre-specified percentage of each other are treated as equal, therefore allowing the qualitative model to take preference if all the final costs are within the percentage.

EXAMPLE

The results of the invitation to tender suppliers' evaluation model are as shown in Table 13.2 with suppliers C and D comprising the final short-list. The results of the suppliers financial evaluation model are supplier C £105 000 and supplier D £100 000.

Table 13.2 Example quantitative financial analysis

Criteria	Max. score	Suppliers A	B	C	D	E	etc.
Totals	1000	632	744	877	845	775	

If the final selection criterion is the lowest cost then supplier D is selected, even though the solution from supplier C was qualitatively better and perhaps preferred by the project team. If, however, a 5 per cent tolerance is allowed, on the assumption that the costs estimates were only accurate to 5 per cent in the first place, then supplier C is selected.

> **CASE STUDY**
>
> BRITISH TELECOM
>
> The final recommendation was a balance between the functional capabilities of the competing products on one side and, on the other, the softer issues like the quality of support and services, how well organized and committed the supplier is to the project. In the words of Lynn Bowring, controller financial systems, 'in the final analysis it is relatively easy to decide the original short-listing on a mechanical functional basis, the final decision, however, is more influenced by subjective factors as we will have to work very closely with the successful supplier for a long time'.

> **CASE STUDY**
>
> BOLTON METRO
>
> The final phase of the evaluation involved extensive formal and informal reference checking of the two suppliers by both the staff and the evaluation panel. At the end of this process, the evaluation panel selected a preferred facilities management supplier, and this conclusion was conveyed to the staff during final comprehensive staff presentations. This was followed by a staff ballot. The staff were invited first, to state their preference: to be part of a facilities management arrangement now, or to remain as an in-house direct service organization, or to state if they had no preference; and second, to vote for one of the two final short-listed suppliers, or to state if they had no preference. The result was an 85 per cent vote in favour of facilities management now and an almost unanimous vote in favour of the supplier recommended by the evaluation panel. The reasons for this are different and complex. The evaluation panel's judgement was more commercial and influenced by their views of the companies' credibility and financial proposal, whereas the staff vote was more influenced by their perception of the suppliers, their personal employment terms and conditions and pension arrangements and how they would be treated.

Approving the recommendation

The options available to the steering committee when evaluating the recommendation of the project team are to approve it and proceed with preparing the capital request, refer it back to the project team for further work or reject it. The first function of the steering committee is to quality assure the recommendation from the project team. The second function is to apply the critical success factors:

- Has the project team fully considered the organizational impact of the project?
- Has the project team considered all the personnel and training ramifications of the project?

- What change management issues does the project raise?
- Have we considered all the risks?
- Did the project team select the best suppliers for the final short-list?
- Did the evaluation model help the project team to identify the issues and differentiate between the suppliers?
- Have we identified all the costs?
- How accurate are the costs?
- Is the recommended supplier committed to the project?
- Does the recommended supplier understand our business objectives?
- Has the project team recommended the optimum cost solution?

Capital request

Critical success factors

Critical success factors when preparing, approving and authorizing the capital request are:

- Do we need the benefits?
- Can we achieve the benefits?
- What is the risk?
- Are we achieving the benefits at optimum cost?

Format of the capital request

The capital request is an updated business case that is submitted to management for a decision. This decision will normally be to proceed, defer or refer the capital request for further consideration, or reject the capital request. The capital request includes seven key elements:

1. Management summary
2. Statement of the business need
3. Summary of requirements
4. Recommendation
5. Costs

6. Benefits

7. Risk analysis.

1 Management summary

A management summary introduces the capital request, stating the nature of the decision required from the steering committee and corporate management, the timetable, and the management issues arising.

2 Statement of the business need (see Chapters 5 and 9)

In this section the business need is clearly stated and categorized accordingly, i.e.

- Cost driven
- Infrastructure improvement
- Key business ratios
- Market driven
- Organizational
- Risk management
- Volume driven.

3 Summary of requirements (see Chapters 6 and 10)

- Scope
- Functional requirements
- Common requirements and characteristics
- Technical requirements
- Operational requirements
- Implementation considerations
- Personnel considerations
- Management considerations
- Supplier requirements (see Chapter 11).

4 Recommendation (see above)

The recommendation consists of an introduction, details of the final short-listed suppliers and the recommended solution with its supporting arguments.

5 *Costs* (see above)

This section brings forward the costs from the recommended supplier's financial model plus any other costs that are relevant to the project but were not relevant to the comparative suppliers' financial evaluation model, i.e.

- Consulting fees
- Legal fees
- Personnel and training
- Internal IT services
- Change management
- Organizational impact
- Project management (10-15 per cent)
- Overall contingency (10-25 per cent).

6 *Benefits* (see Chapters 5 and 9)

This section schedules the tangible and intangible benefits and *owning* users and management. It is normal to quantify tangible benefits, but in doing so the assumptions used to calculate the benefits must be stated. It is not normal to quantify intangible benefits.

7 *Risk analysis* (see Chapter 9)

This is an assessment of the risks, impact and consequences associated with the proposal.

Capital request evaluation models

A variety of models are used to evaluate capital requests. Tables 13.3-13.5 are three of the most common: payback, average rate of return and discounted cash flow. Each of the methods has its advantages and disadvantages. The decision as to which method to use is outside the scope of this book and is normally established as a corporate policy. The models illustrated are very simple. In practice models for large projects are complicated and need to be built using either a spreadsheet or a specialized decision support package.

Payback is the simplest method and calculates how long it will take to pay back the investment. In Table 13.3 the investment of £100 000 is repaid in year 4 when the cash flow becomes positive.

Table 13.3 Payback over 4 years (£000)

Years	0	1	2	3	4
CASH OUT					
Capital	100			10	
On-going costs		12	12	12	13
TOTAL	100	12	12	22	13
CASH IN					
Initial benefits		40			
On-going benefits		10	45	45	50
TOTAL	0	50	45	45	50
Net cash flow	−100	38	33	23	37
Cumulative net cash flow	−100	−62	−29	−6	31

The payback method does not take into account any future returns on the investment. The second method extends the model over the life of the project and then calculates the average rate of return. In Table 13.4 the return is £162 000 over the seven-year life of the project, giving an average rate of return of 23 per cent (i.e. 162 000/100 000/7 × 100 per cent).

Table 13.4 Payback over 7 years (£000)

Years	0	1	2	3	4	5	6	7
CASH OUT								
Capital	100			10				
On-going costs		12	12	12	13	13	13	13
TOTAL	100	12	12	22	13	13	13	13
CASH IN								
Initial benefits		40						
On-going benefits		10	45	45	50	55	60	55
TOTAL	0	50	45	45	50	55	60	55
Net cash flow	−100	38	33	23	37	42	47	42
Cumulative net cash flow	−100	−62	−29	−6	31	73	120	162

The average rate of return overcomes the objection to the simple payback method by taking into account the life of the project. However, this does not take into account the *value* of the return. In order to do that then future values need to be discounted to their present-day value.

Discount tables are available for different rates over any period of time. For example, the discount rates of 10 per cent for one year is 0.91, two years, 0.83, three years 0.75, etc. Applying these rates to Table 13.4 and then recalculating the average rate of return comes up with a different answer.

Table 13.5 Payback using discounted cash flow over 7 years (£000)

Years	0	1	2	3	4	5	6	7
CASH OUT								
Capital	100			10				
On-going costs		12	12	12	13	13	13	13
TOTAL	100	12	12	22	13	13	13	13
CASH IN								
Initial benefits		40						
On-going benefits		10	45	45	50	55	60	55
TOTAL	0	50	45	45	50	55	60	55
Net cash flow	−100	38	33	23	37	42	47	42
Discount factor at 10%		0.91	0.83	0.75	0.64	0.62	0.56	0.51
Net cash flow discounted at 10%		35	27	17	24	26	26	21
Cumulative net discounted cash flow	−100	−65	−38	−21	3	29	55	76

In Table 13.5 using discounted cash flow the return is now £76 000 which, over the seven-year life of the project gives an average rate of return of 11 per cent (i.e. 76 000/100 000/7 × 100 per cent).

Preparing the capital request

Most of the information needed for the capital request is now available. The capital request is an updated business case plus the recommendation and an updated suppliers financial evaluation model in the form of a capital request model (see above). The project team now has two areas to complete:

1. Review and update the original business case
2. Build the capital request model.

Review and update the original business case

The business case is built on the business needs, the requirements to meet them and the benefits. What has changed since these were prepared? Do these changes alter any of the underlying foundations of the business case? Two of the key factors reviewed when the original business case was prepared are the impact of the project on the organization and risk analysis (see Chapter 9). Are they still valid?

Build the capital request model

After the original business case is reviewed the capital request model is built based on the recommended suppliers' evaluation model. This model compares solutions and, as such, contains only the costs directly and indirectly associated with the suppliers' proposal. To complete the capital request model all other costs are added and the quantified tangible benefits agreed by their *owning* users and management.

The last item is to consider the financial impact of the project.

- How will it be accounted for?
- Will it affect any previous accounting decisions?
- What is the depreciation policy?
- Are there any tax ramifications?
- How does it affect the balance sheet?

Approving the capital request

The options available to the steering committee when evaluating the capital request are to forward it to corporate management for authorization, refer the capital request back to the project team for further work, or reject the capital request altogether. When evaluating the capital request the steering committee reviews the first three of the fundamental decision-making criteria (see Chapter 9).

Do we need the benefits?

- Are the business needs still relevant to our current business objectives and corporate priorities?
- Do we need the benefits?
- Does the business case move the organization forward? Are the underlying assumptions radical enough? Do we need to apply business process re-engineering before going any further?
- What happens if we do nothing?

Can we achieve the benefits?

- Have the benefits been agreed by the *owning* users and management? Are they achievable? How accurate is the costing? What is the margin of error?
- What is the commitment to the project? Is management committed? Are the users committed? Is the IT department committed? Is the project team committed?
- What is the level of expectation? Is it achievable? Is it set correctly for management and users?

What are the risks?

- Project management:
  - Is the scope of the project defined correctly?
  - Do the requirements accurately reflect our business needs?
  - Have we selected the right supply options and suppliers?
  - Do we understand the technical risks associated with any hardware or software?
  - Do we understand the risks associated with the project, i.e. size, complexity, duration, phasing, difficulty?
  - Does the project have a viable plan?
  - Can we adequately resource the project?
- Has the project team fully considered the organizational impact of the project? Personnel and training ramifications? Change management issues? Management issues?
- Have we considered all the risks? Has anything changed that affects risk?

Then the steering committee addresses the fourth and last of the fundamental decision-making criteria, namely, *are we achieving the benefits at optimum cost?*

- Have we considered the organizational impact of the project?
- Have we considered the personnel and training ramifications of the project?
- What change management issues does the project raise?
- Have we identified all the costs?
- How accurate are the costs?
- Is the recommended supplier committed to the project?
- Does the supplier understand our business objectives?

Authorizing the capital request

The options available to corporate management when evaluating the capital request are to authorize the capital request, refer the capital request back, or reject the capital request altogether. When evaluating the business case corporate management primarily applies the first of the fundamental decision-making criteria—*do we need the benefits?* The decision factors associated with it are:

- Are the business needs relevant to our current business objectives and corporate priorities?
- Do the benefits represent a reasonable return on investment?
- What will be the impact on the organization?
- How will the project be viewed externally?
- What is the risk?
- Can we afford it?
- What happens if we do nothing?

Supply agreements

CHAPTER 14

Critical success factors

Critical success factors when negotiating and finalizing supply agreements are:

- Do we understand the strengths and weaknesses of our position?
- Do we understand the strengths and weaknesses of the supplier's position?
- Do we have the necessary technical, purchasing and legal skills?
- Are we approaching the negotiations to conclude a win/win agreement with the supplier?

Best and final offer

The most appropriate time to invite best and final offers is at the end of the evaluation before finalizing the suppliers' financial evaluation model. By this time the costs of the suppliers' solution should be clear to the project team, any questions and queries arising from the suppliers' invitation to tender response sorted out and an implementation plan built with the suppliers. The format of the best and final offer will depend on the nature of the procurement. The ground rules are:

- Limit all direct communication with the suppliers to one clearly defined channel during the negotiation step. If the negotiations cover an extended period then this policy can have a down side. One of the critical success factors in implementing an IT solution is a sound long-term working relationship with the supplier. The right time to start to build such a relationship is during the evaluation and cement it by negotiating a win/win agreement. This process can be hindered if the project team is not allowed to communicate with the suppliers or support the negotiations. This is especially the case if the only contact the suppliers have is with a hard-nosed negotiator who may not have the long-term interests of the project in mind and who probably will have no long-term involvement in the project;

- Agree at least the outline terms and conditions with the suppliers before inviting best and final offers
- Agree with the suppliers precisely what they are quoting
- Clearly state that this is the last round, that best and final offer means just that and that the recommendation will be based on the suppliers' quotations
- Clearly state that the suppliers must include all costs.

CASE STUDY

PRUDENTIAL ASSURANCE

All IT supply agreements are negotiated by the specialist IT procurement group. One of their fundamental rules is that during the negotiating period all contact between the Prudential and the suppliers must be via this group. This is to ensure that the best possible terms and conditions are negotiated and at the same time stopping interesting parties confusing the issue.

Negotiating

The objective of any negotiation is to achieve a win/win agreement that is good for both parties. If the final result is one-sided then it will adversely affect the agreement. IT solutions are frequently complicated, require a high degree of expertise to make them work and normally have plenty of scope for discussion and disagreement. If one side or the other believes that they have ended up with a poor deal then either the customer will try to get more out of the supplier than the supplier is expecting to give or the supplier will try to get more out of the customer than the customer has budgeted. Neither is a good starting point for what should be the beginning of a long and satisfactory working relationship. However, it is a fact that the prices paid for similar IT solutions have varied greatly and that negotiating is an essential part of the selection process.

The objective of the best and final offer is to ensure that the costings used to make the recommendation are as accurate as possible. Final final negotiations take place after best and final offer! The objective is to agree the best possible terms and conditions with the preferred or recommended supplier.

In order to conclude the final round of negotiations as quickly and as satisfactorily as possible it is important to prepare carefully. The following is a checklist of things to do before starting negotiations:

- Decide who is responsible for the negotiations, what are their limits of authority and understand your own internal procedures for confirming the negotiations, formalizing and signing agreements and purchase orders

- Find out the suppliers' negotiating procedures, limits of authority and who is responsible for accepting new orders and agreements on their behalf. This is particularly important when negotiating with a representative, agent or dealer of a hardware manufacturer or software author. They will be restricted in their ability to negotiate, especially on terms and conditions, and there is little point in negotiating terms and conditions that the representative, agent or dealer cannot deliver
- Prepare best-case and worst-case scenarios
- Consider the outcome if you cannot proceed
- Identify your weak and strong points
- Identify the supplier's weak and strong points
- Prepare a list of items to discuss and notify the supplier in advance
- Identify any issues that the supplier will raise
- Consider what benefits you can offer the supplier
- Is leasing a viable option? It is possible to include all initial capital costs, including software, and five years' hardware and software maintenance charges in a lease. However, it is essential to balance the risks of committing and effectively prepaying for future services against the cost savings that might be negotiable from the supplier. Put another way, it is no good prepaying for services in five years' time if, come the time you do not want them or the supplier cannot deliver, you will probably not get your money back.
- How can you improve your negotiating position?
- Facts to consider when negotiating include:
  - Budget
  - How important is the solution to you? How important does the supplier think it is to you?
  - How important is the deal to the supplier? How important do you think it is to the supplier?
  - The size of the deal
  - The number of products involved and multi-product discounts
  - The number of sites involved and multi-site discounts
  - Options that might be required in the future
  - Future potential to the supplier
  - The term of the deal and cancellation options
  - Risk sharing.

Agreements

Introduction

The starting point for contract negotiations depends on a number of factors, i.e. the size of the procurement, who you are and whether you have a tried and tested contract, the nature of the procurement and the view of the supplier. In practice, most software is licensed on the suppliers' standard agreement or a variation of it. More complicated turnkey agreements and system integration agreements might be based on a standard agreement from the Chartered Institute of Purchasing & Supply or based on the suppliers' or on a specially prepared agreement. Facilities management and outsourcing agreements are more likely to be specially prepared because of the complexity and the high value of the agreement. When negotiating and drafting one-off agreements an important point is who controls the paperwork. When the agreement is based on a suppliers' original or a pro forma from, say, the Chartered Institute of Purchasing & Supply then this is not so important. But in the case of complex turnkey, system integration, facilities management and outsourcing agreements then an effective method of keeping control of the paperwork and ensuring that negotiations start from your draft agreement is to include a sound draft in the invitation to tender.

Turnkey agreements and software licences

Turnkey agreements typically include computer and telecommunications hardware, software and services. Hardware can be depreciated and disposed off like any normal asset. Software, on the other hand, is different. Software products are normally licensed to be used under strict terms and conditions. Because of this it is essential that the use of the software both now and in the future is anticipated by the project team. Renegotiating software licences can be both time consuming and expensive. The reason software products are licensed and not sold is that the cost of development of the software normally far exceeds any one licence fee and therefore no rights of ownership are transferred to the user. Whereas software products are licensed to users and owned by the authors the same is not necessarily true of bespoke software. When the full development cost of the software is paid for by the user then it is reasonable that the software is then owned by the user. If this is the intention then it must be clearly stated in the agreement.

A difficult area is amendments to application packages that are fully funded by one user. Two problems can arise. First, when the amendment gives the user a competitive advantage, how can the software authors be restrained from releasing the amendment to other and potentially competitive users? This can only be resolved by negotiation up-front before the amendment is commissioned. Second, should the funder of the amendment be reimbursed by the author for future sales of the amendment? This is a more difficult issue as frequently amendments are subsequently rolled into future releases of the package and therefore the value of any one amendment is impossible to access. Generally, it is better to negotiate a simple up-front arrangement than get involved in complex deals that are difficult to monitor and in practice are not likely to make a significant return.

Supply agreements cover the initial supply of product and services and on acceptance are complete, subject to any on-going warranties. They are complemented by maintenance agreements that cover the future support of the solution once the supply has been accepted. It is possible to include the supply and maintenance agreements in one combined agreement. However, for drafting reasons it is preferable to separate them. There are frequently several points of overlap between the supply and maintenance agreements that can cause confusion. First, there is the hardware warranty. The warranty in the supply agreement might be less generous than the support arrangements in the maintenance agreement, i.e. the supply agreement warranty might be 90-days' return to supplier, whereas the maintenance agreement is 4-hour response on-site support. Second is the software warranty. Software is normally licensed with a 90-day bug-fixing clause but the software maintenance agreement will provide a more comprehensive service. Once the software is accepted it will normally take months before the software is live. The question to resolve with the supplier is when the software maintenance agreement comes into effect. Normally it is on acceptance of the software as the project team will need access to the full range of services offered by the software maintenance agreement.

The following is a checklist of items to be considered. The list cannot be inclusive for all circumstances and in any case professional negotiating and legal skills should be retained by the project team before concluding any agreement.

Supply agreement(s)

Computer configuration
Communications configuration
Environmental requirements
Bespoke software specification
Software products with version numbers
Software amendments specification
Specification of *futures*

Specification of services
Project team training
User training
Software licence conditions
   -Ownership
   -Usage rights? By type or size of processor? By number of users? By site(s)? For standby processing?
   -Transferability? To another company? If taken over? To a facilities management or outsourcing supplier?
   -Period of the licence
   -Renewal options
   -Future upgrades
   -Warranties
   (Note: It is necessary to consider the licence conditions for each supplier and perhaps each product, e.g. operating system, systems software, utilities, applications software.)
User responsibilities
Service levels
Delivery and acceptance procedures, performance criteria and payment terms for each of the following:
   -Computer hardware
   -Communications hardware
   -Bespoke software
   -Software products
   -Software amendments
   -Software futures
   -Services: fixed price and variable
   -Training
   -Escrow arrangements
Change control procedures
Options in the future to upgrade either hardware or software at pre-agreed prices or conditions
General terms and conditions
Appendices
   -Specifications of computer hardware
   -Specifications of communications hardware
   -Detailed specifications of bespoke software
   -Detailed specifications of software amendments
   -Invitation to tender
   -Suppliers' response to the invitation to tender.

Maintenance agreement(s)

Specification of computer hardware maintenance service

Specification of communications hardware maintenance service
Specification of software maintenance service
Service-level agreements
Start date
Period
Payment terms
Renewal options
Cancellation options
Price reviews
Product changes (e.g. fixes, new releases, upgrades)
User responsibilities
Change control procedures
(Note: In a turnkey agreement one supplier may contract for all the maintenance services, perhaps subcontracting part of them; or maintenance agreements entered into directly with the original suppliers; or maintenance agreements entered into with independent third-party maintenance suppliers.)

Facilities management and outsourcing agreements

Whereas turnkey supply agreements and software licences can normally be agreed very quickly (perhaps a matter of a few days) facilities management and outsourcing agreements are much more complicated and normally take months to negotiate. Further turnkey supply agreements and software licences are frequently negotiated and executed without legal advice, which is not the same for facilities management and outsourcing agreements.

CASE STUDY

BIRMINGHAM CITY COUNCIL
Between May and July the formal agreement was negotiated between the City and the supplier. The City retained a private solicitor to help them with the negotiations and to prepare the agreement. The agreement was then double-checked by the City's legal department before signature. The agreement itself is 30 pages but with the various schedules and appendices is two inches thick. The agreement is made up of three separate agreements:

1. Transfer assets
2. Buy back services
3. Lease for the data centre building.

These agreements were supported by schedules containing the service-level agreements and appendices containing the software licences. Most of the system software licences were transferred to the supplier, whereas most of the application software licences were retained by the City as they were deemed personal to the City and not transferable by the licensor. The application software owned and developed by the City was only licensed to the supplier and ownership retained by the City. With respect to the hardware, the agreement encompasses both outsourcing and facilities management. The IBM mainframe computers were transferred to the supplier under a classical outsourcing arrangement. The ICL and Bull mainframe computers were retained by the City, because of the leasing conditions, and are managed in a classical facilities management arrangement by the supplier.

The agreement was for five years. The City retains the right to vary the agreement and procedures; add, drop and change schedules; with an arbitration clause to sort out any disputes.

CASE STUDY

BOLTON METRO

A seven-year agreement, with an option to terminate after five years, was negotiated by the finance director and the IT manager with the help of a private solicitor. The agreement is made up of three separate agreements and runs to about 50 pages:

1. Transfer of assets
2. Provision of services including model service-level agreements
3. Lease for buildings.

CASE STUDY

TRENT REGIONAL HEALTH AUTHORITY

The negotiations of the supply agreement were driven by Trent RHA who retained expert legal advice. The agreements took three months to negotiate, resulting in seven agreements:

1. Transfer of the assets of the RCC
2. Service agreements between the supplier and the RCC customers (the detailed supporting service-level agreements took another three months to negotiate)
3. Software licences for crown software
4. Software licences for consortia software developed by the RCC in conjunction with its customers
5. Premises lease
6. Short-term telephone lease
7. Consultancy agreement for the staff who did not transfer.

Points of interest arising from the negotiating process were:

- Instruct and control the solicitors carefully and retain control of the paperwork
- The agreement did not include due diligence
- Assess the risks of transferring undertakings previously carried out by internal staff. An example is that the agreement includes fraud insurance cover as the supplier is conducting transactions on behalf of its customers (i.e. BACS money transfers)
- Watch out for conflict of interest during the negotiation process between the employees of the RHA and the RCC and their personal future
- The agreement includes a right of audit by the RHA.

I am grateful to Rory Graham of Bird & Bird for supplying the following outline of an outsourcing transfer of assets agreement. (Note: the agreement has a front sheet and a list of the parties, as well as a recital setting out what the agreement addresses. Notes on the operative provisions of the agreement only are set out below. Schedules to the agreement would set out assets to be transferred to the service provider, list any employees to transfer and other relevant information.)

1 Definitions

(Note: it makes the agreement easier to follow if the defined terms are set out at the start.)

2 Agreement for sale and transfer

(Note: this recites the fact that the IT activities of the customer, or a defined part of them, are to be transferred to the service provider as if they were a going concern.)

3 Consideration

(Note: usually the service provider makes a payment to the customer to reflect the value of the assets being transferred. This clause deals with this payment and related VAT and other tax issues.)

4 Completion

(Note: this sets out the date and timing of the transfer of the assets.)

5 Transferred contracts

(Note: this deals with the assignment or novation of those contracts with third-party suppliers (e.g. software licensors) which are in the name of the customer but which are to be transferred to the service provider. This will address the responsibility for obtaining any consents necessary from such third parties to the transfer and division of responsibility between customer and service provider for actions before and after the transfer.)

6 Employees

(Note: this sets out the respective responsibilities of the parties with regard to those of the customer's employees deployed within the in-house service, its content being largely dependent on whether or not TUPE (the Transfer of Undertakings (Protection of Employment) Regulations 1981) applies. If applicable, terms for incorporation will include, for example, the allocation of risk in relation to, respectively, pre- and post-completion liabilities to transferring staff. This is best dealt with by way of mutual indemnification. Similarly, the service provider will probably wish to address liabilities to employees who may as a matter of law transfer to the service provider, but whom by design or oversight the parties have not contemplated will be transferring; and liabilities to certain former employees of the customer which may transfer automatically to the service provider. The customer, for its part, may seek, for example, reimbursement of any redundancy costs in respect of transferring employees, should TUPE later be held not to apply.)

7 Pensions

(Note: a record is often made here of the pensions terms, if any, the service provider intends for transferring employees.)

8 Premises

(Note: if the service provider is to be granted property rights to any of the premises of the customer – e.g. to a computer building – this clause will cross-refer to the lease to be signed on completion.)

9 Liabilities, obligations and apportionment

(Note: this usually sets out that the customer remains responsible for acts and omissions relating to the activities being transferred prior to that transfer and that the service provider is responsible for everything after transfer. It may also deal with apportioning responsibility for payment for e.g. leased lines, which relate partly to the period prior to transfer and partly to the period afterwards.)

10 Warranties

(Note: if included, this will cross-refer to a schedule in which the customer gives some basic warranties about the assets being transferred, e.g. that it owns the assets it is selling. If these warranties prove to be false, the service provider can sue for damages, subject to any conditions and limitations contained in the clause.)

11 Access to information

(Note: this gives the customer the right to require information about the transferred assets which it needs post transfer, e.g. access to books and records for tax and audit purposes.)

12 Guarantee

(Note: depending on the financial soundness of the service provider, it may be asked to provide a guarantee of its obligations from its parent company.)

13 Confidentiality

(Note: it would be normal for the parties to agree to keep confidential information each learned about the other and there may be reasons why the facts and terms of this agreement should also be kept secret.)

14 Costs

(Note: normally this would provide that each party bears its own legal and other costs connected with the agreement.)

15 General

(Note: this would include 'boilerplate' clauses common to most contracts, for example dealing with the giving of notice and governing law.)

Service-level agreements

Service-level agreements are between suppliers, either internal or external, and the users. They may be standalone or part of, say, a facilities management or outsourcing agreement. The following is a checklist of items to be considered that obviously cannot be inclusive for all circumstances. Each service-level agreement only covers one service. Therefore if more than one service is used then a separate agreement is required for each service.

Definition of service (e.g. computer processing, communications services, software development, software maintenance, training)
Definition of support and escalation procedures (e.g. helpdesk, how support calls are prioritized)
Definition of the users
Period of the agreement
Renewal options
Cancellation options
Change control procedures
Warranties and liquidated damages
Environmental requirements
User responsibilities

Delivery and acceptance procedures
Performance criteria
Fee structures
Payment terms
General terms and conditions.

I am grateful to Rory Graham of Bird & Bird for supplying the following outline of an outsourcing services agreement (Note: the agreement has a front sheet and a list of the parties, as well as a recital setting out what the agreement addresses. Notes on the operative provisions of the agreement only are set out below. Schedules to the agreement would set out the services to be performed, the service levels, the charges and other relevant information.)

1 Definitions

(Note: it makes the agreement easier to follow if the defined terms are set out at the start.)

2 Commencement and duration of agreement

(Note: this deals with the date the agreement comes into force and the ability of the parties to terminate on notice after an agreed period. It is not usual to have a fixed term with a 'drop dead' date but instead to allow notice to be given at any time after the initial period (typically, three to five years) has expired. The commencement date will usually be the same date as the transfer of assets agreement comes into effect.)

3 Provision of services

(Note: this clause sets out the basic obligation to provide services: the defined term 'services' will cross-refer to the schedules where the services and service levels will be set out. The date of service commencement will sometimes differ from the date of commencement of the agreement, for example if there is to be a period of migration to a new system on the service supplier's site.)

4 Access to sites

(Note: this deals with the right of the service provider to enter onto the customer's sites in order to provide the services and any restrictions on this—e.g. as to hours of access. There would also usually be a right for the user to refuse access in certain circumstances and an obligation on the service provider to comply with safety and security requirements. This section does not deal with any rights of exclusive occupation which may have been granted to the service provider under the Transfer of Assets Agreement, e.g. a lease of the computer room.)

5 Staff

(Note: this sets out an obligation on the service provider to use suitable staff and any obligation to obtain approval of new staff from the customer.)

6 Changes to the services

(Note: this crucial clause sets out the procedure for the customer to request new services or major changes to the existing services. Generally, minor changes or volume-related issues would be dealt with in a schedule. The customer would wish to have freedom to market test the provision of new services and to set out the basis of charging for such changes.)

7 Contracts

(Note: this deals with any new contracts with third-party suppliers which the service provider wishes to enter into in order to provide the services. These might include the procurement of leased lines or new software. Some customers may wish to have a right to input on the terms of such contracts. The clause also deals with any agreements with such suppliers that are in the name of the customer but which the service provider will deal with as part of the services. There should be an obligation on the service provider not to do anything that would put the customer in breach of such agreements, backed up with an indemnity.)

8 Prices and payment

(Note: this will generally refer to a charging schedule for the sums payable to the service provider and address the ways in which the charges can be increased, e.g. by indexation.)

9 Quality of services and credits

(Note: this will oblige the service provider to meet the service levels set out in the schedules and provide for the payment of credits against charges for failure to do so.)

10 Insurance

(Note: this will set out the levels of insurance, e.g. professional indemnity insurance, which the service provider will be obliged to maintain.)

11 Reporting, consultation and dispute resolution

(Note: this will set out the frequency of liaison meetings between the parties' representatives and also escalation procedures for disputes.)

12 Performance review

(Note: this provides for major reviews, usually once or twice a year, to identify problems and to discuss strategy.)

13 Confidentiality, data protection and security arrangements

(Note: this will cross-refer to security procedures set out in a schedule and also deal with compliance with data protection legislation. It will also give the customer rights to audit the provision of the services and to enter the service provider's premises to do this.)

14 Termination

(Note: this sets out the parties' rights to terminate and the triggers for exercise of such rights, for example breach of a material term of the agreement or insolvency of one party. This should not be confused with the right to terminate on notice at the end of an agreed minimum period without fault, as described in Clause 2.)

15 Consequences of termination

(Note: this sets out the principles governing the unwinding of the outsourcing contract and the transfer of the service provision to a new company or back in-house. The rights of the parties will depend on the reason for termination and on whether one party is at fault. Typically, it will deal with the transfer of, for example, software licences back to the customer as well as other practical rights to enable as smooth a transition as possible to take place.)

16 Force majeure

(Note: this sets out the circumstances in which a failure to perform will be deemed to be outside a party's reasonable control so as to avoid liability for that failure. Typically, it would allow a right to terminate if a *force majeure* event lasted for a significant period.)

17 Intellectual property rights

(Note: this deals with ownership of data processed by the service provider and software and other material produced by the service provider.)

18 Limitation of liability

(Note: it is normal for the service provider to be able to cap its liability to the customer for breach of contract and to allow exclusion of liability for consequential loss. This clause always requires careful thought to reflect a fair allocation of risk between the parties.)

19 Assignment and sub-contracting

(Note: this deals with the parties' rights to assign the contract and the ability of the service provider to subcontract any of its obligations.)

20 Parent company guarantee

(Note: depending on the financial soundness of the service provider, it may be asked to obtain a guarantee of its obligations from its parent company.)

21 General

(Note: this would include 'boilerplate' clauses common to most contracts, for example dealing with the giving of notice and governing law.)

CHAPTER 15

Implementation considerations

Introduction

The systematic process described in this book should ensure that the right building blocks are in place when implementing the solution. First, the original business case is built on a sound analysis of the business needs and the scope of the requirements to meet those needs. Second, the selection process involved the users, the IT department and management setting the right levels of expectation and commitment. Third, the risks associated with the project are understood and are quantified by the project team. Fourth, an implementation plan is built with the supplier who should be totally committed to the solution. Finally, the benefits of the project are quantified and agreed with their *owning* users and managers.

Critical success factors

Critical success factors when implementing the solution are:

- Define what success is!
- Review and redefine the roles, responsibilities and terms of reference of the project team
- Review and redefine the roles, responsibilities and terms of reference of the steering committee
- Manage the internal levels of expectation and commitment
- Manage the supplier
- Manage the benefits.

Define what success is!

This may seem simple but can vary enormously. Once the solution has been chosen then it is very easy for the project team to get bogged down in the detail of the project and lose sight of the objective. The objective is normally the original business need, i.e. reduce costs, improve competitive position. Sometimes the objective and measure of success is less tangible but equally important.

EXAMPLE

Two separate organizations licensed the same general package about the same time. One was a large private sector company that already had a good general ledger and management information system. It wanted to improve its system and at the same time reduce the cost of ownership of the system by moving from an in-house-developed to a package solution. The other was a large public body that had a poor in-house solution. The package they both selected was flexible and capable of meeting almost any requirement. The measure of success by the large private company was to replace and improve upon the present system and reduce the cost of ownership. The measure of success by the large public body was to implement a ledger solution that balanced. By focusing the project teams accordingly, both organizations succeeded in their objectives. Had the public body not focused the project team then there was a real danger that the project team would have been captivated by the possibilities of the package, raised the level of expectations of the users beyond their capability and failed completely.

Review and redefine the roles, responsibilities and terms of reference of the project team

Once the solution is selected, the nature of the project changes. The pre-feasibility, feasibility and selection phases normally have a high level of management involvement as the project is testing out ideas and moving the organization forward. Implementation, on the other hand, normally has less senior management involvement, involves more people and is more detail than conceptually oriented. These factors need to be taken into account when planning for the implementation. Questions to address are:

- Implementation strategy and priorities
- Managing and resourcing the implementation
- Particularly with facilities management and outsourcing projects, it is essential to retain sufficient expertise to manage both the transition and the on-going relationship with the supplier.

Review and redefine the roles, responsibilities and terms of reference of the steering committee

Once the solution is selected, the responsibilities and duties of the steering committee change. The steering committee will still comprise management representatives of the interested user departments and IT management as well as general management representing the organization itself.

Setting up the implementation project:

- Decide on the membership of the project team and their training requirements
- Agree terms of reference with the project team
- Agree reporting arrangements with the project team
- Agree critical success factors with the project team
- Agree the project plan with the project team.

Monitoring the implementation project:

- Managing the scope of the project
- Ensuring that the project has a viable plan
- Has anything changed that affects risk?
- Is the project meeting its objectives?
- Is the project on time?
- Is the project following its quality plan?
- Is the project on budget?
- Is the project adequately resourced?

CASE STUDY

YULE CATTO

The first implementation in Holland, which is the home of Baan International, went very smoothly. However, the second implementation in the UK ran into problems. It was only after restructuring the support to the operating companies from both the supplier and the IT department's implementation team that the difficulties were resolved. The successful formula parallels the support from Baan and the Yule Catto IT department to the operating companies. Both organizations now have a three-tier structure: international, country and at operating company level. Support is available to the operating companies from both Baan and the Yule Catto IT department. Coordination is maintained at site, national and international levels by formal regular progress meetings that set clear unambiguous targets with action plans and follow-up procedures.

Manage the internal levels of expectation and commitment

This is probably the most important aspect of the implementation. Success is relative to expectation! Commitment can vary depending of how much the project is perceived as benefiting the individual players. Managing the levels of expectation of the end users, user management and senior management is therefore critical to the success of the implementation. By the end of the evaluation expectation levels may be achievable or totally unrealistic. A good way of resetting them is via a conference room pilot with the supplier. The conference room pilot also has another benefit of reviewing the implementation plans that were prepared as part of the evaluation. They are quite likely to change for a number of reasons. First, business needs and priorities may have changed. Second, users will develop their requirements as they become more familiar with the solution. Third, as the users and the team move from deciding what to do to actually doing it, an air of reality normally concentrates the minds on meeting the key objectives, letting some of the more esoteric requirements fade away.

EXAMPLE

A major retail and distribution company needed to implement a new accounting system in five months in order to give flexibility to senior management to reorganize the company. The company processes millions of transactions each month. The scale of the project was enormous but the deadline very real. The project was a success for two reasons. First, the project met its deadline, which pleased senior management. Second, the project was well received by the users even though the implementation involved a lot of work for them and delivered no immediate benefits. The reasons for this were that the project team invested a lot of time explaining why the project was essential to the company and at the same time deliberately setting a low level of expectation for the end users for the first release of the new system. The actual delivered system was slightly above the expectation level and the project team followed up with a positive plan for a second release that did deliver benefits to the users.

Manage the supplier

Once the solution is selected, the supplier, who until then has been competing for the business, is now your partner in achieving the solution. How the relationship develops is a direct result of the efforts of both parties. As discussed above, a conference room pilot is an effective method of reviewing the implementation plans, setting expectation levels and starting to work with the supplier as a partner.

CASE STUDY

BIRMINGHAM CITY COUNCIL
The City appointed a senior operational manager to be responsible for managing the contract with ITnet. This person works in parallel with the department within the City responsible for IT strategy. The agreement between the City and ITnet is managed and monitored on a weekly, monthly, quarterly and annual basis.
    The weekly meetings are operational and concern themselves with day-to-

day matters. The monthly meetings with ITnet are preceded by meetings with the user departments collecting input and feedback. The monthly meetings with ITnet then look back on the service levels achieved, look forward to the requirements of the coming month, and review technical plans. The quarterly meetings are between the senior officers of Birmingham City Council and the board of ITnet and take a more strategic view. The annual review is a formal report to the council members.

Manage the benefits

The post-implementation benefit review is the main vehicle by which the benefits realized are compared against the projected benefits in the original business case and the capital request. However, in order for that to be possible the benefits need to be assessable. This implies that the pre- and post-situation can be measured.

Tangible benefits, by definition, can be quantified. Reductions in working capital can be quantified; compliance can be recorded; cost containment, cost reduction and productivity improvement measured; profitability measured; and service levels monitored.

Intangible benefits, on the other hand, are more difficult to quantify and are not normally quantified in the business case or capital request. However, their importance is not undiminished by this, and careful thought needs to be given as to how their realization can be recorded.

With many intangible benefits the simple fact that the project has been successfully implemented is all that is needed. However, for other intangible benefits then the effect can be measured even if the bottom-line results are impossible to quantify. How an organization is viewed externally can be monitored using market research and customer surveys. How an organization is viewed internally can be monitored by staff-retention statistics, staff surveys and annual reviews.

Why projects succeed

There are many reasons why projects succeed and below are seven of them.

1. The project has the commitment and support of the whole organization. Senior management is involved, problems are dealt with quickly and no one user or department is allowed to undermine the project
2. Expectation levels are realistic and achievable
3. The project is adequately resourced
4. The priority is to deliver the project on time, even if this means going

over budget, rather than being late or, worse still, late and over budget

5. The project is user-led

6. The implementation is phased and planned to deliver early benefits and winners. When planning the implementation priority is given to implementing in the sequence that delivers the most benefit rather than the logical sequence or the sequence that is most convenient to the project team.

> **EXAMPLE**
> When implementing a financial system of accounts payable and general ledger the probability is that the general ledger by providing management information will deliver more benefit than the accounts payable. If this is the case then it is better to implement the general ledger first even if it means building a temporary bridge to the old accounts payable system.

7. The start of each phase of the implementation is dependent on the successful completion of the previous phase.

Why projects fail

There are many reasons why projects fail, some of which are the opposite reasons to those above. Discussed below are seven of them.

1. The project does not enjoy the support and commitment of senior management. A typical scenario is that the project is authorized as result of pressure from users and middle management. Senior management is not committed or involved in the project and the original needs and benefits are rather vague. The project team finds it difficult to focus on the real objectives, the users and middle management endlessly debate what is required and time slips by until someone says enough is enough.

2. The project does not enjoy the commitment of the users, typically, when the solution is hoisted onto the users by the IT department who did not consult the users about what they really wanted, or when the normal concerns about introducing a new system are not properly addressed.

> **CASE STUDY**
> CASE STUDY B
> Business pressures had reduced the time scale to three months to implement the new system. This was unrealistically short but the project team agreed to do their best and started work without a project plan and only an outline business requirement ... the development of the application continued as it had started with no clear requirements document. Infrequent meetings were held with the users and the first release of the new application delivered late. To this day the

project is still on-going ... according to the new head of IT, who was brought in from a line management function ... many lessons have been learnt from this experience. Users are now given ownership of their own projects.

3. The levels of expectation are unrealistic.

EXAMPLE A residential training school contracted for a new bespoke booking and reservations system. The old system was manual and savings were anticipated by introducing an integrated system capable of booking students on courses, allocating bedrooms and classrooms, billing and accounts receivable. The problems arose because neither the management or staff had any idea of how to specify, accept and implement the solution. They simply expected it to happen! Needless to say, relations between the supplier and the school quickly deteriorated with each side blaming the other for lack of progress. Once the responsibilities and duties of the school and the supplier had been sorted out and the staff understood what they had to do, the project was completed successfully.

4. The project is inadequately resourced. This happens all too often because either the cost of the products is higher than budgeted and insufficient funds are left for the implementation, or the selection process overran and the implementation timetable was reduced to make up for the lost time. Neither scenario is a good starting point for the implementation. Implementation costs are approximately one third of the total project. There is little point in selecting a solution if you cannot afford to implement it!

5. The project is unnecessarily overcomplicated.

6. The environment within which the project was working was too rigid and inflexible to accept change.

7. The implementation plan was too risky and too fast.

EXAMPLE A reputable supplier bid for a turnkey control system using tried and tested application software. However, the specification demanded resilient computing which at the time was not available. The supplier decided to build resilience into the solution by linking two computers together and amending the application software to automatically back up the data from one computer to the other. It pushed the supplier into unknown technical territory that was both difficult to quantify and manage. The result was that the solution was very late and the supplier had to resolve many unforeseen technical problems.

Post-implementation reviews

CHAPTER 16

Introduction

There are two post-implementation reviews: the system review and the benefits review. The system review is commissioned by the steering committee about one month after each phase of the project is completed. The benefits review is commissioned about six months after the total project is completed. The objectives of the reviews are to monitor what has been achieved on the basis of *what gets monitored gets done* and to give the organization the opportunity to reflect and learn from its experiences.

Critical success factors

The critical success factors for post-implementation reviews are:

- Create an environment where the objectives and benefits of the post-implementation reviews are understood by all concerned so that the reviews are conducted in a positive atmosphere
- Give clear terms of reference for the reviews
- Conduct the post-implementation reviews independently and impartially
- Act on the results of the post-implementation reviews.

System review

The terms of reference and objective of each system review are different. If the project is phased and the commencement of the next phase dependent on the success of the previous phase then the reviews will affect the operational decisions of the steering committee. If, on the other hand, the project is relatively short and not phased then the review will influence what comes next by way of follow-up to the project. In both circumstances the review will add to the organization's experiences and help future projects.

The nature of the review will depend on whether this is the first review, one of a series of reviews and the type and size of the project. Many factors need to be taken into account when planning a system review. The following is a checklist of items to consider.

Terms of reference
The objectives of the review
Time scale of the review
Reporting arrangements
Lines of communication to users and management
Limit of authority
What to review?
The systems and procedures used by the project team?
The systems and procedures used by the supplier?
The current deliverables?
   -What were the objectives?
   -Were they the correct objectives?
   -Did anything change that altered the objectives?
   -Have they been achieved?
   -What is outstanding?
   -Are there any unexpected results?
   -Are there any knock-on effects?
   -What has been learnt?
The project management
   -Did the project team have a viable plan for this phase?
   -Did anything change that affected the risk?
   -Did this phase of the project complete on time?
   -Did the project team follow their quality plan?
   -Is the project on budget?
   -Is the project adequately resourced?
   -Did the project maintain good internal and external communications?
Who to review and consult?
The project team?
The users?
The steering committee?
The IT department?
Management?
The supplier?

How to review?

The first step is to request the project manager to complete a project review stating the project objectives, what has been achieved, what is outstanding, issues arising from the implementation and lessons learnt. Then consider what to review, who to review and how to achieve the reviews. Reviews are normally carried out by either structured interview or questionnaire. The choice of which is better depends on the objective. Questionnaires are good at quickly gathering feedback from a large number of people. They are especially helpful when conducting satisfaction surveys and checking what has been functionally delivered and what is outstanding. Interviews are better when comments and suggestions are required and fewer people are involved. The distribution list for a questionnaire includes the project team, the steering committee, users, the IT department and the supplier.

Format of the system review report

The system review report essentially consists of four sections:

1. The introduction outlining the terms of reference of the systems review, the current phase of the project and whether this review relates to any other previous reviews
2. Details of what was reviewed, how it was reviewed and who was consulted
3. Findings of the review
4. Recommendations.

CASE STUDY

BP OIL
The project successfully met the user requirements and rebuilt the lost credibility of the IT department. The lessons learnt according to the project manager Graham Williams are:

- 'The difficulty in forecasting the demand on the server in systems like this when demand is subject to user satisfaction
- The importance of keeping the user community fully informed of progress
- The availability of appropriate structured education, awareness and training sessions was definitely a key element in gaining business acceptance and an understanding of what we were trying to achieve.'

The other major intangible benefit has been 'the rebuilding of morale in the IT department and a consequential significant improvement in service levels'.

Benefits review

The benefits review is far more focused than the system review in that it concerns itself with measuring only the tangible and intangible benefits realized. Further, the terms of reference are less flexible. The objectives of the benefits review are to compare the tangible and intangible benefits realized, some of which may not have been expected, with the anticipated benefits in the capital request. The benefits review is normally carried out about six months after the project has been signed-off, when any disruption caused by the implementation has settled down and it is possible to quantify the changes. The objective of the benefits review is to determine the success, or otherwise, of the project and, as such, the report is for the steering committee and corporate management who authorized the investment.

In order to make the benefits review possible the project team will, during the implementation phase, monitor the changes (see Chapter 15).

CASE STUDY

TRENT REGIONAL HEALTH AUTHORITY

The initial review after one month concentrated on identifying outstanding issues and ensuring that they were followed up by management. This was followed six months later by a benefits/business review. A strict cost comparison between the old and the new is no longer possible as it would not be comparing like with like. However, on a broader front the 14 regional health authorities that existed in 1988 are now being reduced to eight and are being phased out altogether in 1996; from that strategic viewpoint the project has achieved its objectives.

According to Charlie Boylan, assistant commercial director of Trent RHA:

- 'The initial experience was that few cultural problems were encountered as the staff adjusted to commercial life, some went overboard and became too commercial, some found it difficult to adjust but, by and large, common sense prevailed
- The outsourcing agreement needs to be monitored and managed. Even though the RCC was no longer the responsibility of the RHA there are a number of on-going decisions that need to be made. Internal management processes need to change to reflect the new situation and formal commercial, product and service level reviews held monthly with the supplier. Further, as time goes on the goalposts move and new criteria arise that need to be managed
- The other time-consuming management commitment is the initial and on-going selling of the concepts and benefits to the DHAs and hospitals to ensure the success of the new arrangements; setting expectation levels; and sorting out misunderstandings
- The general level of product and service from the outsourcing supplier has increased and significant attention is paid by the supplier to cost containment and cost reduction. One unexpected problem with the original agreement is over software development. The RHA retained ownership of the consortia software but it became obvious to us that there is little incentive for the supplier to invest in the software if the supplier does not enjoy any ownership rights
- An area of difficulty we did experience was in preparing service-level agreements. This was due to an absence of expertise on our side and any

model agreements to build on. The service-level agreements now cover:
- Specification of service, i.e. bureau services, data communications, software development, software maintenance
- Classification and prioritizing of problems
- Service levels
- Terms and conditions
- Fee structures
- Notices and procedures

■ The only other major area to watch out for is data communications. Our decision is to retain ownership of the regional network and use the supplier to manage it for us under a facilities management arrangement.'

CHAPTER 17

Two case studies compared

The following two case studies both set out to select an IT solution. They used very different methods and coincidentally both selected the same database management system but with very different results. Company A was successful and Company B was not (Table 17.1). An analysis of the critical success factors shows why (Table 17.2).

Table 17.1

Case study A	Case study B
Background Company A is a leisure company, part of a major group, and operates leisure facilities in the UK. Turnover in 1993 was nearly £200 million and at peak times operational staff exceeds 4000.	*Background* Company B is a public company in the foods and beverage industry. Turnover is over £100 million and they employ over 500 staff of whom about 20 are in the IT department.
Business need and benefits The marketing system was running on an old mainframe computer that was shared with other group companies and run under a facilities management arrangement. The cost of running the mainframe was shared by the companies using it, so that as one came off the costs to the remaining companies went up accordingly. The marketing system was batch oriented and it was no longer meeting the needs of the business. In the UK, the booking cycle has reduced from months ahead to just 3-4 weeks. In order to respond, the marketing system needed to link daily to the operational bookings system to keep up to date with availability to target short-term marketing campaigns. The tangible benefit of downsizing the	*Business need and benefits* Company B commissioned consultants to review their IT strategy as part of their plan to go public. Their report was accepted by the board and an operational plan prepared to downsize the old mainframe-based applications to an open platform over a period of three years. This was to take advantage of a wider choice of products and anticipated cost savings. The first application to be implemented under the new strategy was the sales information management system.

Table 17.1 cont.

Case study A	Case study B
marketing system from the mainframe to an open solution was a one-year return on investment. The intangible benefits were potentially as attractive. By providing more up-to-date information to the marketing department, better decisions could be made on pricing, advertising, direct mail and telesales campaigns resulting in better margins and sales.	
Project team The project team was IT-led and managed the selection and implementation. The project team members were (figures in parentheses are estimates of how much time they allocated to the project): IT project manager (100%) Financial director (10-15%) IT director (10-15%) IT technician (for benchmarking only) Two users from the marketing department (60% each) Two developers with no previous programming experience (100% each) The Steering Committee consisted of the project team plus the marketing director, a representative from another group company and a representative from the group.	*Project team* The project team was IT-led. The project team members were: Head of IT (project manager) Systems development manager Operations manager.
Planning Feasibility report to the board seeking approval to proceed. Select software: five weeks Select hardware: two weeks Recommendation to steering committee, approved by the company board and group.	*Planning and time scales* Business pressures had reduced the time scale to three months to implement the new system. This was unrealistically short but the project team agreed to do their best and started work without a project plan and only an outline business requirement.

Table 17.1 cont.

Case study A	Case study B
Develop new marketing system: two months Implement new marketing system: two months Overall elapsed time scale: six months The project was planned, monitored and evaluated using a project management package. *Quality assurance* Quality assurance is achieved within the group by the use of standard evaluation models, pro forma business cases and post-implementation reviews. *Requirements* A short one-page requirements document was prepared stating the functional requirements of the marketing system and the key technical criteria, namely that the solution must be developed using a relational database to give access to the data, the environment must offer genuine user access to the data and the solution must be based on a portable platform. *Short-listing options and suppliers* A check of the application package market confirmed that there was not a suitable package available to meet the requirements of the marketing department. It was therefore decided to develop the new marketing system in-house. A request for proposal was prepared. This simply requested potential database management system suppliers to build a test database with defined access paths using the one million records supplied. The potential suppliers were identified as a result of checking through software directories, reading the technical press and input	*Short-listing options and suppliers* Company B has a tradition of building systems in-house. The project team quickly came to the conclusion that the new system could not be satisfied by a package and therefore decided to redevelop it in-house. This meant selecting a relational database and a UNIX-based computer on which to run it. In order to save time the project team selected, in their opinion, the leading database supplier and the leading UNIX computer supplier for evaluation. One of these assumptions was correct!

Table 17.1 cont.

Case study A	Case study B

from professional colleagues. Five potential suppliers of relational database management systems were selected. Hardware suppliers were to be evaluated after the database management system supplier was selected and again five were short-listed to benchmark the recommended database management system.

Evaluation
The five short-listed database suppliers were each given three days to build and load the database. This was then benchmarked against the required extraction performance criteria on a UNIX-based computer lent by one of the manufacturers for the purposes of the evaluation. The assessment of how quickly the database was built, performance, and ease of access by the end users to the data were then input into a price–performance evaluation model that also took into account the support, stability and research and development of the suppliers. The five hardware manufacturers UNIX-based computers were then benchmarked against the recommended database management system now holding one million records. The results were input into a price–performance evaluation model that also took into account product range and scalability, product stability, company size, research and development, support and the supplier's attitude to third-party maintenance support.

Evaluation
The project team immediately got to grips with evaluating their selection. Equipment and software were delivered and the project team started a two-week trial to build a prototype of the new application. As problems arose they contacted the suppliers for support. After two weeks they decided that they liked the computer hardware supplier but were dissatisfied with the technical functionality and support from the database management system supplier. The computer supplier was given preferred supplier status and it was decided to evaluate the next two database management system suppliers on their list. After a one-day overview from each of the database suppliers they opted for one of them and immediately recommenced another two-week prototype build of the application. This went well and after reference visits and financial health checks on the computer hardware and database management system suppliers both were recommended. The supply agreements were negotiated and signed by the head of IT who was also the project manager.

Implementation
Phase 1 which was to replicate the old system in the new downsized environ-

Implementation
The development of the application continued as it had started, with no

Table 17.1 cont.

Case study A	Case study B
ment took two months to develop and two months to implement, which included cleaning up the database. Because the developers were not experienced programmers a consultant was brought in for one day to quality assure the database design, which to this day has stood the test of time. The principle underlying the design and implementation of the new marketing system is that it must be capable of being run on a day-to-day basis by the users, with the IT department only involved if there is a requirement to change the core system.	clear requirements document. Infrequent meetings were held with the users and the first release of the new application delivered late. To this day the project is still on-going.
Post-implementation review According to the IT director of Company A, the lessons learnt are: 'Concentrate as a project director on managing the project and levels of expectation. During this project containing user expectations was difficult and the specification of Phase 1 was enhanced to beyond just replacing the functionality of the old system. Fortunately in this case it did not impact the completion date of the project. However, it does illustrate the potential problem of managing the expectation of overenthusiastic users who might be seeing for the first time the capabilities of IT. As the knowledge of the users grows of what is possible there is a temptation (best resisted) to continually update and enhance the specification before achieving the primary objective of completing the first phase of the development.' Subsequently the original UNIX-based computer has been replaced. When re-evaluating *UNIX boxes* another *box* was found to offer better	*Post-implementation review* According to the new head of IT, who was brought in from a line management function '... many lessons have been learnt from this experience. Users are now given ownership of their own projects and must present a sound business case before any expenditure is authorized. Further, products and services must be evaluated in line with the requirements as determined by the business need, scoped correctly and the evaluation and selection process properly planned.'

Table 17.1 cont.

Case study A

price-performance, which reinforces the IT director's view 'that the hardware has become a commodity but it is vital to form a lasting relationship with your software supplier'. The new marketing system took half of one day to port to the new box.

All the tangible and intangible benefits were realized.

Table 17.2

Critical success factors	A	B
Critical success factors in defining business needs and identifying benefits are:		
■ Are the business needs relevant to current business objectives and corporate priorities?	Yes	Yes
■ Have the benefits been agreed by the *owning* users and management?	Yes	No
■ Do we understand the assumptions made in calculating the benefits?	Yes	No
■ Are the benefits achievable?	Yes	Perhaps
■ Are the benefits measurable?	Yes	Yes
Critical success factors when preparing the summary of requirements are:		
■ Does the project team have the correct balance of skills to define the application, technical and management requirements?	Yes	No
■ Is the scope of the project defined correctly?	Yes	No
■ Do the requirements accurately reflect our business needs?	Yes	Yes
■ Do the technical requirements fit in with our IT strategy?	Yes	Yes
■ Is a quality review part of the preparatory procedures?	Yes	No
Critical success factors when preparing the request for proposal are:		
■ Does the request for proposal (RFP) effectively convey our business requirements to potential suppliers enabling them to respond quickly and efficiently?	Yes	No RFP

Table 17.2 cont.

Critical success factors	A	B
■ Does the suppliers section of the request for proposal adequately reflect our requirements from suppliers?	Yes	NA
Critical success factors in short-listing options and suppliers are:		
■ Have we selected the right options?	Yes	Yes
■ Have we long-listed the right potential suppliers to issue the request for proposal?	Yes	No
■ Have we followed the correct procedures when we issued the request for proposal (particularly important to the public sector and some parts of industry who are subject to EU and GATT regulations)	NA	NA
■ Have the most likely suppliers responded to the request for proposal?	Yes	NA
■ Do we understand our key requirements well enough to differentiate between suppliers?	Yes	No
■ Will our evaluation model and procedures produce the best initial short-list?	Yes	No
Critical success factors in preparing the business case are:		
■ Are the business needs still relevant to current business objectives and corporate priorities?	Yes	Yes
■ Have the benefits been agreed by the *owning* users and management?	Yes	No
■ Are the benefits achievable?	Yes	Yes
■ Have we selected the right supply options?	Yes	Yes
■ Have we selected the best suppliers for the initial short-list?	Yes	No
■ Have we considered the organizational impact of the project?	Yes	Yes
■ Have we considered the personnel and training ramifications of the project?	Yes	Yes
■ What management issues does the project raise?	NA	NA
■ What change management issues does the project raise?	NA	NA
■ Have we considered all the risks?	Yes	?
■ Is the level of expectation set correctly for management?	Yes	No
■ Is the level of expectation set correctly for users?	Yes	No
■ Are management still committed to the project?	Yes	Yes
■ Are the users still committed to the project?	Yes	Yes
■ Is the IT department still committed to the project?	Yes	Yes
■ Can we adequately resource the project?	Yes	Yes
Critical success factors when evaluating the business case are:		
■ Do we need the benefits?	Yes	Yes

Table 17.2 cont.

Critical success factors	A	B
■ Can we achieve the benefits?	Yes	Perhaps
■ What are the risks?	Yes	?
Critical success factors when preparing the operational requirement are:		
■ Does the project team have the correct balance of skills and available resources to define the detailed requirements?	NA	NA
■ Is the scope of the project, as defined in the summary of requirements, still correct?	NA	NA
■ Is the operational requirement a forward-looking document?	NA	NA
■ Will the operational requirement be checked for consistency (especially important for a large document)?	NA	NA
■ Are all requirements designated either mandatory or desirable?	NA	NA
■ Is a quality review part of the preparatory procedures?	NA	NA
Critical success factors when preparing the invitation to tender are:		
■ Have we selected the best short-list of suppliers to issue the invitation to tender?	NA	NA
■ Does the invitation to tender adequately reflect our requirements?	NA	NA
Critical success factors in producing the final short-list of suppliers are:		
■ Have the most likely suppliers responded to the invitation to tender?	NA	NA
■ Do we understand our key selection criteria well enough to differentiate between suppliers?	Yes	No
■ Will our evaluation model and procedures produce the best final short-list?	Yes	No
■ Are we addressing the fourth of the fundamental decision-making criteria *Are we achieving the benefits at optimum cost?*	Yes	Perhaps
Critical success factors when making and approving the recommendation are:		
■ Have we considered the organizational impact of the project?	Yes	Yes
■ Have we considered the personnel and training ramifications of the project?	Yes	Yes
■ What change management issues does the project raise?	NA	NA

Table 17.2 cont.

Critical success factors	A	B
■ Have we considered all the risks?	Yes	No
■ Did we select the best suppliers for the final short-list?	Yes	No
■ Did the evaluation model help us identify the issues and differentiate between the suppliers?	Yes	No
■ Have we identified all the costs?	Yes	?
■ How accurate are the costs?	Accurate	?
■ Is the recommended supplier committed to the project?	NA	NA
■ Does the supplier understand our business objectives?	NA	NA
■ Have we selected the optimum cost solution?	Yes	Perhaps
Critical success factors when preparing, approving and authorizing the capital request are:		
■ Do we need the benefits?	Yes	Yes
■ Can we achieve the benefits?	Yes	Yes
■ What is the risk?	Yes	?
■ Are we achieving the benefits at optimum cost?	Yes	Perhaps
Critical success factors when negotiating and finalizing supply agreements are:		
■ Do we understand the strengths and weaknesses of our position?	Yes	Yes
■ Do we understand the strengths and weaknesses of the supplier's position?	Yes	Yes
■ Do we have the necessary technical, purchasing and legal skills?	Yes	Yes
■ Are we approaching the negotiations to conclude a win/win deal with the supplier?	NA	NA
Critical success factors when implementing the solution are:		
■ Define what success is!	Yes	No
■ Review and redefine the roles, responsibilities and terms of reference of the project team	Yes	No
■ Review and redefine the roles, responsibilities and terms of reference of the steering committee	Yes	No
■ Manage the internal levels of expectation and commitment	Yes	No
■ Manage the supplier	NA	NA
■ Manage the benefits	Yes	No
The critical success factors for post-implementation reviews are:		
■ Create an environment where the objectives and benefits of the post-implementation reviews are understood by all concerned so that the reviews are conducted in a positive atmosphere	Yes	NA

Table 17.2 cont.

Critical success factors	A	B
■ Give clear terms of reference for the reviews	Yes	NA
■ Conduct the post-implementation reviews independently and impartially	Yes	Not done
■ Act on the results of the post-implementation reviews	Yes	NA

NA stands for not applicable

CHAPTER 18

Case studies: selecting IT solutions

BP Oil

Background

Since 1992 the role of the head office of BP Oil at Moorgate has significantly changed, resulting in a reduction of headcount from over a thousand to around 150. The associated reduction in IT support staff meant that a new approach to the provision of desktop services was needed.

Prior to these reductions, the policy with respect to office automation had been *to give the users what they want*. The result of this practice was five different graphics packages, four word processors and three spreadsheets. Local area networks were mainly used to share printers. Information exchange between individuals within the same building, let alone different geographic locations, was extremely messy and long-winded.

The inherent problems and inefficiencies in managing this technical environment had led to a widespread view that the IT department was *late, useless and expensive*.

Business needs and benefits

The project was initiated by the IT department to improve their efficiency and perhaps their image by creating a better desktop environment for the users in head office. The tangible benefits, supported by a cost-benefit analysis, were to reduce the direct costs of the IT department in licensing, maintaining and supporting such a diverse range of products. The intangible benefits were generally to improve the overall efficiency of head office by standardizing on the desktop and making all data compatible; inter- and intra-communications easier; eliminating the necessity to convert or re-enter data from one system to another; and making it easier and simpler for the head-office team to work electronically anywhere in the world.

As it turned out, the nature of the project changed and it was subsequently viewed as an infrastructure project adding to the overall operating efficiency of head office.

Project team

The project team was IT-led. The project team members were:

- Systems services manager (project manager)
- Two business analysts
- One software designer
- Five project engineers.

There were no users on the project team as it was seen to be only of benefit to the IT department; a contributory reason was the lack of belief in the user community that the IT department could deliver against promises. The project team reported to a high-level steering committee consisting of the IT manager (chairman) and five senior users representing the major departments in head office. The project sponsor was the CEO of BP Oil who appointed the steering committee.

Planning and time scales

June 1992	Feasibility study and selling ideas
August 1992	Business case presented, prototype solutions built
October 1992	Project started
January 1993	Implement phase I
April 1993	Complete full implementation
May 1993	Project sign-off
September 1993	Post-implementation review.

The project was initially planned at an activity level using Hoskyns' PMW and the details filled in as the project proceeded. The project was subject to BP quality assurance procedures.

Requirements

The first task of the project team was to agree the functional requirements with the users. Users were categorized as senior managerial, professional power users or secretarial and administrative support. The first task was to analyse which products were in use. This was followed by user interviews to gather requirements. The scope of the project included word processing, spreadsheet, graphics, electronic mail and groupware. Requirements were classed as either mandatory or desirable by the users, and after discussion any requirement classed as mandatory was included in the final requirement document. To confirm requirements, prototypes were built for each category of user and tested in a workshop environment with the users.

Evaluation

The package evaluation was straightforward. The analysis of current products in use, the need for an integrated solution and the mandatory requirements quickly settled on Microsoft OFFICE and Lotus NOTES running under WINDOWS. Once this had been decided a standard test rig was built to benchmark PCs, workstations, servers and networks. The necessary equipment was obtained on a sale-or-return basis. This evaluation process recommended Dell PCs, Compaq servers and a Novell network.

Invitation to tender

Once the recommendation had been accepted by the executive management team a formal invitation to tender was issued to four value-added resellers for the recommended solution. Responses were then evaluated by purchasing using a price-sensitive model.

Implementation

The implementation was wedge-driven building on the success of the early users. Each user was allowed to control when they transferred to the new system to ensure that no changes were made during peak periods. The implementation was managed in-house with an outside training company being used to build customized user training courses.

Post-implementation review

The project successfully met the user requirements and rebuilt the lost credibility of the IT department. The lessons learnt according to the project manager Graham Williams are:

- 'The difficulty in forecasting the demand on the server in systems like this when demand is subject to user satisfaction
- The importance of keeping the user community fully informed of progress

- The availability of appropriate structured education, awareness and training sessions was definitely a key element in gaining business acceptance and an understanding of what we were trying to achieve.'

The other major intangible benefit has been 'the rebuilding of morale in the IT department and a consequential significant improvement in service levels'.

Castle Cement

Background

Castle Cement Ltd is Britain's second largest cement producer with over 25 per cent of the market, 1200 employees and a capacity of over 3 million tonnes per year. Castle Cement was originally formed in 1982 as RTZ Cement through the acquisition of three cement companies. The new company was renamed Castle Cement in 1986 and then purchased in 1988 by Scancem Group Ltd, a 50:50 joint venture company between Aker a.s. of Norway and Euroc AB of Sweden.

In 1989 the company had five major sites, seven sales ledgers, seven purchase ledgers and nine general ledgers running on a ten-year-old accounting system at two data centres. The maintenance of these systems was dependent on two external contract programmers as the company no longer had any internal expertise. The financial director decided to replace the old systems and recruit an accountant to manage the selection and implementation.

Business needs and benefits

The overriding need was to introduce an up-to-date accounting system that could meet the requirements of the company. The tangible benefits were to reduce the operational costs of running the old accounting systems and the intangible benefits were:

- To improve financial reporting by using a new standardized general ledger coding system, giving the same item the same code across the divisions
- Better credit control by centralizing the sales ledger and reducing the number of ledgers from nine to one, therefore making it possible instantly to get an overall debtor position with major accounts
- General efficiency improvements by using a standard system, e.g. flexibility in relocating and transferring accounting staff from one site to

another; better understanding and appreciation of the capabilities of the new system by the management team.

Project team

The project team was user-led. The project team members were (figures in parentheses are estimates of how much time they allocated to the project):

Management accountant (project manager) (95 per cent)
Accountant (95 per cent)
Two representatives from the IT department (50 per cent)
One external consultant (5 days)

The core project team was represented on, and supported by, four sub-project teams during the implementation:

1. Purchase ledger consisting of three users

2. Sales ledger consisting of six users

3. Standardization consisting of three users responsible for ensuring a standard treatment of costs throughout the company and also how budgets were to be held and flexed in the new system

4. General ledger consisting of six users. This subproject team was also responsible for the key task of devising the new standard chart of accounts to be used across the company.

The project team reported to the financial director, who was the sponsor of the project.

Time scales

September 1989	Project starts in the background, long-list of six suppliers prepared by the IT department, initial short-list of four potential suppliers selected by the project team
February 1990	Evaluation starts
March 1991	Decision
May 1991	Implementation starts, user training, design of the new chart of accounts, build new system
September 1991	Start parallel running
January 1992	Live
September 1992	Evaluate executive information systems
December 1992	Select executive information system
February 1993	Implement new executive information system.

Short-listing options and suppliers

The Castle Cement IT strategy is based on a Digital VAX platform. Sales order processing is viewed as a core system capable of delivering competitive advantage and therefore is an in-house bespoke-developed application. The advantage of this to Castle Cement is that first, the sales order processing meets their exact requirements, and second, as it is under their control it is capable of being enhanced quickly to meet new business opportunities. The financial systems, on the other hand, do not offer such obvious competitive advantage, and, not wanting to reinvent the wheel, Castle Cement decided to evaluate packages. An initial short-list of six potential suppliers was submitted by the IT department to the project team.

Evaluation

The long-list from the IT department was reviewed by the project team and an initial short-list of four potential suppliers produced by reading the suppliers' literature. These suppliers were visited by the project team and after the presentations and demonstrations a final short-list of two suppliers was produced. The selection criterion used to produce the final short-list was informal and based on the experience of the project team and their knowledge of the company requirements. One of the two short-listed suppliers was preferred to the other, and after an intensive period of evaluation, involving three demonstrations, four user visits and 40 users visiting the supplier, this supplier was recommended. The recommended supplier was Coda.

Implementation

Once the supplier had been selected, four implementation teams were set up. The teams were then trained by the supplier using customized training courses that used Castle Cement data. The training policy was *train the trainer*. Once the project teams had been trained and had decided how to use the package they in turn implemented it and trained the end users.

The seven purchase ledgers were reduced to four and implemented by simply phasing in the new ledgers, letting the old ledgers clear themselves down. The seven sales ledgers were reduced to one and open items transferred from the old ledgers to the new sales ledger. The new general ledgers were started at the beginning of a new year, necessitating the transfer of balance sheet items only, budgets were input the next year, and most transactions posted automatically from the feeder systems of purchase ledger, sales order processing, pricing and plant maintenance.

Post-implementation review

Subsequently, due to the recession in the UK and slump in demand for cement, capacity was reduced by 50 per cent in one site in 1991 and a second site closed the same year. Castle Cement now operates two purchase ledgers, one sales ledger and ten general ledgers. In 1993 an executive information system from Planning Sciences was implemented to consolidate the data from the ten general ledgers and prepare the monthly management reporting pack. According to David Braybrook, management accountant and project manager, '... the new system has delivered all the anticipated benefits and allowed us to manage the company through the recession. We are also pleased with our decision to select a software supplier with a strong track record on our chosen computer platform.'

Leicester City Council

Background

In 1989 Leicester City Council found themselves in a situation with their three key financial applications—general ledger, accounts payable and accounts receivable—running on three different computer platforms. Data was taking lots of effort to put in and even more effort to get out in a useful format. A six-month financial management information system study was commissioned from KPMG Peat Marwick that reported in late 1991. This report was accepted and it was decided that a new integrated system was needed to meet the needs of the Council in the 1990s.

Business needs and benefits

The primary need of the Council was to invest in a new management information system to increase overall efficiency and to devolve more financial management responsibility to individual departments. It would also provide the necessary costing information for the Council to comply with the compulsory competitive tendering legislation.

Project team

The selection project team was user-led. The project team members were (figures in parentheses are estimates of how much time they allocated to the project):

Financial control manager (project manager) (80 per cent)

Two representatives from the IT department (60 per cent each)
Four representatives from user departments (20 per cent each)

The sponsor of the project was the city treasurer. The project team reported to a chief officer board.

Planning and time scales

1991	Financial management information system study and report
December 1991	Prepare statement of requirements
January 1992	Start selection process
September 1992	Select suppliers
October 1992	Start implementation
April 1993	Phase 1 general ledger live
April 1994	Purchase order processing and account payable live, commitment accounting and accounts receivable still being implemented

The project is planned and managed using simple bar charts and the evaluation models were built using a standard spreadsheet.

Requirements

A 100-page statement of requirements was prepared in December 1991 in parallel with the technical requirements. The statement of requirements did not state any preferred computer environment and took the form of a functional checklist for general ledger, accounts payable, accounts receivable, purchase order processing, commitment accounting, payroll and personnel.

Short-listing options and suppliers

It was decided to issue an invitation to tender for the complete requirement with the hope of selecting one software supplier who could provide an integrated solution. The software to be implemented in-house in conjunction with the successful supplier and the necessary computer hardware selected after the selection of the software by the IT department.

Evaluation

The statement of requirement was incorporated within an invitation to tender which was advertised in the *EU Journal*. Twenty-eight suppliers responded to the advertisement, 28 invitations to tender were issued and 22 responses received. These responses were evaluated without any contact with the suppliers. Potential suppliers were evaluated based on their size, credibility and track record. The detailed responses to the functional requirements were scored against the checklist model. As a result of this process a long-list of ten suppliers was produced.

Each of the ten suppliers on the long-list was then invited to give a one-day presentation and demonstration of their products. The results from the presentations and demonstrations were input to the evaluation model producing a short-list of six suppliers, one based on a mainframe solution, two on UNIX and three on an IBM AS400. Of the six short-listed suppliers, two bid complete solutions and the other four suppliers had joint bid their accounting solutions with specialist payroll and personnel suppliers. The evaluation model, apart from containing the functional checklist, also took into account technical considerations, how easy the packages were to implement, support and the credibility and financial strength of the supplier.

Further detailed discussions with the short-listed suppliers resulted in a final short-list of two. By now it had become apparent that none of the suppliers could meet the complete requirement. The products of the two suppliers that had bid complete solutions were rejected because it was considered that they were not sufficiently advanced in their development to be worth the risk. The two final short-listed suppliers had both joint bid with payroll and personnel suppliers. It was therefore decided to separate the two requirements and proceed in parallel on the basis of selecting one supplier for the accounting requirement and one supplier for the payroll and personnel requirement, ensuring that both solutions could run on the same computer.

One of the problems that the project team encountered was that from the model's point of view all the short-listed suppliers looked the same! It was only after detailed discussions with two final short-listed suppliers and reference checking that the project team recommended licensing the IBM AS400 versions of the Computer Associates accounting packages, moving the current CYBORG payroll and personnel package to an AS400 and acquiring another AS400 to run the packages.

Post-implementation review

On reflection, the project team now believe that they took too much on trust from the suppliers. A particular problem they found was that it was not possible to verify all the statements of the suppliers with respect to the various environments that they supported, which version numbers of products were available in which environment, when new versions would be available, what features were in what release and the quality control procedures for each new release. This was compounded by the habit of nearly all suppliers to demonstrate the latest version of their product, not necessarily in the environment that is being evaluated or finally chosen.

With respect to the selection process the evaluation model built by the project team erred on the side of generosity. On reflection, the project team believe that by applying better weightings and using stricter criteria a smaller initial short-list would have been produced, potentially saving both their time and that of the suppliers.

Prudential Assurance

Background

The sales department of the Home Service Division of the Prudential employs 7000 representatives, the traditional front-line of the Prudential, knocking on doors and, until recently, collecting money. They generate more than 50 per cent of the Prudential's premium income and are organized into five regions and 180 branches. They were supported by standalone PCs in each branch that were used to produce quotations and reconcile cash. In order to use a PC each salesperson had to come into the office and wait their turn. In practice, of course, this did not happen. The PCs were not connected to any of the back-office systems and they were not significantly adding to the overall sales effort.

Business needs and benefits

There was recognition in the IT department that in order to take advantage of point-of-sale technology an infrastructure creating a new branch platform needed to be built. This would offer the potential of each representative having a portable PC capable of producing instant and accurate quotations linked to the back-office systems. This recognition coincided with proposals to re-engineer the back-office systems from a product to a customer focus. In the past each individual product was supported by its own system. This meant that if a customer had more than one product it was difficult for a representative to get a complete picture of the customer's account, without knowing all the products their customer had purchased and their reference numbers. The re-engineering of the product systems enables a complete picture of a customer to be built up quickly and easily. All this created the potential of building a customer information system (CIS) that could support the representatives. The project, with a total budget of £15 million, is viewed as an infrastructure investment replacing the PCs in the branch offices.

The intangible benefits are first, moving the Prudential into a position to use point-of-sale technology and achieve efficiency benefits by linking the branch and back-office computer systems, and second, increasing sales by providing the representatives with much-improved customer account information leading to more effective prospecting. These conclusions were reached as a result of a prototype CIS tested in the field. The field trial also concluded that a CIS type system was an essential tool for representatives to do their job properly.

Project team

The project team was user-led, full-time and managed the selection and the implementation. The members were:

Business project manager (reporting to the sales director)
IT project manager (reporting to the IT systems development manager)
Four computer-literate users

At its peak, the core project team was supported by a further 30 development and implementation staff.

The project team reported to a delivery board (steering committee) chaired by the deputy sales director and attended by the IT systems development manager and the project manager. The delivery board's terms of reference were to concentrate on meeting the tactical objectives of the project.

Planning and time scales

June 1992	Feasibility and prototyping (two months)
December 1992	Select software and hardware (eight months)
January 1993	Prepare business case
July 1993	Independent review of the business case by Andersen Consulting
July 1993	Start development of new system (six months)
September 1993	Approval
January 1994	Start roll-out to 180 branches (six months)
Overall elapsed time	Two years

The project was planned and monitored using Lucas's ARTEMIS.

Requirements

A detailed requirements' specification was prepared and included:

- Specification of the standard packages required and bespoke developments to build the CIS system
- Specification of system software to build the new client/server branch platform consisting of PC WINDOWS clients and UNIX servers in each branch connected to the back-office IBM mainframe computer
- Specification of the PC clients and UNIX server computers
- Specification of the development tools to build the bespoke application software
- Specification of the system software to manage the new branch platform environment (ensuring that no technical skill was needed in the branch and that the new environment could be managed remotely by the central IT department).

The relevant parts of this requirements document were then handed over to the specialist IT procurement group, who issued a formal invitation to tender to potential suppliers.

Short-listing options and suppliers

Of the various options available, the Prudential decided to:

- Build a bespoke system based on the earlier prototype for the account management, portfolio management and prospecting components of the CIS
- Evaluate packages for the word processing and spreadsheet components of the CIS
- Build and integrate the system management software as it had already been determined that there was not yet a suitable comprehensive package available
- Evaluate and select the database software, tools and hardware necessary to create the new branch platform
- Manage the project in-house and not use a system integrator.

The IT procurement group then short-listed suitable suppliers based on their own experience and on-going research in keeping up with the market.

Evaluation

The product evaluation was managed by the specialist IT procurement group. Each short-listed system software product was benchmarked against each short-listed hardware product using the CIS prototype as a model to simulate the technical requirements. The results of this technical evaluation were then compared with the research and development plans of the suppliers, their track record of delivering new releases on time, quality of new releases, product life cycle expectations, price performance and an overall supplier appraisal. The software products selected were SYBASE, POWERBUILDER and Microsoft OFFICE. Hewlett-Packard servers and PCs were chosen for the hardware.

Negotiating

All IT supply agreements are negotiated by the specialist IT procurement group. One of their fundamental rules is that during the negotiating period all contact between the Prudential and the suppliers must be via this group. This is to ensure that the best possible terms and conditions are negotiated and at the same time stopping interesting parties confusing the issue.

Decision making

The business case, prepared by the project team, was first approved by the delivery board and then taken by the sponsor, in this case the sales director, to the Home Service divisional board. The project, because of its size, then needed to go to head office for approval. This involved an independent quality review by Andersen Consulting before being submitted to the chief executive for signature.

Change management

Once the CIS system had been built the roll-out was at a rate of 20 branches per month. The critical issue was not training the representatives how to use the system, but how to change their way of working so that they exploited and benefited from the system. This was always recognized as being a slow process. *How to* training and usability laboratories were used to build up individual skills. Best practice was then sought and individuals who had quickly appreciated the potential of the new system were encouraged to tell others how it had benefited them.

Post-implementation review

The CIS project was completed on schedule and is now live. The key objective of building a branch platform for now and the future has been achieved. According to Ron Skelley, systems development manager, the success of the project

> ... has been a direct result of building sound long-term vendor relationships. And, of creating the best team in the first place with particular emphasis placed on appointing a project manager who is business led, capable of making decisions, recognizing when they do not know the answer and delegating and bringing in expertise when required.

The biggest problem was

> ... retaining the interest and support of senior management in the project. The project was all about building for the future and as such offered few, if any, tangible short-term benefits. The cost of not going ahead with the project, on the other hand, was potentially very high in loss of competitive position. The lesson learnt is that to successfully manage this type of project requires, first, the commitment of a senior management sponsor, and second, for that commitment to be tested and reinforced regularly.

Yule Catto

Background

Yule Catto Building Products Division has a turnover of about £100 million and is part of Yule Catto. The Building Products Division was built up by acquisition and consists of seven companies in three European countries. These companies had a diverse range of systems running on eight different computers. The larger Speciality Chemical Division of Yule Catto had built up a strong tradition of using standard systems and senior management had appreciated the benefits in terms of both cost saving and the availability of consistent management information.

Business need and benefits

The accounting, sales order processing, stock control, purchasing and costing systems of seven companies within the Building Products Division each had their own local IT staff, thus proving expensive to run and maintain. By 1990 it was clear to the Building Products Division that it would benefit from using standard systems and moving away from a hardware- to a software-led approach. It was decided to standardize on a package for supply chain management and to run payroll on either a local PC or a local bureau.

The tangible benefit of replacing the eight different systems with one package was a significant cost saving. The new system could be supported by a small central team and there would no longer be any requirement for local IT staff. Further, the introduction of an integrated sales order processing and stock control system should realize significant stock reductions.

The intangible benefits of standardizing were consistent reporting to senior management; the knowledge that once a report had been produced by one company it could quickly and easily be produced by another; and the opportunity to better understand the cost structure of the Division to enable senior management to optimize manufacturing throughout Europe.

Project team

The project team was head office- and IT-led who managed the selection and implementations. The project team members were (figures in parentheses are estimates of how much time they allocated to the project):

Chief executive of the Division (5 per cent)
IT director (50 per cent)
IT project manager (100 per cent)
Financial directors of operating companies (who are responsible for IT), who in turn were supported by sub-project teams defining and agreeing their functional requirements (20 per cent).

Planning

Short-list potential software suppliers (one month)
Prepare a 20-page invitation to tender (two months)
Select software package (three months)
Implement the first six companies in three countries (18 months)
Overall elapsed time scale (two years).

Requirements

The 20-page invitation to tender detailed the functional requirements of the various modules required. However, in order to meet the business need the following key requirements were all-important:

- An international package that could meet the varying requirements of the European operating companies
- A modern package that will continue to meet the requirements of the Division in the future

- A UNIX-based solution that could run on Hewlett-Packard, the preferred computer hardware supplier

- A black-box solution, without any bespoke changes, that could be run at each operating company without the need for any local IT staff and backed by a supplier who could support each operating company directly

- A package that could meet the key functional requirements of the building industry in configuring products to customers' specifications

- Flexible software pricing to reflect the differing sizes of the operating companies, i.e. from an eight- to a 64-user licence.

Short-listing options and suppliers

The options had been pre-selected in that an international package was required from a software house with Hewlett-Packard as the preferred computer hardware manufacturer. A long-list of potential software suppliers was drawn up by inviting each operating company financial director to suggest possible suppliers based on their local research. The long-list was reviewed by the head office project team who quickly produced an initial short-list of three software houses based on the key requirements above.

Evaluation

The evaluation followed a traditional approach with the short-listed suppliers invited to present their products followed by a demonstration and five-day workshop. A preferred supplier quickly emerged based on the key requirements. This preference was confirmed by user visits and the strong empathy that developed between the two companies. A significant factor in this was the belief in the project team that Yule Catto could influence the development of the chosen product and therefore avoid bespoke modifications that are expensive to carry forward from one release of a package to another. The product selected was TRITON from Baan International.

Implementation

The first implementation in Holland, which is the home of Baan International, went very smoothly. However, the second implementation in the UK ran into problems. It was only after restructuring the support to the operating companies from both the supplier and the IT department's implementation team that the difficulties were resolved. The successful formula parallels the support from Baan and the Yule Catto IT department to the operating companies. Both organizations now have a three-tier structure: international, country and operating company level. Support is available to the operating companies from both Baan and the Yule Catto IT department. Coordination is maintained at site, national and international levels by formal regular progress meetings that set clear, unambiguous targets with action plans and follow-up procedures.

Nine companies have now been implemented with one outstanding and the original benefits have been realized. There are no IT staff employed by the operating companies as all support is from the supplier and the Yule Catto IT department. The total headcount of the Yule Catto IT department is seven, of whom four support the Building Products Division.

Case studies: IT solutions and business process re-engineering

CHAPTER

19

British Telecom

Background

Managed Network Services is responsible for the business-to-business data networking and messaging products of BT. It is the market leader in the UK, with a turnover of around £150 million and 600 employees. The sector is now very competitive, with new products and suppliers entering the market as a result of the competition policy of the UK government. The Managed Network Services accounting system was an old, heavily modified package that was dependent on downloading information to PC spreadsheets to produce meaningful reports. More importantly, the system was inflexible and had become incapable of producing the range of management information needed to run the business.

Business needs and benefits

In order to react to, and anticipate, competitive pressures Managed Network Services needed to reduce its cost structure and build new management information systems. These systems needed to be flexible and capable of delivering information directly to the line managers to enable them to react quickly in a fast-changing marketplace.

Parallel with the financial systems project a business process re-engineering exercise is being managed by the deputy director. Business process re-engineering identified the four main processes of the business as win business; provide service; provide after-service; and bill and collect. The early results of the business process re-engineering exercise were already demanding a fourth dimension to the general ledger coding system to capture process (or activity) costs as well as a requirement to focus the whole organization more on the customer. This is illustrated by the amount of poor-quality data coming through to the accounts department, generating billing queries and hindering account settlement. Currently the accounts department has to sort it out. This problem of poor-quality data will be overcome by more customer-focused procedures that accurately capture the data once for use by all systems.

The tangible benefits of replacing the old system with a new one were used to build a standard BT business case with a cost-benefit analysis over five years. The overall savings resulting from the implementation of the new financial system and the business process re-engineering will ultimately be a 20 per cent reduction in the finance department, reducing the headcount from 100 to 80.

These tangible benefits were supported by the intangible ones that were not quantified in the business case. The key intangible benefit is to open up the information within the finance department to line managers, enabling them to react faster to the changes in the market, and control costs.

Change management

The management team recognized that it would have to make a significant effort to keep everyone up to date while the company adjusted to the new market conditions. All staff were briefed on the business pressures facing the company and the changes necessary to take advantage of the growing market in data communications. As a result, the finance department is committed to the new system and the benefits it will bring. They also understood the need for the headcount reduction that follows implementation. Fortunately, some of the pain of this reduction is alleviated by the high percentage of temporary staff in the finance department.

Project team

The project team is user-led and managed the selection and now the implementation. The project team members for the selection were (figures in parentheses are estimates of how much time they allocated to the project):

Controller financial systems (project manager 50 per cent)
Financial controller (5 per cent)
Project leader (70 per cent)
Users (5 per cent)
Support from IT department (1 per cent)
Part-time external consultant to advise on planning, preparation of the supplier long-list and also responsible for quality assurance.

The project team reported to a steering committee made up of the financial management team.

Planning and time scales

May 1993	Vision document
July 1993	Statement of requirements
	Preliminary business case
October 1993	Invitation to tender
December 1993	Recommendation
February 1994	Decision
April 1994	Started implementation

The project was planned and monitored using simple bar charts and evaluation models built using a standard spreadsheet.

Requirements

A 20-page statement of requirements was developed on a consensus basis with the user departments. This mainly took the form of a functional checklist.

Short-listing options and suppliers

The old system was running in a Hewlett-Packard UNIX environment and the decision was taken to continue in this environment with ORACLE as the BT standard database management system. The evaluation process was therefore to select an application package, running in this environment, to be implemented by the project team in conjunction with the successful supplier.

A long-list of 12 potential suppliers was drawn up based on the personal knowledge of the project team members, analysis of *The Software Users Year Book*, independent research and advice from the external consultant. These 12 suppliers were issued the invitation to tender and given three weeks to reply.

Evaluation

In parallel with issuing the invitation to tender an evaluation model was prepared to score the responses. Each item on the invitation to tender was allocated a weighting that was scored between 0 and 10 depending on the functionally match and its availability, i.e. 7-10 available in the current release, 2-5 due in the next release, 0 not available. The total scores for each section were then reduced to fit into the overall model:

Common requirements	(13 per cent)
Technical requirements	(10 per cent)

Reporting requirements	(16 per cent)	
Security requirements	(5 per cent)	(44 per cent)
General ledger	(12.5 per cent)	
Accounts receivable	(12 per cent)	
Accounts payable	(9 per cent)	
Fixed assets	(7.5 per cent)	
Cash book	(5 per cent)	
Project management	(10 per cent)	(56 per cent)
Total		(100 per cent)

The mechanical scoring of the responses to the invitation to tender produced an initial short-list of four that was reduced to a final short-list of two after supplier presentations and updating the evaluation model accordingly.

Further demonstrations and workshops were arranged with the two final short-listed suppliers. Checklists of areas for discussion were prepared and given to both suppliers. These were then scored. At this stage both suppliers could satisfy the functional requirements. The objective of the workshops was to establish the closest fit to the functional requirements. Implementation plans were built with both suppliers and three reference visits undertaken. The final recommendation was a balance between the functional capabilities of the competing products on the one hand, and on the other, the softer issues like the quality of support and services, how well organized and committed the supplier is to the project. In the words of Lynn Bowring, controller financial systems, 'in the final analysis it is relatively easy to decide the original short-listing on a mechanical functional basis, the final decision, however, is more influenced by subjective factors as we will have to work very closely with the successful supplier for a long time'. The software recommended was Oracle FINANCIALS.

Negotiating

Before the recommendation was made the two final short-listed suppliers were invited to submit best and final offers. These were then used to negotiate the final deal with the preferred supplier Oracle.

Implementation

At the time of writing the implementation of the new system is current. The plan is for each individual department within finance to own its part of the implementation. This plan was agreed with Oracle during the evaluation and was a factor in the decision-making process. The individual departments are in turn supported by the small finance department project team of four responsible for planning, coordination, integration and integrity. The project team can call on the IT department for additional technical support if required.

Pepe Jeans

Background

Pepe Jeans is a very successful 21-year-old company. Based in London, Pepe Jeans created a world brand image in a competitive, fast-moving consumer goods market. Turnover rose to over $200 million and Pepe Jeans was recognized as being among the top ten jeans companies in the world. The Pepe Jeans formula is to be sales and marketing driven, sell via traditional retail outlets, design their own products but subcontract manufacturing. In 1992, however, the company was almost bust. Overexpansion and a world recession combined with overconfident management resulted in losses for two consecutive years in excess of $25 million. De-listing and new owners followed. A new management team was recruited committed to turning the company round.

Business process re-engineering

The old company was decentralized. Each country in Europe acted independently running old standalone systems. The new management team reviewed the European operation and decided that the most efficient way to run the company was to centralize everything except sales and customer service. Pepe Jeans is a sales and marketing company. It is therefore essential that the sales and customer service departments are as close as possible to the customer to meet local market demands and satisfy local terms and conditions. Design, marketing, procurement, distribution and finance and accounting were centralized in London. The business processing re-engineering cut out two levels of management and reduced the total headcount of the company in Europe from over 350 to 250.

Business needs and benefits

The business need was to reduce significantly the operational costs of running of the company by restructuring and implementing new integrated systems. The tangible benefits of implementing an integrated system and changing the way people work are to reduce the operational costs by eliminating the labour effort necessary to maintain system interfaces, and to dispense with the role of the information provider by providing management information directly to the end users. The intentions were to halve the size of the accounting department and completely do away with the IT department, as it is not core to Pepe Jeans' business.

Project team

The project team was user-led and its members were:

Chief financial officer (chairman)
Chief operating officer (part-time)
User project manager (full-time)
Technical project manger (full-time for eight months)

The core project team was European and multi-lingual, consisting of a Dutchman, an Englishman, a German and a Scot (which sounds like the start of a bad joke!).

The project team was supported by five subproject teams defining functional requirements, i.e. sales order processing, warehousing, sales administration, procurement, finance and accounting. Each subproject team had two or three active members out of a total five or six. The subproject teams were made up of representatives from the European operating companies. The project was sponsored by the European chief executive officer and reported to a management steering committee.

Planning and time scales

1992 and early 1993	Preliminary research by old IT department
May 1993	Issued invitation to tender to 12 suppliers
July 1993	Short-list of four suppliers
November 1993	Decision
July 1994 to January 1995	Roll-out to 13 European sites

A very detailed project plan was developed by the two project managers with in-built quality control procedures.

Requirements

A detailed specification of requirements was prepared, the critical requirements being:

- A sales order processing system to meet the requirements of the textile trade
- A standard off-the-shelf package operating in a computing and communications environment that could be facility managed
- An international package that could meet the requirements of the European operating companies
- Multinational support from the supplier, obviating the need for an IT department to support the solution
- An integrated solution.

Evaluation

Preliminary research had identified about 50 packages. A long-list of 12 suppliers was selected by reading the suppliers' literature, interviewing potential suppliers and applying the key criteria of the requirement. These twelve were issued the invitation to tender. Nine satisfactory responses were received and an initial short-list of four selected after each supplier had given a half-day presentation to the project team.

Eventually the project team and users were equally divided between the two suppliers on the final short-list. One supplier was quite small but with a very good sales order processing package developed for the textile trade and the other was an incumbent supplier. The deciding factor was user satisfaction. This was tested during the reference visits by some searching questions and an open and frank discussion with the suppliers' senior management. The decision was for the UNIX- and PROGRESS-based package from Option Systems Ltd. Once the software supplier had been selected a very quick hardware evaluation selected NCR with AT&T as the facility's manager for the computer and communications network.

Post-implementation review

The project has been very successful to date. The size of the accounting department has reduced from 100 to 45, the IT department from 16 to two and the company is back in profit. Rob de Meij, the chief financial officer of Pepe Jeans, has some very clear views on why the project has been so successful:

1. 'The project was well planned, a prototype of the application was built before it was rolled out, the users were involved throughout the project owning their part of the implementation
2. Having a multi-lingual European project team, an English-speaking-only

team would have been a disaster as they would not have understood the different European cultures and would not have been able to communicate effectively

3. Building a sound working arrangement with the suppliers coordinated by the Pepe Jeans' user project manager

4. Selecting a software supplier who is totally committed to our solution, if we fail, he fails.'

Rob de Meij also believes that preparing the invitation to tender should have only taken two months and that the evaluation would have been quicker and easier had they taken up references earlier.

SmithKline Beecham

Background

The Chemical Division of SmithKline Beecham has five major production sites around the world and a number of smaller sites all working continuously. These sites were using a mixture of in-house-developed applications and packages for their maintenance management systems. However, they all faced the same issues of compliance with regulatory bodies; interfacing their maintenance management systems with condition base monitoring systems, financial systems and other systems; as well the introduction of total productive maintenance. In 1989 a worldwide project team was set up to decide an overall approach to engineering systems.

Business process re-engineering

Parallel with this project a Divisional team was also looking ahead and applying business process re-engineering techniques. One of the areas being looked at was the relationship between the operators of the plant and the tradesmen and craftsmen maintaining it. A number of the management team had visited Japan and were struck by the sense of ownership by the Japanese operators of their equipment. The Japanese operators took a wider view of their job and consequently were more efficient, as they could quickly sort out many of the jobs that in the UK required a craftsman. This was in stark contrast to the traditional way of working in the UK plants that had a strong demarcation between the duties of the operators and tradesmen. The project team concluded that by multi-skilling the operators, providing them with the necessary training and tools, a lot of the work previously carried out exclusively by craftsmen could be done by the operators with big productivity gains.

Business needs and benefits

The project team evaluated the options available to the Division and recommended that a standard solution be selected for each site to implement in its own time. The team recognized what was good and what was bad in each site and evolved a strategy to ensure that each site benefited from the best practice in the Division. Once the core solution had been selected each site would be responsible for developing a key subsystem, and its interface with the core system, for the benefit of the other sites (e.g. expert systems, interfaces with monitoring equipment, multimedia diagnostic systems). The benefits of this approach were:

- The maintenance management solution will integrate with the company-wide business re-engineering programme and total productive maintenance programme

- Use of a common system throughout the world will make comparisons between different plants easier, particularly in the case of the sites already using an independent efficiency audit

- The total solution, including the subsystems and their interfaces to the core system, would have to be validated only once by the regulatory bodies. This is potentially of great significance as thereafter only the use of the system at each site would need to be validated compared with current practice, which is to validate both the use and the design and integrity of the systems, which is very time consuming. (Note: validation in the chemical and pharmaceuticals industries is an in-house process requiring specially trained staff and subject to audit by the regulatory authorities.)

Once the core product had been selected by the project team and recommended to the Division it was then up to each operating site to prepare its own internal capital request, showing the return on investment, to justify the expenditure.

Project team

Works engineer (chairman) (5 days)
Engineering planning manager (project manager) (60 days)
Five user representatives from the sites (20 days each)
One representative from corporate IT (10 days)

Time scales

Mid-1988   Irvine site in Scotland decides to evaluate maintenance management packages

Late 1988	Idhammer maintenance management package selected
Early 1989	Core Idhammer package implemented at Irvine
June 1989	Worldwide review of engineering systems
August 1989	Decision to select a worldwide solution, a second evaluation of packages and comparison with in-house alternatives
November 1989	Idhammer package reselected
July 1994	Four sites live, with three yet to be implemented.

Requirements

A functional checklist of about 100 items for the core maintenance management systems was prepared and distributed to each site. This document served two purposes: first, to form a consensus as to the worldwide requirement, and second, to find out which of these functional items were available in the local in-house systems. This second part was then used to select the in-house system with the most functionality for comparison with the preferred package solution.

Other more general requirements were identified of more importance than the individual functional items:

- The ability to interface with the IBM AS400-based financial and manufacturing packages

- A solution that could be used worldwide and be flexible enough to integrate with the key subsystems to be developed by each site

- Worldwide support by the supplier

- Multi-language versions

- Satisfy the requirements of the regulatory authorities.

Evaluation

The first phase of the evaluation was to revisit the package selection. Twelve packages were identified from the software directories and after reviewing sales brochures a short-list of three was produced. The Idhammer maintenance management package was reselected after a formal evaluation.

The Idhammer package was then compared with the best of the in-house systems. The final recommendation was in favour of the package for the following reasons:

- The Division did not want to be committed to development work outside of its core business

- Previous experience of in-house-developed systems that had been hindered by lack of resources, resources being transferred to higher-priority work at critical times and the general belief that an external supplier would be more committed and would allocate more resources to the project
- Future functionality with a package was more assured, as was the ability to maintain interfaces with current and new subsystems
- The availability of multi-language versions and worldwide support
- A belief that the regulatory authorities have a preference for package solutions
- A view that the best of the in-house systems was inflexible and designed for planners and stores, not for end users
- The availability of multi-site discounts and user-based licences that was of particular importance to some of the smaller sites only requiring a five-user licence.

Change management

The decision to change the method of working of the plant operators and craftsmen at the Irvine site needed careful planning to train the operators in their wider roles. Critically, it was essential to win the cooperation of the craftsmen, who currently had all the skills, to help with the skills transfer. This was achieved by team working and the realization that their craft skills would also be enhanced as part of the initiative. Once the right atmosphere had been created, the craftsmen relaxed and cooperated with helping to produce the multi-video tools necessary to train and help the operators in their wider role.

Another ramification of the business process re-engineering was the need to upgrade the IT systems with the resultant increase in IT staff. At the Irvine site the central IT *cell* of eight is responsible for strategy and coordination and competes with external suppliers for departmental business. Two of the key outcomes of the business process re-engineering are to flatten the organization and to devolve routine decision making to empowered workers. Fundamental to achieving these are information systems that can deliver the necessary information directly to the empowered worker, bringing only exceptions to the attention of management.

An interesting side effect of this is that management are not normally included in the information flow for the simple reason that the decision making has been devolved downwards and they did not need the information. It is essential therefore to implement a change management programme for management to adjust to the new way of working and the very different management responsibilities.

Implementation

The implementation strategy is to devolve responsibility for subsystems of the total system to individual sites and for these sites to become the lead site in their subsystem and support other sites when they implement it. The objective of this strategy is to be able to move the whole process of building and implementing the new system forward in parallel, therefore reducing the total elapsed time. A key secondary benefit of the strategy is to gain a sense of ownership and commitment in the new system by the major sites of the Division.

Responsibility for the multimedia subsystem to be used by the operators was allocated to the Irvine site in Scotland. A WINDOWS-based system has been built using simple select and click mouse-driven routines. For example, if an operator wants to diagnose a problem, the part of the plant is selected followed by the machine. Options are then presented to the operator that include diagnostics, faults, repairs, routine maintenance, manuals, parts. If diagnostics is selected common faults on that machine will be presented. More detail can be selected giving possible causes and actions to take; these are supported by information from manuals (that have been scanned into the system), locally made sound videos (made during routine maintenance) that talk the operator through the problem, diagrams and warning messages.

Post-implementation review

According to Gerry Flavelle, site engineer at the Irvine plant and a driving force behind this project, the key factors in a project like this are:

- 'Look at what you want to achieve, not how you think you are going to achieve it

- Look to the future when specifying your requirements and do not just duplicate old systems

- Concentrate on your core requirements. Leave the new system for six months before making any changes and then make sure you differentiate between nice to have and needed requirements.'

The Irvine site has been one of the plants subject to an independent efficiency audit as part of its continuous monitoring and improvement programme. During the life of this project the rating has improved from 47 per cent in 1989, which was then viewed as slightly above average, to 89 per cent in 1992.

Case studies: facilities management and outsourcing

CHAPTER 20

Birmingham City Council

Background

In 1988 Birmingham City Council found itself with a large central IT unit of 200 staff and significant concern among the senior management team of the City Council about its performance. Birmingham City Council is one of the largest authorities in the UK and the largest individual city authority. Already the larger departments in the City had their own IT unit and had always been responsible for their own PCs and workstations. In order to achieve greater flexibility the city treasurer, with the support of the council members, decided to outsource the computer operations, communications network and the central development operations of the City.

Business needs and benefits

The tangible benefits to the City of this decision were to reduce the on-going running costs of these services and receive a capital injection for the sale of the assets. The intangible benefits were to:

- Anticipate the government's intentions to introduce compulsory competitive tendering throughout the public sector
- Improve the level of service to the user departments within the City, particularly for systems development
- Create a situation whereby the City could begin to divest from its old COBOL-based mainframe systems and utilize newer technologies, downsize applications where appropriate, and use more packages
- Devolve the responsibility for IT to the user departments
- Reduce management time in running a large and complicated technical department.

Project team

The project team was independent of the central IT unit. The team members were (figures in parentheses indicate the percentage of time spent on the project):

IT auditor (project manager and full-time)
City treasurer (15 per cent)
Two user representatives from the social services and housing departments (full-time)
One independent consultant responsible for quality assurance (20 per cent)
Two representatives from the IT strategy department (one full time and the other 20 per cent)
Purchasing officer (20 per cent)
Plus co-opted members as necessary

The sponsor of the project was the city treasurer and the project team reported to a subcommittee of council members.

Planning and time scales

September 1988	Project set-up and the invitation to tender prepared
November 1988	Invitation to tender issued to four short-listed suppliers
January 1989	Answer queries on the invitation to tender
February 1989	Receive suppliers' responses to the invitation to tender
March 1989	Evaluate responses
	Staff vote on suppliers
	Short-list of two suppliers
April 1989	Recommendation of selected supplier agreed by council members
May to July 1989	Negotiate terms and conditions of staff contracts and the agreement between the City and the supplier
August 1989	Implement
July 1994	Original five-year agreement extended for another three years

The project team focused on commercial issues. In parallel with the project team was a committee looking at the project from the staff point of view. This staff committee consisted of six staff representatives who were supported by the city treasurer's personnel section, their trade union and an expert on pensions.

Hoskyns' PMW was used to plan and manage the project which was originally planned as a purchasing exercise. However, the planning of the project was difficult as this type of exercise had not been previously undertaken by the City. The project turned out to be a lot more complicated than even a complex procurement with many processes running simultaneously.

Requirements

A requirements document was prepared which was turned into a 150-page invitation to tender with standard terms and conditions. The invitation to tender scheduled the assets and staff to be transferred and the services that the City wished to buy back.

The hardware specification included the IBM, ICL and Bull mainframe computers as well as the communications network. It was the intention to transfer the systems software and applications software licences to the supplier. It was also the intention to license the successful supplier to use the software that had been developed by the City council but for the City to retain ownership. The only other major item was the leasing or rental arrangements for the building that housed the data centre. The services that the City wished to buy back were:

- Mainframe operations, network management and laser printing
- Hot-line support and helpdesk
- Some systems development but the amount was not guaranteed as the successful supplier would have to compete for work with internal and external resources.

The invitation to tender clearly stated that the City Council wished to transfer all the staff in the central IT unit and that all bids for services had to be priced separately.

Short-listing suppliers

The project team selected an initial short-list of four potential suppliers to whom to issue the invitation to tender. These suppliers were short-listed based on their capability and credibility using the judgement of the project team.

Evaluation

Commercial

The invitation to tender was issued to the four short-listed suppliers allowing one month to respond. In practice this was extended by one month as it took a month to answer all the suppliers' questions arising from the invitation to tender. The City was expecting the responses to be in two parts: first, the suppliers' valuation for the transfer of assets and second, a quotation for the services requested. In preparation for this the project team valued the assets to be transferred on a written-down basis and no value was placed on the business or staff to be transferred. In practice, the four short-listed suppliers used four different cost structures on which to base their bids. It took a month of questions and answers with the suppliers to sort out the detail before a financial model could be built of the four bids. Using this model, two of the suppliers were rejected primarily on cost grounds, leaving a final short-list of two. These two final short-listed suppliers were then invited to make a presentation to a committee of interested council members.

The selection criteria for the final choice included:

- The supplier's attitude and approach to integrating the staff within their own organization
- How well prepared the supplier was to take on the job
- How well the supplier had anticipated the effects of the new arrangements on the staff and the City both during and after the transfer
- Service levels offered
- Capital transfer value, cost structures for services brought back and length of agreement
- Arrangements for leasing the data centre building
- The supplier's quality procedures
- The supplier's operational contingency arrangements.

Staff

In parallel with the commercial evaluation the staff committee invited the four short-listed suppliers to present their case to the staff of the IT unit. This was followed by a period of negotiations with the suppliers on the terms and conditions of the transfer of the staff and their terms and conditions on subsequent employment with the successful supplier. During this period the committee was supported by the City treasurer's personnel section, their trade union and an expert on pensions.

The staff committee was negotiating on the basis that all the 200 staff in the central IT unit would be transferred. However, in practice only 180 out of a total of 200 did actually transfer. The twenty who did not transfer were either near retirement or administrative staff who transferred to other departments within the City.

A vote of the staff was then taken organized by the Electoral Reform Society, each member of staff having a single transferable vote. The results of the ballot were then published. The staff voted according to their perception of the supplier, conclusions reached after the supplier presentations, feedback from the negotiations of the staff committee and their own personal dealings and experiences with the suppliers.

The results of the staff ballot were in line with the commercial evaluation and in April ITnet was recommended to and accepted by the Council members as the supplier.

Supply agreements

Between May and July the formal agreement was negotiated between the City and the supplier. The City retained a private solicitor to help them with the negotiations and to prepare the agreement. The agreement was then double-checked by the City's legal department before signature. The agreement itself is 30 pages but with the various schedules and appendices is two inches thick. The agreement is made up of three separate agreements:

1. Transfer assets
2. Buy back services
3. Lease for the data centre building.

These agreements were supported by schedules containing the service-level agreements and appendices containing the software licences. Most of the system software licences were transferred to the supplier, whereas most of the application software licences were retained by the City as they were deemed personal to the City and not transferable by the licensor. The application software owned and developed by the City was only licensed to the supplier and ownership retained by the City. With respect to the hardware, the agreement encompasses both outsourcing and facilities management. The IBM mainframe computers were transferred to the supplier under a classical outsourcing arrangement. The ICL and Bull mainframe computers were retained by the City, because of the leasing conditions, and are managed in a classical facilities management arrangement by the supplier.

The agreement was for five years and the City retained the right to vary the agreement and procedures; add, drop and change schedules; with an arbitration clause to sort out any disputes.

Post-implementation review

The City appointed a senior operational manager to be responsible for managing the contract with ITnet. This person works in parallel with the department within the City responsible for IT strategy. The agreement between the City and ITnet is managed and monitored on a weekly, monthly, quarterly and annual basis.

The weekly meetings are operational and concern themselves with day-to-day matters. The monthly meetings with ITnet are preceded by meetings with the user departments collecting input and feedback. The monthly meetings with ITnet then look back on the service levels achieved, look forward to the requirements of the coming month, and review technical plans. The quarterly meetings are between the senior officers of Birmingham City Council and the board of ITnet and take a more strategic view. The annual review is a formal report to the council members.

At the end of the first year most of the anticipated benefits had been realized. Operational cost savings had been achieved and the development service had improved considerably. In subsequent years the City believe that it is still receiving a value-for-money service. This is despite the fact that demands for mainframe services has gone up and not down as had been expected, with a resultant increase in costs. The City is also beginning to make use of newer technologies and is using more application packages. It regularly tests the market to ensure that the pricing structures within the agreement are competitive. This is achieved by going out to tender for all major development work and by using consultants to review the costs of operational services.

In July 1994 the original five-year agreement was extended for another three years. The main reason for extending the contract without going out to tender is the current level of uncertainty in the local government sector. Birmingham City Council do, however, believe that the optimum length of time for an outsourcing or facilities management arrangement is five years. Five years is a balance between the conflicting pressures to test the market as often as possible; the costs and disruptive effect of retendering; and the natural desire to use a satisfactory service for as long as possible once a good working relationship has been achieved with the supplier.

According to Gerry McMullan, original project manager and now head of computer management services, responsible for managing the contract with ITnet, the lessons learnt are:

- 'The importance of having a well-documented agreement that is not too rigid and allows for the changes that will arise in the normal course of business

- The management of a major outsourcing contract is not easy and is a full-time job. Examples of day-to-day things that need to be sorted out are: refereeing minor disputes; managing the networks; apportioning costs to the users; capacity planning; and guiding the supplier on what decisions the supplier can make, what decisions have to be referred to the City and making decisions on behalf of the City when appropriate

- Clearly define what has to be done and establish priorities with your management and users

- Understand the attitude and approach of your supplier

- Beware of the consequences of outsourcing your communications network. The supplier is most likely to take a tactical view and extend the network on demand without taking a longer-term strategic view of the possible consequences

- One of the benefits of outsourcing in the public sector is that it is possible to achieve objectives that would be very difficult to achieve within it. This, of course, leaves senior management to reflect whether the changes could have been achieved internally without the major restructuring involved with outsourcing!'

Bolton Metro

Background

Bolton Metro is a local authority in north-west England. It employs 12 000 staff and has a revenue budget of £200 million. It had a central IT unit of 70 staff managed as a business unit within the finance department. Bolton Metro is politically stable, has a strong tradition of openness and consensus management and a policy to devolve authority away from the centre to the operating departments. By 1993 Bolton Metro found itself with the central IT unit offering traditional services, based on an ICL mainframe, and departments with their own IT staff developing their own new systems and controlling their use of PCs and workstations. The total IT budget is about £6 million with about two-thirds accounted for by the central IT unit and one-third by the departments. Paradoxically, whereas the new systems are being built as departmental systems, demand on the existing mainframe systems is growing.

Options

During the 1980s Bolton Metro had tried to develop an IT strategy, without much success. In 1991-2 a chief officer group, chaired by the finance director, reviewed IT strategy and considered three options:

1. Centralize all IT activities into one unit run as a direct service organization
2. Decentralize IT, make each department totally responsible for its own IT, with a small central standards and coordinating team
3. Continue with the status quo.

The decision was to continue with the status quo. However, by spring 1993 this decision was reconsidered in the light of the government's compulsory competitive tendering regulations due to take effect in 1996. Coopers & Lybrand were invited to undertake a short ten-day study of the competitiveness of the central IT unit. Their report confirmed that the central IT unit offered a good-quality service but was at risk under compulsory competitive tendering. This created a situation that was potentially difficult for the council members of Bolton Metro as their policy is one of no compulsory privatization. Soundings of members and staff were taken and a decision reached to explore the potential benefits of facilities management. The staff were assured that during this process they would have the right to veto and stop the process at key checkpoints. At this stage facilities management was defined as transferring the staff and the delivery of the service, but not the assets; the scope of the services to be transferred was left open. The evaluation of the in-house prospects indicated:

- A high operating cost of the mainframe computer compared to a facilities management supplier
- Difficulty in matching the flexibility of processing and development requirements of the users in the future
- Likely staff reductions, to match staffing to the workload in the future, might make the unit too small and therefore not viable, and in any case, might not still be enough to win a competitive tender in 1996 due to anticipated intense competitive pressure.

Business needs and benefits

The business need was to anticipate the consequences of compulsory competitive tendering. The tangible benefits were to protect the interests of the staff and make significant revenue savings for Bolton Metro. The

FACILITIES MANAGEMENT AND OUTSOURCING

intangible benefits were to achieve more flexibility in the delivery of IT and to gain advantage from being the first authority in the North-west to set up a facilities management arrangement.

Project team

The core project team was (figures in parentheses are the estimated time spent on the project):

Finance director (chairman 30 per cent)
IT manager (40 per cent)
Coopers & Lybrand consultant (part-time)
Staff panel: Six representatives from the IT unit
Evaluation panel (figures in parentheses are the estimated time spent on the project during the critical periods in early 1994):
   Finance director
   IT manager
   Representative from the housing department (15-20 per cent)
   Representative from the social services department (15-20 per cent)
   Chief personnel officer (10 per cent)
   Representative from the legal department (5 per cent)
   Member of staff from the IT unit (30 per cent)
The sponsor of the project was the finance director.

Timetable

July 1993	Fact finding
September 1993	Two-day staff consultations
October 1993	Report to council members
	Formal decision to evaluate facilities management
	Advertisement in *EU Journal*
November 1993	21-page pre-tender questionnaire issued to 24 companies who responded to the advertisement in the *EU Journal*
January 1994	13 responses received to the pre-tender questionnaire
	Invitation to tender issued to five suppliers on the initial short-list
March 1994	Four responses received to the invitation to tender
April 1994	Final short-list of two suppliers
May 1994	Preferred supplier selected
	Staff consultations and staff vote

June 1994	Report to council members
	Sign agreement
July 1994	Agreement starts

Requirements

The requirements were to transfer the IT staff of the IT unit and buy back computing, networking and system development services for an agreed period of time. The requirements from the supplier were:

- Financial stability
- Undertakings to honour the staff terms and conditions and to guarantee employment until 1996
- Facilities management experience in local government
- Relevant technical competence.

Evaluation

The 24 suppliers responding to the advertisement in the *EU Journal* were issued a pre-tender questionnaire. The responses to the questionnaire were evaluated by a panel using a 30-line model of requirements. The intention of the model was to produce an initial short-list of facilities management suppliers who were well established and had the necessary local government and technical experience. The evaluation was completed without any contact with the suppliers and produced an initial short-list of five suppliers. These five suppliers were then issued with the invitation to tender which included a draft facilities management agreement from a private firm of solicitors that formed the basis of the final agreement. Four responses were received.

In preparation for the final short-listing step the evaluation panel built, with the help of Coopers & Lybrand, a more detailed evaluation model. The model was weighted and ran to about four pages. The main sections of the model scored the short-listed suppliers on financial proposals, staff provisions, service provision and subjective analysis. The financial section included an analysis of the financial proposal, financial flexibility, software royalties and miscellaneous income. The staff section included terms and conditions, staff preferences, staff prospects and pension arrangements. The service provision section included disaster-recovery contingencies, account management, implementation planning, software development plans and working arrangements, local authority knowledge and relevant technical experience. The subjective section included the quality of proposal, reference sites feedback, change-over plans and future flexibility.

The four suppliers on the initial short-list were then invited to make presentations to the evaluation and staff panels. These presentations were followed by further detailed meetings and the model was then scored for each supplier. The result was two clear frontrunners, who became the final short-list.

The final phase of the evaluation involved extensive formal and informal reference checking of the two suppliers by both the staff and the evaluation panel. At the end of this process, the evaluation panel selected a preferred facilities management supplier, and this conclusion was conveyed to the staff during final comprehensive staff presentations. This was followed by a staff ballot. The staff were invited first, to state their preference: to be part of a facilities management arrangement now or to remain as an in-house direct service organization or to state if they had no preference; and second, to vote for one of the two final short-listed suppliers or to state if they had no preference. The result was an 85 per cent vote in favour of facilities management now and an almost unanimous vote in favour of the supplier recommended by the evaluation panel. The reasons for this are different and complex. The evaluation panels' judgement was more commercial and influenced by their views of the companies' credibility and financial proposal, whereas the staff vote was more influenced by their perception of the suppliers, their personal employment terms and conditions and pension arrangements and how they would be treated. The selected supplier is CFM Ltd, a subsidiary company of ICL.

Supply agreements

A seven-year agreement, with an option to terminate after five years, was negotiated by the finance director and the IT manager with the help of a private solicitor. The agreement is made up of three separate agreements and runs to about 50 pages:

1. Transfer of assets
2. Provision of services including model service-level agreements
3. Lease for buildings.

Post-implementation review

Fifty-five of the available 67 IT staff transferred to CFM as part of the agreement. Those who did not transfer were the data preparation unit and the three members of the new internal client-support unit set up to manage the agreement. According to Peter Horrocks, IT manager of Bolton Metro and now manager of the new client support unit:

1. 'The whole exercise has been an example of good communications and leadership in proactively addressing a difficult problem
2. The operational savings to Bolton Metro will be over 20 per cent per year after taking into account what was considered possible by way of a managed reduction to prepare the unit for compulsory competitive tendering
3. We believe that we will benefit by being the first authority in the Northwest to commit to a facilities management arrangement as CFM are basing their new northern regional office in Bolton.'

Trent Regional Health Authority

Background

The year 1988 saw the start of the changes in the National Health Service initiated by the government. Until then the regional computer centre (RCC) had been funded by the regional health authority (RHA) offering a computing, system development and communication service to the RHA, district health authorities (DHAs) and hospitals. The RCC turnover was about £4 million per annum. The service included a number of packages that had been developed on a consortia basis by the RCC for use within the region (e.g. accounting, payroll, supplies, patient administration). A situation was building up where, on the one hand, the RHA was reluctant to invest in the RCC because it was no longer considered a core activity. On the other hand, the RCC customers wanted to take ownership of their own IT and some of them were beginning to build up their own local IT expertise. The RCC was experiencing problems in retaining junior staff and was also being encouraged to compete for its work within the RHA. It was being hindered by not having the flexibility to change pay structures, nor being allowed to compete for work outside of the region and a lack of investment.

The regional general manager decided to investigate alternative funding arrangements for the RCC as the RHA was not prepared to invest any more money in it.

Options

During the last few months of 1988 various options were explored and considerable effort was put into finding a partner. However, these came to nothing as the RHA was not prepared to share the risks and rewards nor was it empowered to set up a joint company. It was therefore decided to sell (or outsource) the computer operations and systems development of the RCC to a suitably qualified purchaser but to retain ownership of the data communications network. Consideration was given to a management buy-out. However, this option was rejected as it was felt that the new company would need strong management, marketing and sales skills to survive, which were not present in the RCC.

Business needs and benefits

In 1988 the total number of staff in the region was about 100 000 of which about 1500 were employed directly by the RHA. The government had signalled its intentions to radically change the structure of the National Health Service and core to that was the concept of purchaser and provider. Trent RHA took the view that running the RCC as a service for the benefit of the DHAs and hospitals was not part of its core responsibilities.

The tangible benefits of selling the RCC were compliance with the government's intention; an immediate capital income from the sale of the RCC; and the avoidance of future capital expenditure and management responsibilities in running a complicated technical service. The intangible benefits were:

- Protecting the long-term job interests of the employees of the RCC, as their future under the RHA was very uncertain

- Improving the quality of service to the DHAs and hospitals by investment in the software packages and computing facilities by the new owner

- Speeding up the development cycle by taking a more commercial approach to the packages and not developing on a consortia basis, which tends to move at the speed of the slowest

- Increasing the long-term choice to the customers of the RCC, as the new owner would have to compete for business, the DHAs and hospitals having no obligation to continue to use the services of the RCC.

Project team

The project team was business-led and members were (the figures in parentheses indicate the percentage of time spent on the project):

Commercial director (project manager and 70 per cent)
Assistant commercial director (100 per cent)
Regional computer services manager (40 per cent)

The core project team was supported by an independent private solicitor, management consultants Coopers & Lybrand and various subproject teams as required.

The project team reported to a steering committee consisting of the chairman of the RHA, the regional general manager and the financial director. In turn the steering committee was accountable to a sub-committee of the RHA comprising the chairman of the RHA and two members.

Planning and time scales

November 1988	Take soundings and explore options (three months)
January 1989	Agree terms of reference with regional general manager
	Prepare a profile of the RCC covering assets, liabilities, employees, customers, computer hardware and software (this took six months to complete but most information was ready by May)
February 1989	Agree a long-list of eight potential suppliers
March 1989	Invite proposals from suppliers on the long-list
April 1989	Agree final short-list of two suppliers
May 1989	Staff meet with the final two short-listed suppliers
	Issue invitation to tender
July 1989	Recommendation to RHA
	Preferred supplier meets with customers of the RCC
September 1989	Construct legal agreement (three months)
November 1989	Final negotiations
February 1990	Execute agreements

The project was particularly difficult to plan as this was an unprecedented step in the National Health Service. The first phase of the project was simply exploring the options available and ascertaining the positioning of the outsourcing suppliers as to what and what not they were prepared to offer. Consequently the planning was iterative with each next step very dependent on the outcome of the previous one. The overall structure of the project was, however, clearly defined. The selection process encompassed three parallel actions: a commercial selection process that would produce a short-list of recommended suppliers; staff meetings with the short-listed suppliers to take soundings; and finally meetings between the preferred supplier and RCC customers.

Requirements

The terms of reference agreed between the project team and the regional general manager clearly laid out the requirements in order to meet the objectives of the RHA. These were:

- Put the interests of the staff of the RCC first when selecting a solution
- Protect the position and interests of the customers of the RCC, the DHAs and hospitals, on price, quality of service and commitment of the supplier
- Not to make any on-going or future business commitments
- Select a supplier who will invest in the RCC and develop the software packages
- Select a supplier who will buy the RCC as an on-going business and take over its commitments
- Select a supplier who understands the health market
- Select a supplier with strong sales and marketing.

Evaluation

A long-list of eight suppliers was prepared based on the research previously undertaken by the commercial (purchasing) department. Proposals were invited from these suppliers and, using the key requirement criteria above, an initial short-list of three suppliers produced. This was reduced to a final short-list of two, one being rejected as too small. The evaluation then divided into two.

The commercial evaluation continued and an invitation to tender issued to the two final short-listed suppliers based on the profile of the RCC. One of the issues facing the project team was how to value the RCC. On the advice of the consultants a notional profit and loss account for the RCC was built and, using appropriate P/E ratios, its commercial value calculated. The detailed responses to the invitation to tender were then evaluated against the following factors:

- The approach of the suppliers to the existing RCC staff
- Their view of the business opportunity, growth and investment
- Future fee structures
- Flexibility on service-level agreements
- Commercial terms and conditions (e.g. bid for the assets to be transferred, rent back arrangements for premises, software royalties).

In parallel the staff had been kept up to date with progress but as yet had not met any of the suppliers. Once the short-list was confirmed the final two short-listed suppliers were invited to give presentations to the staff and discuss terms and conditions. Consideration was given to what would happen if some members of staff did not want to transfer. As it turned out, 88 out of the 93 staff of the RCC did transfer, one retired, the others staying on the RHA payroll but being contracted back to the supplier.

The results of the staff soundings after the consultation process with the short-listed suppliers and the commercial evaluation was a unanimous recommendation in favour of AT&T Istel. The preferred supplier was now introduced to the RCC customers to gain their commitment to continuing to use the services of the RCC under its new ownership.

Supply agreements

The negotiations of the supply agreement were driven by Trent RHA who retained expert legal advice. The agreements took three months to negotiate, resulting in seven agreements:

1. Transfer of the assets of the RCC

2. Service agreements between the supplier and the RCC customers (the detailed supporting service-level agreements took another three months to negotiate)

3. Software licences for crown software

4. Software licences for consortia software developed by the RCC in conjunction with its customers

5. Premises lease

6. Short-term telephone lease

7. Consultancy agreement for the staff who did not transfer.

Points of interest arising from the negotiating process were:

- Instruct and control the solicitors carefully and retain control of the paperwork

- The agreement did not include due diligence

- Assess the risks of transferring undertakings previously carried out by internal staff. An example is that the agreement includes fraud insurance cover as the supplier is conducting transactions on behalf of its customers (i.e. BACS money transfers)

- Watch out for conflict of interest during the negotiation process between the employees of the RHA and the RCC and their personal future
- The agreement includes a right of audit by the RHA.

Post-implementation review

The initial review after one month concentrated on identifying outstanding issues and ensuring that they were followed up by management. This was followed six months later by a benefits/business review. A strict cost comparison between the old and the new is no longer possible as it would not be comparing like with like. However, on a broader front the 14 regional health authorities that existed in 1988 are now being reduced to eight and are being phased out altogether in 1996; from that strategic viewpoint the project has achieved its objectives.

According to Charlie Boylan, assistant commercial director of Trent RHA:

- 'The initial experience was that few cultural problems were encountered as the staff adjusted to commercial life, some went overboard and became too commercial, some found it difficult to adjust but, by and large, common sense prevailed
- The outsourcing agreement needs to be monitored and managed. Even though the RCC was no longer the responsibility of the RHA there are a number of on-going decisions that need to be made. Internal management processes need to change to reflect the new situation and formal commercial, product and service level reviews held monthly with the supplier. Further, as time goes on the goalposts move and new criteria arise that need to be managed
- The other time-consuming management commitment is the initial and on-going selling the concepts and benefits to the DHAs and hospitals to ensure the success of the new arrangements; setting expectation levels; and sorting out misunderstandings
- The general level of product and service from the outsourcing supplier has increased and significant attention paid by the supplier to cost containment and cost reduction. One unexpected problem with the original agreement is over software development. The RHA retained ownership of the consortia software but it became obvious to us that there is little incentive for the supplier to invest in the software if the supplier does not enjoy any ownership rights
- An area of difficulty we did experience was in preparing service-level

agreements. This was due to an absence of expertise on our side and any model agreements to build on. The service-level agreements now cover:
- Specification of service, i.e. bureau services, data communications, software development, software maintenance
- Classification and prioritizing of problems
- Service levels
- Terms and conditions
- Fee structures
- Notices and procedures

- The only other major area to watch out for is data communications. Our decision is to retain ownership of the regional network and use the supplier to manage it for us under a facilities management arrangement.'

Author's postscript

Managing IT projects is an essential skill for today's managers. I hope that this book has broken down some of the mystique and will enable IT projects to be managed like any other. Success is a result of effort, application and a little luck. The process described in the book gives you the way forward, the effort is up to you. Good luck!

I would appreciate hearing about your experiences in selecting and implementing IT solutions and any comments or criticisms that you have about the process described in this book. My email address is "100540.3066@compuserve.com".

Index

Agreements:
  facilities management/outsourcing, 166-169
  service level, 140-143
  software licences, 166-169
  turnkey, 166-169
Andersen Consulting, 107, 210, 212
Approving:
  business case, 109-110
  capital request, 160-161
  recommendation, 154-155
ARTEMIS, 210
AT&T, 20, 143, 223
AT&T Istel, 244
Authorizing capital request, 161-162

Baan International, 180, 215
Benefits, 54-58, 100, 108, 157, 182
Birmingham City Council, 56, 105, 169, 181, 229-235
Bolton Metro, 49, 55, 57, 124, 126, 154, 170, 235-240
BP Oil, 17, 187, 200-203
British Telecom, 52, 89, 127, 145, 153, 217-221
Bull, 170, 231, 233
Business case, 95-110
Business needs, 49-54
Business process re-engineering:
  case studies, 217-228
  general, 3, 58-60

Capital request, 155-162
Case study:
  A, 65, 110, 190-199
  B, 11,65,190-199
  business process re-engineering, 217-228
  facilities management, 229-246
  outsourcing, 229-246
  selecting IT solutions, 200-216
Castle Cement, 53, 66, 203-206

CFM, 57, 239
Champion, 13
Change management, 15-17, 101-102, 149, 155, 161
Client/server, 12, 29, 140, 211
Coda, 205
Commitment, 9, 180-181
Compaq, 202
Computer Associates, 208
Computer Users Year Book, The, 87
Conference room pilot, 70-71, 117-118, 137
Conflict, 15-20
Consultants:
  approach, 15
  function, 85,
  role, 15
  use of, 10, 23, 44, 69, 80, 87, 190, 212, 234, 242
Coopers & Lybrand, 49, 236, 238, 242
Corporate management:
  function, 27, 98, 149, 161
  responsibilities, 7-8, 45, 96, 109, 162, 188
  role, 6-7
Costs, 72, 76, 100, 125, 152, 157
Critical success factors:
  business case, 95
  business needs and benefits, 48
  capital request, 155
  comparison of case studies A and B, 195-199
  evaluation, 129
  general, 8-10, 29
  implementation, 178
  invitation to tender, 120
  operational requirement, 113
  options, 81-82
  post-implementation reviews, 185
  recommendation, 149
  request for proposal, 72
  summary of requirements, 65

INDEX 249

supply agreements, 163
CYBORG, 208

Decision maker, 14
Decision making, 4, 29, 149-162
Definitions:
  benefits, 54
  business case, 98
  business need, 49
  invitation to tender, 120
  operational requirement, 113
  request for proposal, 72
  solutions oriented, 4-6
  summary of requirements, 66
Dell, 202
Digital (DEC), 66, 205

EDI, 3
EU, 10, 23, 28, 81, 88, 97
EU Journal, 94, 127, 207, 238
Evaluating:
  business case, 108-109
  invitation to tender, 138
  product, 138-143
  request for proposal, 91-94
  services, 143-145
  supplier, 146-148
Evaluation, 129-148
Expectations, 9, 180-181

Facilities management:
  agreements, 169-173
  case studies, 229-246
  conflict, 19
  definition, 84
  evaluation, 130, 133
  legal, 23
  legislation, 28
  options, 80-81, 84
  planning, 33, 38-39, 133
Feasibility phase, 46-48
Format:
  business case, 99-100
  capital request, 155-157
  invitation to tender, 121
  operational requirement, 113-116
  recommendation, 150-151
  request for proposal, 73
  summary of requirements, 66-68

Gartner Group, 87
GATT, 10, 23, 28, 81, 88, 97

Hewlett-Packard, 89, 212, 215, 219
Hoskyns PMW, 210, 231

IBM, 86, 110, 170, 208, 211, 226, 231, 233
ICL, 49, 170, 193, 231, 233, 239
Idhammer, 226
Implementation, 178-184
Institute of Chartered Accountants, 87
Interviews, 62-63
Invitation to tender, 120-128
IT department, 1, 15, 22-23
ITnet, 181, 233

Keeling Partnership, The Dennis, 87

Legal department, 14, 22, 23, 163, 233, 237
Legislation, 28, 52
Leicester City Council, 58, 94, 127, 142, 206-209
Lotus Notes, 202
Lucas, 210

Microsoft, 202, 212
Models:
  decision-making process, 96
  evaluation:
    capital request, 157-159
    invitation to tender, 133-136
    recommendation, 152
    request for proposal, 88
  feasibility phase, 47
  quality flow chart, 45
  selecting options and suppliers, 79
  selection phase, 112
  selection process, 5

NCR, 20, 143, 223
Negotiating, 164-165
NOVELL, 202

Offer, best and final, 163-164
OFFICE (Microsoft), 202, 212
Operational requirement, 111-119
Option Systems, 19, 223
Options, 82-86
Oracle, 89, 145, 219, 220
Outsourcing:
  agreements, 169-173
  case studies, 229-246
  conflict, 19

definitions, 84
evaluation, 130, 133
legal, 23
legislation, 28
options, 80-81, 84
planning, 33, 38-39, 133

Pace, 29
Pepe Jeans, 18, 19, 22, 55, 102, 116, 143, 146, 221-224
Planning:
  application software, 34-35
  evaluation, 120-133
  facilities management/outsourcing, 38-39
  invitation to tender, 126-128
  operational requirement, 116
  overall, 21-22
  request for proposal, 77
  systems software, 36-37
Postscript, 247
POWERBUILDER, 212
Preparing:
  business case, 101-107
  capital request, 159-160
  invitation to tender, 128
  operational requirement, 116-118
  request for proposal, 77-78
  summary of requirements, 69
Price Waterhouse, 2
Priorities, 28
Procedures, evaluation, 136-137
PROGRESS, 19, 223
Project management tools, 40, 202, 210, 231
Project manager, 10, 21-22
Project team, 7-8, 24-25, 28
Prudential Assurance, 22, 50, 58, 86, 101, 104, 107, 146, 164, 209-213
Purchasing department, 22, 23, 78, 88, 128, 164

Quality, 29, 43-45, 71, 118-119

Recommendation, 149-155
Re-engineering, 81
Request for proposal, 72-78, 88
Resourcing, 28
Reviews:
  benefits, 187-189
  operational requirement, 117
  system, 185-187

Risk, 28, 93, 102-106, 157, 161
Roles, 13-15

Selection phase, 111-113
Service level agreements, 173-177
SmithKline Beecham, 51, 61, 117, 224-228
Software licences, 166-169
Solutions oriented, 4-6
Sponsor, 13, 27, 62, 104, 107
Steering committee:
  composition, 25
  function, 25
  responsibilities, 7-8, 45, 96, 108-109, 154-155, 160-161, 179-180, 185-188
  role, 6-7
Summary of requirements, 65-71
Suppliers:
  identifying, 86-87
  final short-list, 148
  initial short-list, 94
  long-list, 87
Supply agreements, 166-177
SYBASE, 212

Technicians, 14
Third-party maintenance, 2, 84, 169
Training, 28
Trent Regional Health Authority, 53, 86, 110, 127, 170, 188-189, 240-246
TRITON, 215
TUPE, 23, 28, 171
Turnkey agreements, 166-169

UNIX, 1, 12
UNIX Software Directory, 87
Users:
  approach, 15
  reactions, 15
  responsibilities, 23
  role of, 2, 14
  skills, 23

WINDOWS (Microsoft), 86, 202, 211, 228
WORD (Microsoft), 6
Workshops, 63

Yule Catto, 54, 66, 89, 101, 126, 180, 213-216